Jeremiah

PAIN AND PROMISE

Jeremiah

PAIN AND PROMISE

◖◗

Kathleen M. O'Connor

Fortress Press
Minneapolis

JEREMIAH
Pain and Promise

First Fortress Press paperback edition 2012

Cover image: *Dead Tree, Gray Sky* © iStockphoto.com / Mike Elliott
Cover design: Joe Vaughan
Author photo: Scott Chester
Book design: PerfectType, Nashville, TN

ISBN 978-0-8006-9930-7
The Library of Congress cataloged the hardcover edition as follows:

Library of Congress Cataloging-in-Publication Data
O'Connor, Kathleen M.
Jeremiah : pain and promise / Kathleen M. O'Connor.
p. cm.
Includes bibliographical references and index.
ISBN 978-0-8006-2040-0 (alk. paper)
1. Bible. O.T. Jeremiah—Criticism, interpretation, etc. I. Title.
BS1525.52.O26 2011
224'.206—dc22   2011009347

Manufactured in the U.S.A.

CONTENTS

PREFACE

This book is not a commentary on the biblical book of Jeremiah. It is an interpretation of aspects of Jeremiah using insights drawn from contemporary studies of trauma and disaster. Trauma and disaster studies investigate how overwhelming violence and debilitating losses afflict minds, bodies, and spirits. In Jeremiah every passage anticipates disaster, speaks about it, or searches for ways to cope with its enduring consequences. A full-throttle response to a multi-leveled calamity, the book of Jeremiah addresses the victims of the Babylonian assaults on Judah in the sixth century B.C.E., including invasions, displacements, and deportations. Trauma and disaster studies examines the impact of such violence and the less visible wounds upon the life of the community that come inevitably in its wake.

Writing this book was both painful and promising. It was painful to write because its subject is how to survive pain, physical and spiritual, communal and individual. Writing was painful also because somewhere deep in my spirit the sufferings depicted in Jeremiah distantly evoke my life in ways beyond words. And mostly, it was painful because I have tried to write it for a wide audience, for students of the prophet, preachers and ministers, clergy, caregivers, and for anyone who has experienced loss, displacement, and brokenness. It would have been much easier to write only for my colleagues in biblical studies, and, yes, I am trying to persuade them that trauma and disaster studies illuminate the book of Jeremiah in startling ways.

But writing about Jeremiah and disaster was also promising because trauma and disaster studies have explained so many problems I have had with Jeremiah, especially with his portrait of a violent, angry God and the book's entry and reentry into violent images, metaphors, and relationships. I vigorously searched the literature to discover how these features of the book might have helped the people of Judah carry on after the Babylonian assaults.

I discovered how Jeremiah's artistry lifts violent destruction into worlds of poetry and symbol where horrible pain and loss can be seen, taken in, and acknowledged without overwhelming its victims anew. I saw how Jeremiah's potent images, metaphors, and dramatic scenes enact on a small stage the plight of the nation. I rethought how the life of the prophet embodies the fate of the people, the threat to their life, their public humiliation, their approaching death, and always miraculous escape.

I discovered how Jeremiah promises a future beyond the death of the nation, a future that is uncertain, open-ended, and just over the horizon. That future will come because God, whom they thought had punished them, failed them, or left them, was still there, still loving, and still yearning for them. Jeremiah does not explain suffering in any satisfactory way, at least to me (no biblical book does), but the book pledges that God will make a future and points the way toward it. Jeremiah's literary artistry is a mode of survival, an expression of hope, even when the words themselves are hopeless.

Because violence saturates the world of the readers, Jeremiah sees violence in every sphere of life, even within God's own being. This literary violence offers victims of disaster language to speak about their experiences, a capacity of expression brutally undermined by the violent events themselves. The tears of Jeremiah, God, the people, and the earth itself flow across the book, promising to awaken hearts turned to stone by brutality. Jeremiah's portrait of an angry God promises, first, that God is alive even though every faith tradition of the past had been smashed to pieces like their environment, and, second, there is a cause and effect in the world, order in the mist of utter chaos.

Viewed from this perspective, Jeremiah is a work of resilience, a book of massive theological reinvention, and a kind of survival manual for a destroyed society.

In its poignant beauty, the literature transforms memories of violence, reframes them, and gives them coherence—partial and momentary—to lead victims and their offspring through the turbulent morass that is disaster. Because the book of Jeremiah is a work of art, it can reach out to embrace other sufferings, losses, and doubts of the world. This is the book's promise.

I am writing this preface as disaster strikes Japan in earthquake, tsunami, and nuclear hazard, as Libya and other parts of northern Africa boil up in violence and warfare, as Israelis and Palestinians continue struggling over the land, and the United States and western powers occupy Iraq and Afghanistan. If nothing else, Jeremiah mirrors the plight of these peoples and invites those of us in more tranquil places to understand and perhaps to act.

ACKNOWLEDGMENTS

When the Henry Luce III Foundation granted me a fellowship for 2004–2005, they not only gave me the gift of time to begin research on this book, but they also validated the project as worth doing. I am immensely grateful to them. This is only the beginning of my gratitude.

Jeremiah: Pain and Promise was born because a community supported me, inspired me, and loved me for the embarrassing number of years it took to write it. My thanks are due first to Walter Brueggemann, giver of praise, thinker of new thoughts, and poet of the Word who blew upon the little idea-flame I had to bring it to high heat. Daniel Smith-Christopher's studies of Ezekiel prompted the first flash of new insight into Jeremiah, when he used trauma and refugee studies to insist that biblical books from the Babylonian Period reflected vast amounts of traumatic suffering, often ignored or underplayed by interpreters.

At the root of all my experiments with Jeremiah has been ongoing conversation with two profound thinkers and dear friends, Pete Diamond and Louis Stulman. Year after year we met to talk about our troublesome prophet. We lamented scholarship that left Jeremiah in historical dust and, together over good food and drink, sought new ways to interpret it. So many ideas in my work come from them that it is hard assign authorship to any one of us. This is a rare joy.

The ever-creative Carol Newsom encouraged me to keep digging into other people's fields of study, and she and other members of the Atlanta Consortium of Feminist and Womanist Scholars continue to support me with laughter and camaraderie.

Then there is the Old Testament Colloquium that meets yearly, first at Conception Abbey in Conception, Missouri, and now at St. John's Abbey in Collegeville, Minnesota. Its members—Irene Nowell, Gale Yee, Dale Launderville, Leslie Hoppe, Tom McCreesh, Gregory Poland, Corrine Carvalho, Steve

Ryan, Roberta Salvador, Mark Smith, Christopher Frechette, and the late Larry Boadt—endured paper after paper from me about Jeremiah and disaster and even let me find trauma in their texts whether it is there or not.

When my husband, Jim Griesmer, and I left New York for me to take a teaching position at Columbia Theological Seminary in Decatur, Georgia, it felt like moving to a foreign land. But Columbia has been a wonderful place for me. Its tradition of strong biblical scholarship and colleagueship make it a rarity among academic institutions. The give and take, challenge and respect, and hilarious good times spurred my work, and I remain deeply thankful for my life here. Among my colleagues, Christine Yoder deserves special thanks as co-teacher, organizer, scholar, and dear friend. Bill Brown has brought intellectual energy and wonder into our midst.

Librarians are a special breed. Director Sara Myers, Erica Durham, Mary Martha Riviere, and Griselda Lartey, in particular, are most gracious super-sleuths who seem able to find anything with the tiniest bit of information. I thank the students at Columbia Seminary for their questions, resistances, and insights, especially those in classes where I thought my way through this book.

Friend and poet Jim Mengert helped me draft my book for a wider reader-ship, and Kari Pelegrino worked meticulously on the bibliography. Thanks to both of them. Many colleagues and friends have talked with me about traumatic experiences or about studies that have greatly helped my work. Even though I cannot name them all, I am thankful.

My husband, Jim, teaches me how to live. His love, support, and good humor provide the music of my days, and our friends keep us both surrounded by love and laughter.

This best thing about writing this book has been the circle of community that helped me keep going and loved me into being. This I value more than anything.

Introduction

Wounds without Words

I became a student of the book of Jeremiah because the prophet's first-person prayers, called the "confessions," touched something very deep within me. I had no words for that meeting of life and text then, but I continued to pursue this difficult work throughout my life as a teacher and interpreter. But despite my own involvement with the book, I found it harder and harder to teach it. In one class for pastors and ministers at Columbia Theological Seminary, I met strong resistance to Jeremiah even before we had studied five or six chapters of the book. These students found the prophet's angry, punishing God nearly unbearable. They said that Jeremiah's theology blamed the victims, was deeply sexist, and was not useful for their churches today. When their lives met the biblical text, the results of the encounter were toxic. Since I could discover little help for these theological and pastoral problems, I let the book lie fallow for a long time, at least in the classroom. Avoidance seemed a good, if temporary, solution.

Several years later, I taught Jeremiah again to a class of mixed degree students who had very different responses from the previous classes. This time, the book of Jeremiah called forth stories of their lives, stories of deep suffering only partially visible to them, of pain still alive within them. What had changed in the intervening years? What made it possible for this biblical book to connect with students' lives?

Perhaps the primary difference was that my perceptions of the book of Jeremiah had deepened. I began approaching it differently, teaching it from another angle, framing its confusions, conflicts, and harsh rhetoric within different frameworks—informed by my study of trauma and disaster. Rather than pursuing

1

matters of the history and origins of the book, I became interested in how the book addressed its readers as survivors of traumatic and disastrous historical events. Trauma and disaster studies help me to refocus my attention from questions of the book's creation—such as which words belonged to Jeremiah, which were words of later writers and editors—to the matter of why these words were kept alive at all. These studies, gathered from an interdisciplinary conversation about the impact of traumatic violence and catastrophe upon individuals and communities, enabled me to think about how the book may have helped the people of Judah after the Babylonian Empire destroyed the nation in the sixth century B.C.E.

Trauma and Disaster

Trauma and disaster studies arose from the bloody smear that was the twentieth century. Central to these loosely connected investigations are the long lasting effects upon victims and their offspring of the Holocaust, or Shoah—the systematic destruction of European Jewry and others by the Nazis during the Second World War. But the list of modern disasters is broad and sweeping. It includes the Armenian genocide at the beginning of the century, two world wars, the dropping of the atomic bombs on Hiroshima and Nagasaki, and numerous smaller devastations in Europe, Asia, and Central America, as well as bloodbaths in the Congo, Rwanda, and Bosnia, merely to begin the list that expands into the twenty-first century. Trauma studies, in particular, have led to the growing recognition that war, rape, and abuse inflict lingering consequences upon victims, even to the next generations.

This interdisciplinary conversation around the effects of trauma and disaster draws from diverse fields of study. They include cognitive psychology, counseling, sociology, anthropology, and literary criticism. The shared hope of these investigations is to gain further understanding of the life-destroying effects of violence upon people and ultimately to find processes that help people to endure, survive, and perhaps eventually thrive.

From Trauma to Disaster

Trauma comes from the Greek word for "wound." In classical medical language, trauma refers to the violence that inflicts injury, not to the injury itself.[1] To "be traumatized" is to receive a blow, to become the victim of sudden and perhaps repeated assaults in one form or another whether physical or emotional. To "be traumatized" is, by necessity, expressed in the passive voice because trauma reduces victims to a passive state. Victims are acted upon rather than actors who chose what happens to them. Injury from violence can afflict people in a number of ways yet not traumatize them, but for most people, trauma inflicts wounds without words. Such wounds are often called today by the awkward title "post-traumatic stress disorder" (PTSD). Although I do not use this odd collection of adjectives and nouns, and I also avoid medical models of individual recovery related to PTSD, the study of individual trauma—and its next of kin, disaster—helps show how violence afflicts people and, in my work, how the book of Jeremiah addresses these wounds.

Trauma refers to the impact of violence upon individuals. But when traumatic violence reigns down upon a whole society, trauma becomes a public disaster. When suffering and loss heaped upon one person is no more than a miniscule moment in the massive destruction of a society and its habitat, violence magnifies its effects in uncountable ways. It creates a kind of mental vacuum. It so overwhelms the capacities of victims to take it in, that the violence cannot be absorbed as it is happening. Traumatic violence comes as a shocking blow, a terrifying disruption of normal mental processes, distorting reality, even as it becomes the only reality.

Disasters brought about by traumatic violence disturb what people think, feel, and believe. They distort perceptions and shut down ordinary life. Memories of the violence imprint themselves in the brain like a powerful ghost that returns again and again, repeatedly disordering daily life. Human beings cannot absorb extreme violence as it occurs; they simply cannot take it in. The consequence of this shutting down of the mind is that memories of traumatic events become fragmented, even as they take up residence in the mind where they have a life of their own. Contradictory though it may seem, these memories can be neither forgotten nor escaped, even though they exist as shattered moments of experience. They become what literary critic Cathy Caruth calls "unclaimed experience," a hidden "story of a wound that cries out," of a hurt that is not fully assimilated and that both demands our witness even as it defies the possibility of being witnessed.[2] The wounds are unspeakable.

The unutterable nature of the wounds is a second form of violence and related to fragmented memories. Often it is impossible for victims to tell what happened to them, to name their experiences, or to depict in words the terrors that have overwhelmed them.[3] Traumatic violence eludes expression in language; it is "unspeakable."[4] Words to tell what happened, to set events into a story, and to explain why they happened simply disappear. "There are no words!" is the frequent cry of survivors of disasters as they try to report the cataclysm that has engulfed them. Trauma and disaster suppress language and can even bring people into a state of muteness.

A third effect of traumatic violence is that it automatically shuts down feelings and turns off human responses to overpowering shock.[5] And when emotions and cognition turn off in the face of violent blows, when people lock violent experiences away in a form of self-protection, they also lose access to knowledge of their own pain, loss, and grief. They become stuck, unable to move toward recovery or to flourish as vital human beings. Life can continue but as a kind of half-life, a form of endurance in a barren, affectless landscape.

A fourth effect, equally serious for individuals and societies but less visible, is that trauma and disaster destroy or at least undermine trust in God, other people, and the world. Trauma and disaster can leave people feeling betrayed and God-forsaken.[6] Beliefs and traditions, what Louis Stulman might call the society's "symbolic tapestry,"[7] those interlocking ideas and institutions that once secured them firmly on the earth and kept them grounded in daily life and communal identity—these no longer seem reliable. After all, God did not protect them, nor did prayer comfort them, nor is worship any longer possible because the gods of chaos rule the cosmos. No longer is there a stable, secure foundation upon which to stand.

Trauma and Jeremiah

When I began to apply insights from trauma and disaster studies such as these to the teaching of Jeremiah, what happened in the classroom, among church groups, and in my own perceptions of the book was astonishing. Not only was Jeremiah more accessible and acceptable to the students, it also elicited from them their own stories of violence and trauma. Many students related to passages from Jeremiah in visceral, personal ways. Here are a few of those stories, told with permission.

Walter Baer, an Episcopal priest from New Orleans, remembered taking a walk with relatives in Berne, Switzerland, where he came upon watermarks on the sides of buildings from a recent flood. It was that sight that catapulted him back into the tumult of life in New Orleans and its devastating waters after Hurricane Katrina many months earlier. Until that walk he had gone on without stop after the catastrophe, trying to help people in his community, cleaning up, trying to cope. His delayed reaction caught him by surprise.

Another student, Wylie Hughes, returned from a third tour of duty as a Marine in Iraq and attended a memorial service for one of his fellow soldiers, but few of his friends in the Corps were able to attend. They could not face the memories of violence and death they brought home with them. Wylie speaks of the moment when the vehicle in which he was travelling with other Marines hit a roadside bomb. His friend was sitting next to him when the explosion hurled them in opposite directions. His friend died and Wylie lived. Upon return to the base, the debriefing of the incident followed standard military protocols. Each

Marine retold events according to a kind of check list: what happened at impact, where each person's body, weapons, and equipment fell, what each saw, the estimated time each element of the violence took to unfold. Emotion was necessarily absent, discouraged, not permitted, probably not even yet available. After all, no matter how they felt, they had to get up and face the same terrors the next day.

During one class session, a third student, Yvonne Thurmond, remembered a painful incident from her childhood. I provoked the remembrance by my remark that a parent's inexplicable slapping of a small child was a "relatively small illustration" of the impact of violence on a life. Yvonne corrected me immediately, and she was right to do so. Such a blow is not small, not trivial. Its traces can follow one through life. I might have said more accurately that this scene could serve as a "common illustration" of the lasting pain of violence, not a trivial one. My example not only triggered gentle protest from Yvonne, it also created space for her story of being aggressively intimidated in childhood, a story she was able to piece together decades later to explain fears that lingered well into adulthood.

In the same Jeremiah class, Dan Jessop told about the shocking suicide of a teammate on his high school football squad. Dan has not been able to forget the event not only for the sadness that will not leave him but also because he continues to wonder what he might have done to prevent it.

These scattered accounts have in common the experience of varying degrees of traumatic violence, violence that inflicts bodily, emotional, and spiritual harm. Each of these people in my class has their suffering imbedded in their bodies. It is part of them, never to be forgotten and somehow to be assimilated into their larger lives. Now when I speak about and teach the book of Jeremiah, similar stories emerge without my asking, sometimes privately, sometimes shared with a larger group, always humbling, always a moment of human communion across differences.

As the class unfolded and the student's stories came out, I recognized something else about Jeremiah that before had been only an unarticulated hunch. The book did more than give voice to the afflicted. It was and is a most effective instrument of survival and healing. I know because I witnessed it working this way among my students in their encounter with the book.

Many scholarly interpreters of Jeremiah already know the profound devastation underlying the book and reflected in its pages, and many see the book's healing capacity in its potent rhetoric and lyrical appeal to readers. Trauma and disaster studies add to Jeremiah interpretation a recognition that the book's powers to lead toward rebirth of the shattered people of Judah lies in the very fire and brimstone that turned off my modern, ethically engaged students several years ago.

With my own eyes opened anew by these studies and moved by students' stories, I began to consider more deeply the original audience of Jeremiah's book and to wonder what stories they would tell, if they could narrate the historical events of the Babylonian invasions. I wanted to imagine what it would be like to live through the disaster and traumatic violence that produced the book of Jeremiah in the first place.

I tell those stories in the next chapter, where I attempt to set the prophet's work into its historical context, not to show how the book was composed but to imagine the destroyed world in which the book intervenes like a survival manual for people wavering between life and death. Then I tell more about the effects of trauma and disaster upon its victims in the third chapter. The fourth chapter and all the subsequent ones reflect on selected sections of Jeremiah, trying to show how the book seeks words for festering wounds for which there are no words.

1

Imagining Lives

Historical Context

A disaster is marked by what it takes away. It takes away nearly everything. The nation of Judah underwent a series of unfolding disasters in the sixth century B.C.E. The Babylonian Empire (centered in present day Iraq) invaded Judah three times, occupied it for close to fifty years, and with each invasion deported some of the nation's leading citizens to Babylon. These events brought Judah to the brink of extinction, a point long embraced by Jeremiah's interpreters.

Imagining Little Stories of Disaster

To set the background for the book of Jeremiah, I want to imagine what it might have been like to live in Jerusalem when the mighty Babylonian Empire breached the city walls of Jerusalem, Judah's capital city. But before presenting Judah's larger historical narrative, I begin by inventing small stories of families living in Jerusalem during the second invasion (587 B.C.E.). I take the drastic step of inventing lives because I think Shoshana Felman is correct when she writes: "So much historical coverage of history functions to empty it from its horror."[1] Felman means that the writing of history usually eliminates human suffering—the blood, the pain, and the horrors—from its reports about the past. Too often it dehumanizes victims and overlooks the horrible consequences of events for real people.[2]

Historians, of course, are properly cautious not to overstate what the evidence allows them to report. Yet the suffering depicted in biblical texts arising from the Babylonian Period contrasts sharply with most modern historical accounts of the time.[3] From the point of view of trauma and disaster studies, the "facts" simply do not convey the full tragedy that accompanied Babylonian aggression.[4] This prompts me to wonder what stories victims of this disaster might tell if they had been in my class?

With apologies to Gary Herion, who writes about the "Great" and "Little" traditions of monarchic Israel,[5] I want to enter into the great events of Judah's history by way of small ones, by telling little stories of families rather than of nations. I am encouraged to do so by the book of Jeremiah itself, because it also speaks about the massive historical disaster through little stories about the prophet, stories that seem to gather up elements of the whole thing. Perhaps by imagining the human toll of the Babylonian assault upon Judah, these stories may help readers experience the vibrant power of Jeremiah's beautiful, difficult words.

Because such stories do not exist in any of our historical sources, I have to make them up. But fiction, too, can be a mode of truth-telling. It can help us think and feel our way into lives of others on a more human scale than some historical reports. Since life in ancient Judah centered upon the extended families and upon community rather than individuals, my four stories of violence and survival are situated within family households.

The Asher ben Jacob Family

When the Babylonian army broke through the fortified walls surrounding Jerusalem, the siege of the city had been going on for nearly two years. Hoped-for help from Egypt or from anywhere else has not arrived. News recently reached the city that outlying towns to the south were no longer returning signals to the Judean army, so the Babylonian forces were turning their full attention to Jerusalem. For their whole lives, Asher ben Jacob's family had lived in a two-room house, built adjacent to one of the walls of the city that were to protect it from attack.

Noises of troop movements and battle preparations disturbed the days and nights in the neighborhood. The Babylonian army was building siege ramps up to the wall of the high-perched city with less and less opposition from the demoralized and exhausted Judean army. But the noise was growing more deafening. Babylonian soldiers were using battering rams to pound against the city wall a short distance from Asher's home.

On this summer day in July 587,[6] Asher did not return from his duties as a guard outside the king's palace. Asher's wife, Peninah, was in the house with their five children, Asher's mother, and two female cousins. With no sign of Asher or any other male relative in sight, the women and children faced the army's onslaught alone. Loud crashing sounds near the wall and fearful screams of neighbors filled Peninah with paralyzing fear. The Babylonians must have breached the wall because soldiers were pouring into the street, and no Judean defenders were in sight. With the help of her two cousins, she gathered, grabbed, and pushed her five children and mother-in-law out the door and down a path toward her father's house a short distance away.

When they got there, her father's household was in chaos. The women and her elderly father were throwing pieces of fruit and grain into a burlap sack, along with a cooking pot. Everyone was shouting at once. Their intent was to run for their lives. Babylonian soldiers with spears and swords were shouting in a foreign language and bashing down doors at the far end of her father's street. Soldiers were invading homes in search of men who might resist them, of booty, and, Peninah knew, of women to rape. She ran with members of both households as they scrambled down back alleyways and through neighbors' gardens, trying to stay together and keep track of her children. Terrified neighbors crushed upon them, and an elderly aunt fell in the crowded melee. They lost her in the rush, and Peninah soon lost track of her two oldest children among the throngs of people also running to escape the soldiers. Shrieks and confusion built as the stampeding crowd grew larger.

The two youngest children, an infant and a toddler, had been screaming but eventually grew quiet from fear and weakness as they made their way out of the city. None of her immediate family had eaten much since the Babylonians made camp outside the city nearly two years earlier, but in the past weeks the food was cut off completely. Throughout the siege, Asher had been able to supply them with bits of fruit and grain from the palace, but three days earlier he had come home empty-handed. Food was scarce even in the king's household. On the road out of the city, Penninah's family tried to stay together. Eventually they made their way north with a stream of refugees to the city of Mizpah in Benjamin. Perhaps it would be safer there, even though they had no family to take them in. Perhaps there would be food, shelter, and less violence.

Asher never rejoined his family. Although he was only a soldier—neither royalty nor priesthood—he was a strong man and a potential resister. When Babylonian soldiers captured him, they executed him on the spot, though Peninah and the family would never know what happened to him, nor to her aunt or her two oldest children.

The Micah ben Nahor Family

Less fortunate than Peninah, Deborah, wife of Micah, lived in another small house near the market stalls outside the temple where she sold fruit for a rich farmer. Her husband had been killed in the first siege of Jerusalem ten years earlier and two of her sons had been taken away by the king's men to serve in the army. Now Babylonian soldiers surrounded the temple. They set it on fire along with the outbuildings and small businesses around it. Deborah escaped the burning neighborhood with four children and some neighbors and found a temporary hiding place in a shed for animals at the large estate that belonged to a wealthy, influential family. They were hiding there only a few hours when Babylonian soldiers came to the big house and began dragging out the occupants. Deborah and the children had to flee again. A good distance away they found refuge in a small cave in a hillside where other people were also hiding, including a few more of her stunned neighbors.

When the city grew quiet some days later, she and three others slipped out in search of food. As they surveyed the ruined streets, they feared further violence from bands of Babylonian soldiers guarding the city, but hunger—the children's and their own—forced them forward. What they found was a landscape of destruction. Streets were unrecognizable, filled with stony rubble from destroyed buildings. Corpses of citizens lay unburied, and animals and birds seemed to have disappeared completely. They began searching for food in the half-standing buildings, desperate for anything to bring back to feed the children. They met others also ransacking empty, half-destroyed buildings for food or for valuables to trade. Deborah became obsessively focused on accumulating whatever she could carry.

She and a few companions hobbled back to the cave and managed to hide with their children for several weeks, making forays into the devastated streets only late at night. When the turmoil in the city began to diminish, some of the cave dwellers set out in search of a place to live. They came to the house of the wealthy family where Deborah and her children had first hidden and found it empty except for a few old indentured servants who now lived in the big house. With some of their loot, they were able to bribe the servants for fruit from the scraggly trees in the garden and for shelter in the shed now empty of animals.

Deborah's children were hungry all the time. Her two young sons went to gather wood and her daughter to draw water from a nearby well, but other Judeans were demanding payment for these basics of survival. Rumors reached them daily of girls being raped and of young men being rounded up and forced to grind grain or carry wood and water. Three of Deborah's children watched as soldiers hung two Judean princes by their hands.[7] Her youngest son and her daughter now sat in the corner. They stopped speaking. Life was a misery and survival a daily challenge. She could not pray, nor even weep. Nothing made any sense.

The Noach ben Amoz Family

Noach and his extended family used to live in the big house where Deborah, her children, and their new companions came to find shelter. Noach was a "servant" of the king, a highly placed officer in charge of the treasury and an overseer of tax collections. Although his position afforded his family many privileges and a wealthy way of life, he greatly disliked what it required of him. Palace intrigues made his situation precarious and left him guarded and suspicious of everyone around him. And he had to extract taxes from the people. His neighbors hated him for the strenuous collection tactics he oversaw in the city, as greater and greater amounts of their harvests, their animals, and their treasure were demanded or taken forcibly from them.

For decades, the Judean kings were compelled to pay increasingly high tribute, first to Assyria, then Egypt, and now to Babylon. According to one of Noach's fellow court officers, the king's decision to stop paying tribute probably precipitated the invasions by the Babylonian army to attack them in the first place. But the people and the land had already been wrung dry under the tax system.

Now Noach, his wife Abigail, their four teenage sons, three younger daughters, two elderly parents, and numerous cousins were being herded off with other families of the king's officers and priests who had survived the invasion. Babylonian soldiers treated them like cattle. They cut off their hair, stripped some of them, shackled them together, and forced them to march, while they insulted them and threatened them with whips. They had not gone far when Noach's father fell, and a soldier killed him for hindering the march. The walking was strenuous and, even for the most able-bodied, the physical discomfort was enormous and the shame beyond bearing. These once-powerful families, along with some of the king's relatives and friends, were being marched around the Fertile Crescent to Babylon, where, if they survived, they would be sent to labor in the fields or to work in the cities. Survival seemed unlikely.

The Eli ben Levi Family

Among the deportees was a priest named Eli and his family. Eli was relieved that some of his priestly brothers seemed to have eluded the soldiers, or at least he hoped that was what their absence meant. But he was devastated by the violence he had witnessed. He felt as if he were going crazy. Even though he had long expected the triumph of the invaders over the rabble that was left to defend Jerusalem, he could not believe it was actually happening. That the Babylonians had dared enter the holy city of God and destroy God's temple outraged him. How could this happen? How could the temple built by Solomon, the place where God promised to live with them forever, be burned to the ground by these barbaric heathen? He had no words for this unspeakable indignity to his people and to their God. Watching the temple invaded by foreigners was like witnessing a rape. Seeing the blood of his fellow priests spilled in the sacred place was a pollution and an abomination. Where was their God?

Difficulties of Imagining the Past

My flat-footed stories of families caught in the siege convey only the barest approximations of the terrors these historical times wrought in Judah. Modern, Western readers cannot climb far into the lives of ancient peoples; our worlds are too different. We hold vastly dissimilar beliefs about the roles of family and individuals, about government, religion, God's role in history, and even of what is important about the past and how best to tell it. But the ancient people of Judah were thinking, feeling human beings connected with us by common humanity, by desires and hopes, pain and loss, love of family and friends, and by faith in God. Communication between our disparate worlds must be possible.

By imagining lives of families caught in the vortex of historical forces over which they have no control, I hope to suggest the contexts out of which arose the searing power of Jeremiah's words and to coax the book from its confinement in the closed container of the past. Perhaps in the corners of our vision, we may glimpse some of the horrors Shoshanna Felman finds missing from the writing of history.

Imagining the Great Story

The larger narrative of Judah's history indicates that the national catastrophe began a century before and continued for decades more. That means among other things that the disaster was an enormous, enduring set of destructive events, and it is these that gave birth to the book of Jeremiah.

In the century before the Babylonian invasions, Judah's situation was already precarious. Old Testament historian John Bright describes matters this way: "Seldom has a nation experienced so many dramatically sudden reversals of fortune in so relatively short a time."[8] The first major reversal of fortune came from the aggrandizing incursions of the Assyrian Empire (more or less present day Syria). In 721 B.C.E., this cruel, aggressive empire destroyed Israel, Judah's sister-nation to the north. Twenty years later, the Assyrians also invaded Judah, and only the capital city of Jerusalem escaped destruction (Isa 36:1—37:38). The Assyrians demanded heavy tribute from Judah, a tribute that imposed crippling taxes upon the population, hindered the economy, and interfered in Judah's internal affairs.

When Assyria finally weakened, Judah faced new dangers from Egypt in the South. Trying to fend off the Egyptian advance, Judah's long-reigning King Josiah died in battle in 609 (2 Kings 22:1—23:30; 2 Chron 35:2-24).[9] His death sent shock waves through the nation.[10] Egypt then appointed a king, Jehoiakim, from among Josiah's sons. In 605 Babylon, also called "Neo-Babylon" or "Chaldea," defeated Egypt and became the dominant power in the region.

This brief survey shows that even before Babylon appeared on the international horizon, Judah had been attacked, defeated, and dominated by another imperial power. Judah's own life was severely crippled.[11] But the subsequent rise of Babylon at the end of the seventh century B.C.E. would bring disaster upon Judah.

The First Invasion

Judah's King Jehoiakim may himself have provoked the first Babylonian attack upon the nation. Although he had cunningly switched allegiance to Babylon when it gained supremacy over Assyria, he rebelled against them a few years later. The Babylonian response was swift. On 16 March 597 B.C.E., the empire attacked Jerusalem and deported the new king, Jehoiachin (Jehoiakim had died), along with other prominent citizens and treasures from the Jerusalem temple.[12]

The Second Invasion

Seeking a more compliant Judean on the throne, Babylon's ruler, Nebuchadnessar, appointed Zedekiah to be king (Jer 32:7; 2 Chron 36:10). The book of Jeremiah presents Zedekiah as a weak, vacillating leader (chaps. 37–38), but eventually he too withheld tribute, and nearly a decade after the first invasion, Nebuchadnezzar's armies invaded Judah again. This attack was devastating. Babylon incapacitated outlying towns and blockaded Jerusalem. When the city tried to defend itself, it held off the army for nearly two years, but food supplies dwindled, famine and disease spread, and help from Egypt never came.

In 587 the Babylonian army broke through the walls of the weakened city, razed the palace and the Temple, and deported more Judean leaders to Babylon. King Zedekiah tried to escape with his sons, but Nebuchadnezzar captured them and executed the sons before the king's eyes; then they blinded him (Jer 52:7-11). The nation's leadership was destroyed along with the infrastructure, economy, and daily life in the city and its environs.

The Third Invasion

Babylonian efforts to stabilize the conquered land were not fully successful. They appointed a Judean official named Gedeliah as a kind of governor of the occupied people. He operated in a town called Mizpah in the northern region of Benjamin (Jer 40–41).[13] But as often happens in imperial invasions, an insurgency arose. This one was led by a survivor of Judah's ruling family named Ishmael. He and his followers assassinated Gedeliah and slaughtered a large group of Judahites. To quell the uprising, Babylon invaded again in 582 B.C.E. and deported more people.

How Little We Know

In recent years, biblical historians have disputed nearly every aspect of this historical account. They do not agree about the number of people deported nor about how many remained in the land after the invasions. They quarrel over processes of Babylonian rule, the extent of destruction in Judah, and how bad it was for the survivors remaining in the land or in sent into exile. Because ancient sources of information about the period are sparse, there is broad scope for disagreement about this history. At the heart of the debate is the problem of the Bible's reliability as a source of history.

Why We Know So Little about the Times

Much of what we know about the history of Judah during the Babylonian Period comes from the Bible, but the Bible is not history in the modern scientific sense. It does not present objective, chronological reports of what happened. Rather than simply reporting what happened, biblical texts interpret events in light of God's engagement with the world. And because the texts speak to people who lived in the thick of the struggles in question, it was not necessary to report the historical conditions in which they lived and breathed. The audience of the biblical books needed interpretation and explanation, inspiration and hope. When the biblical texts do present memories of the past, they are already engaged in interpretation of events for the people trying to cope with them.[14] The ancient authors show little interest in the pure facts for their own sake.

Complicating matters further, biblical texts often contradict each other and sometimes themselves, making it hard to know what occurred and when. The books of Kings, Chronicles, and Jeremiah, for example, report differing numbers and times of deportations, obscuring an accurate picture of the time.

Beside the Bible, we also have historical information gleaned from Babylonian records and from archeological study of material remains, but these bring their own problems of interpretation. The Babylonian Chronicles provide one example. These are royal inscriptions (writings) that record deeds of Babylonian kings.[15] Because they were written by the king's scribes, they tend to "maximize" the rulers' achievements, skewing accounts to make their employers look good.[16]

Other archeological sources, such as the remains of material culture, are also limited in what they can show us. Material culture refers to physical remains of a society such as architecture, pottery, stamps, seals, or inscriptions on stone. These remains can show that destruction has taken place, but they often keep secrets about who did the destroying. The remains may show that a population lived in a place for a time, to be replaced later by people with different types of pottery, buildings, or writing. But estimates often are crude, and much uncertainty lingers.

Such limitations on the sources of information mean that, to uncover what happened, biblical historians must do what historians always do. They must weigh evidence, adjust for biases of their sources, and speculate about ancient happenings, their causes, and their consequences. Then, they draw conclusions humbly and provisionally.

How Bad Was It?

Despite many difficulties in reconstructing Judah's history during the Babylonian Period, most scholars agree that the nation experienced a major disaster, and much interpretation of the book of Jeremiah recognizes that the collapse of the nation brought with it unspeakable suffering. The invasions left major devastation in their wake, vastly interrupted ordinary life, and left the survival of the Judean people in serious doubt. Here is a brief survey of some of that destruction as biblical historians present it.

The Babylonian assaults drained away the population through deaths in battle, starvation, disease, deportation, and by the creation of internal refugees in the wake of warfare. And even if only a small number of Judean elite were dragged away to Babylon, the exile of political leaders, owners of land and businesses, judges and priests would have caused immense social and economic disruption.[17] Other citizens who were not deported became internally dislocated, escaping to Benjamin in the north and scattering around the land. Even those who remained in the city of Jerusalem were probably displaced by the crumbling of life around them.[18]

Archeological excavations point to major physical destruction of towns and villages in the southern part of Judah. Life may have been easier in the northern region where there had been less destruction,[19] but population increases there suggest that internal refugees from the south came into the area bringing other burdens.[20]

It is uncertain whether Jerusalem itself was settled during the years after the invasions.[21] Archeologist Lisbeth S. Fried believes that the land itself "lay desolate" because the destruction of the Temple and palace buildings would have affected badly the flourishing economic life upon which the wider society depended.[22] And because both the Temple and palace were major symbols of relationship with God, their destruction called Judah's identity as God's people into serious question.

David Vanderhooft, who studies Babylonian history and archeology, confirms the picture of disastrously interrupted life in Judah under Babylonian rule. In his view, the Babylonians governed their occupied territories with practices as brutal and cruel as those of the notorious Assyrians before them.[23] They disrupted trade, stopped imports, destroyed the economy, and made "periodic military appearances" to insure "the delivery of tribute."[24] If these assessments are even partially accurate, the people of Judah underwent traumatic violence for decades.

Testimony to Disaster

Although biblical books associated with the Babylonian Period do not provide a systematic history of the times, they offer something better. They preserve stunning testimony that the people of Judah experienced an historic catastrophe. Testimony is speech from the inside of events;[25] it does not seek to prove something but to portray and interpret the experience from the inside.[26] The prophetic books of Jeremiah, Ezekiel, and Second Isaiah, and the book of Lamentations testify in poetry and prose to the specter of life destroyed during this period.[27] The book of Ezekiel, for example, with its shocking imagery and "spaced-out" prophet, expresses the thoroughgoing traumas of the people deported to Babylon.[28]

Similarly, the book of Jeremiah is run through with language of annihilation, lament, and struggle explicitly associated with Babylonian political and military realities. Second Isaiah later seeks to comfort the exiles in Babylon, a people battered, scattered, and broken. Finally, the book of Lamentations, also associated with the prophet Jeremiah, provides detailed complaints about life in the occupied land and ends on the brink of despair.[29]

Life under Occupation

Lamentations' five poems weep about the destroyed city, about the suffering of occupants young and old, and about the "eclipse of God."[30] The last lament in the book presents life as a state of continuing terror (Lam 5).[31] It decries the fate of the children, starving in the streets; tells of once ruddy and healthy nobles, now unrecognizable among the walking dead; and expresses shock that the most compassionate mother, desperate for food, cannibalizes her children. Under these conditions, the poem declares the dead to be better off than the living, for strangers occupy their homes and demand payment for water and food. Fathers have vanished, women are raped, and the youth stagger under the heavy burdens of forced labor (Lam 4–5). Lamentations concludes in bitter doubt of God's intentions toward them:

> Restore us to yourself, YHWH, and we will return,
> renew our days as of old,
> unless you have utterly rejected us
> and are angry with us forever (Lam 5:22, my translation).

Lamentations and the other literary works from the period offer poignant witness to the suffering, confusion, and despair that the catastrophe brought upon Judah. They testify that the Babylonian Period was disastrous for the nation and resulted in what Louis Stulman calls a "cosmic crumbling."[32] Although we do not know the exact historical details of the disaster, the biblical literature witnesses from within the continuing traumas to what the people of Judah underwent simply to stay alive.

Trauma and disaster studies can help us imagine further the profound displacements from which the book of Jeremiah emerges and show how the book searches for life in the overwhelming presence of death. They show that Jeremiah's theology, for all its harsh bitterness, its prophecies of terror, and its weeping cries—even because of these things—is profoundly life-affirming. The book is a work of resilience, a moral act for the rebuilding of the community from the ashes of catastrophe. It is a kind of survival manual for victims of disaster and their offspring. These discoveries have opened up the book for me, something like discovering the secret spiritual life of an acquaintance one had known for years, never suspecting the depth that lay hidden there.

2 Hearts of Stone

Disasters and Their Effects

Many Jeremiah scholars have shown exquisite sensitivity to the suffering expressed in the book, but both the literature's terrifying violence and its tender hope receive further illumination with insights from trauma and disaster studies. I am an expert in neither trauma nor disaster nor its related fields, and although I can speak of traumatic moments in my life, such experiences do not dominate my interior landscape or my life in the world. Yet the realities these studies explore have opened my eyes to the physical, spiritual, and psychological collapse that underlies the book of Jeremiah in the most visceral ways. They explain why so much of the book depicts brutal scenes, portrays a punishing, violent God, and overflows with suffering and weeping. They show the long, intertwined process involved in survival and create renewed appreciation for the hope-filled beauty of this book. Trauma and disaster studies have turned me from a somewhat ambivalent reader into Jeremiah's enthusiastic defender and promoter in our disaster-afflicted world.

The words of Jeremiah burst alive in the midst of cataclysms and extreme suffering today. Anyone who has served as pastor, lay minister, or clergy person, who works in fire or police departments, as a counselor, military chaplain, or missionary, as a teacher, a nurse, or a paramedic, among the homeless, with victims of domestic violence, with service organizations, foreign missions, or non-government organizations, or who are merely friends of the suffering— all encounter stories of traumatic violence time and again in their daily work. Confronted with such radical suffering, kind, helping people must also come to terms with their own powerlessness and relative ignorance about both how to help and how to avoid being traumatized themselves by the violence they witness. What should one say or do? How is it possible to offer help that neither creates further pain nor glosses over the depth of the losses involved? And what has all this to do with faith in a God who loves and cares for the world?

The book of Jeremiah does not answer these pastoral questions for us directly, but it does intervene in the chaos and points to processes for coping with it and moving through it. With help from the books of Lamentations, Ezekiel, and Second Isaiah, Jeremiah enables the people of Judah to survive. Fraught with depictions of a world reduced to shards, the book presents a fertile field for disaster and trauma studies. By attending to the traumatic effects of the Babylonian assaults upon Judah in the sixth century B.C.E.,[1] these studies not only explain many puzzling features of Jeremiah and expose deeper dimensions of the scholarship about it, but they also suggest ways the biblical text meets life today. According to Cathy Caruth, they may also help us discover ways we have all been dislocated from ourselves,[2] even if not in such wrenching fashion. And Smith-Christopher expands that lens to include the dismal displacements of global politics.[3]

Trauma and disaster studies are, of course, merely heuristic devices for interpreting Jeremiah, that is, they suggest ways to "find" how the book addresses its audience in the churning aftermath of violent events. They are tools for finding what we did not see so clearly before, something like a pair spectacles to discover what lies hidden beneath the hard surfaces of suffering encoded in the book.

Disasters and Their Effects

Disasters involve more than the sad or tragic events that occur in ordinary human life; they overwhelm everything. Whether disasters are human-made, an event of nature, or a complex mixture of the two, they disrupt life on a vast scale.[4] Daniel Smith-Christopher underscores the enormity of devastation involved in disasters by observing that a disaster is "disastrous only when events exceed the ability of the group to cope, to redefine and reconstruct" their world.[5] Disasters turn life upside down and shake the world apart in unimaginable and unspeakable ways. They destroy daily existence and shatter its meanings. They leave people stunned, isolated, and hopeless.

Disasters appear in many varieties. There are so-called "natural disasters" like the tsunami in South East Asia, Hurricane Mitch in Central America, or Hurricane Katrina on the Gulf Coast of the United States and the floods that followed in New Orleans, the earthquakes in Haiti and Chile. There are disasters caused by human conflict and malevolence like genocides, bombings, invasions, military occupations, terrorism, forced displacements of people. But usually natural disasters and human-made ones overlap and infect one another.

Negligence, mismanagement, power struggles, and greed nearly always compound the problems of recovery after destructive events of nature like droughts, famines, floods, and earthquakes. And human-made disasters like bombings, invasions, and military occupation, and the oil spill in the Gulf of Mexico, inflict harm on the environment, the infrastructure, and the food supply.

Disaster's Lingering Presence

No matter what causes disasters, their long-term effects are similar and long-lasting. Despite important cultural differences in ways communities respond to and recover from disasters, and despite the uniqueness of each disaster, their impact usually follows the same contours. And even when victims of violence regain some physical safety and a "new normal" appears, these less visible consequences can endure indefinitely.

To Be Overwhelmed

The word "overwhelming" may be the most frequently employed English term to describe disasters. Disasters overwhelm nearly everything:

> They overwhelm human capacities and resources.
> They inflict injury on human bodies and spirits, on the environment that supports them,
> and on the symbolic worlds that give meaning to individual and communal lives.[6]
> They overpower the senses and crush normal human responses.
> They devour a sense of safety and decimate the routines of daily life.[7]
> They incapacitate social resources and threaten social instability and unrest.[8]
> They create conditions of hunger, fear, and greed that prompt robbing and looting.
> They create crises in communication.
> They disrupt "systems of meaning" within a community.

It is clear from this drumming, partial list of consequences that distinctions between disaster and its effects do not exist; the effects are the disaster.[9]

The floods in New Orleans, for example, not only destroyed lives, homes, and land, but they also disrupted the social fabric of the city in profound ways, displacing many people, devastating the economy, and breaking down social life. On a narrower geographic scale, 9/11 created its own forms of havoc, and its impact on the character of the United States is still unfolding. On a global scale, the long reach of disasters multiplies beyond calculation. Consider the earthquake, tsunami, and nuclear threat in Japan, the earthquake in Haiti, the invasion and occupation of Iraq, the melt-down of life in Sudan, Kenya, the Congo, Afghanistan, the devastation in Palestine, and countless other contemporary scenes of ongoing disaster.[10] In such overwhelming cataclysms, physical and economic destruction are only the beginning of what happens. On top of those material disruptions, layer upon layer of social, psychological, and spiritual malaise can be crippling and enduring, while recovery—if it is possible at all—is often equally protracted.

Hidden Effects of Disaster

Beyond physical destruction and the disruptions it causes, less visible features of disaster can vastly inhibit a society's chances of survival and recovery. Disasters leave people isolated, embedded in their own suffering,[11] contributing to the breakdown of communal life. They are made numb by the violence and left without adequate language to tell of it or to interpret it. At the same time, memories of violence remain alive and repeatedly return to overwhelm victims, as if the violence were still occurring. To protect themselves from memories of violence, people "turn off" in an emotional and spiritual deadening. Amid such destruction of life, trust in God, the world, and other people becomes unsupportable.

These interrelated consequences of disaster and trauma appear to have been central among the afflictions Judah faced in the wake of Babylonian invasions. At least, that is my hunch, considering the intersections of these effects and the literary intervention that is the book of Jeremiah. Directly or indirectly, the book addresses all of these consequences of disaster.

Fragmented Memories of Violence

Violent events often take possession of their victims. Trauma survivors can experience the violence as a kind of stunning non-event, or more aptly, as such an overwhelming experience that they cannot receive or assimilate it into consciousness. By that I mean victims cannot absorb, understand, or grasp violence as it is happening because traumatic violence overwhelms the senses. The result is that violent experience typically fragments in their minds like broken glass. Memories of it fracture, turn into splintering glimpses of horrors that get stuck in the brain. When this happens, when people cannot take violent events into consciousness, or assimilate them, or interpret them, the violence clamps down thinking and distorts reality. The effect is that splintered memories of the terrors reside in the mind and will not go away, or they disappear briefly and pounce again later, triggered by the smallest sight, sound, smell, or encounter. The memories return to haunt the victim in a "mute repetition of suffering."[12]

In the face of harrowing violence, thinking and feeling turn off automatically. This closing down of normal human responses is a self-protective survival strategy. It prevents the mind from receiving shocking events as they occur so as not to short-circuit it and destroy it.[13] Trauma, then, is "a wound of the mind," a "breach in one's experience of oneself."[14] When violent memories shatter into pieces in the process, according to some neurobiologists, they "engrave" themselves physically on the mind. They become etched upon the brain like a plow-furrowed field.[15] In this way, memories of violence stay alive and return to haunt the victims. A sound, a smell, a slant of light, or any number of events can trigger them and evoke the whole universe of fear and pain, too enormous to see all at once.

Survivors of child abuse speak of the recurrence of shocking memories late into adulthood. Soldiers report how haunting memories of war interrupt their efforts to return to normal life. Survivors of natural disasters recall the screams that will not leave their minds in the night. During the original ordeal, an invisible shield shuts down thinking and feeling in a blessed form of protection. People turn off so they can keep going. But afterwards, without warning, fractured memories can return with the force of the original experience. They agitate and stomp around in the mind like menacing ghosts with a will of their own. Victims find themselves right back there as if in a permanent, default mode of consciousness. Memories retraumatize victims.

To be traumatized, then, is not just to be frightened. It is to be "possessed by the past" in a "mute repetition of suffering."[16] Memories invade and occupy the mind and can easily become "a dominating feature of the interior landscape."[17] How can a whole society immersed in disaster bear its fragmented memories and escape their death grip?

Breakdown of Language

Besides leaving victims with recurring memories of horrors, a second consequence of trauma and disaster is that they take away speech; they silence victims' capacity to talk about what happened. According to Elaine Scarry, physical and emotional pain destroys language because severe pain is "unsharable."[18] In Shakespeare's *King Lear*, the wordlessness of the old king's shock makes his entrance with his dead daughter Cordelia in his arms so pitiful. All he can say is "Howl, howl, howl"—unbearably expressive and beyond words.[19] Pain does not merely resist being put into language; it destroys both language and power to think symbolically. In a kind of "unmaking" of speech, pain reduces its victims to a pre-language state,[20] to groans and screams disconnected from traditional, culturally accepted meanings.

W. G. Sebald provides a telling example of the disappearance of language after catastrophic events. He writes about the fire bombings of the German city of

Dresden and other German cities by the United States and Allied Forces during World War II.[21] His starting point is the fact that the firebombing was vast and horrifying. Yet, despite the unprecedented degree of violent assault upon Dresden, Sebald notices a near silence about it in German records, literature, and lore. The disaster was hardly mentioned among German survivors, nor was it much written about in German history and literature. The firebombings only existed in German historical memory as "vague generalizations," because as Sebald so aptly puts it, the events were an experience incapable "of public decipherment."[22]

There are many reasons for German reticence to speak about what happened; in particular German shame for the Holocaust and other atrocities of World War II. But a major cause for the silence, according to Sebald, was that the catastrophe destroyed language. Eyewitnesses who escaped with only their lives gave erratic, disturbed, and discontinuous accounts. Most lapsed into cliché: "It was an inferno"; "It was like hell"; "it was beyond words." Finally, victims became mute because there were no suitable words to tell of the destruction. Instead, after the war, there was a kind of "individual and collective amnesia," an obscuring of a world that no one could present "in comprehensible terms."[23] The terrors of firebombing could not emerge in language able to convey "the reality of total destruction, incomprehensible in its extremity."[24] And Sebald continues with excruciating precision,

> The death by fire within a few hours of an entire city, with all its buildings and its trees, its inhabitants, its domestic pets, its fixtures and its fittings of every kind must inevitably lead to overload, to paralysis of the capacity to think and feel in those who succeed in escaping.[25]

Overload and an accompanying paralysis of thought and feeling cause the breakdown of language. Words remain, of course, but they do not fit "events."[26]

Contemporary studies of the effects of trauma on the brain show that "the part of the left hemisphere responsible for translating personal experiences into communicable language (is) turned off" by experiences of violence.[27] Victims lose the capacity to "define a situation through traditional understandings," through symbolic ways of thinking and speaking.[28] Under these conditions, reality itself is "up for grabs," and people are left confused and rudderless.[29]

And, in a snow-balling effect, community itself collapses. Because catastrophic experiences cannot be put into words, communal relationships disintegrate and, even when people undergo similar experiences, they can become alienated from one another by their inability to speak about what they have experienced.[30] Nor do they wish to speak since they are shut down with neither ability nor desire to do so. But how is it ever possible to speak about such things? Efforts to create language to talk about traumatic experiences can reactivate horrible memories all over again. Better not to think about it. Better to put it out of mind for it might return, and this time one might not "have the power to endure." [31]

To Become Numb

A third impact of traumatic violence upon victims relates to the first two. Because trauma and disaster usually make people emotionally numb, grief and anger become unreachable. Extreme pain shatters emotional responsiveness. Becoming numb, of course, is a normal, adaptive strategy, an automatic defense mechanism that protects people from feeling unbearable violence, hurt, and loss. They shut down to live through it and survive. In a progressive withdrawal from emotion and from one another, victims of traumatic violence often become "dead to the world." [32] And when people grow numb, when feelings disappear, or when feelings are so riotous as to short-circuit the capacity to feel, then people cannot begin to recover from their many losses. Inability to speak or to feel "forecloses the grief process." [33] The people live, instead, in a shut-down, half-alive state, in a condition where, to use biblical language, their "hearts turn to stone," and they no longer fully live in the world.

Although victims may function normally on some levels, if they are bereft of feeling, passion, and desire, they cannot flourish nor contribute to society, nor connect with God, be worshippers of God. Relationships collapse or fade like an ever flattening line on a heart monitor. Such sealing off of inner life can happen in circumstances other than traumatic violence, [34] of course, but as a permanent condition of life, numbness breeds a seemingly unalterable inner life of despair and hopelessness. When disasters turn hearts to stone, they devastate basic tissues of social life and damage bonds attaching people to families and communities.

Time itself can sometimes heal, of course, and in western societies, professionals can help, and in other societies, traditional community systems of support can lead individual victims toward a more thriving life. [35] But what can heal a whole society? How can a benumbed community create endurance and energy to survive and to begin to rebuild? How can a society nourish resilience that it may survive? Religious traditions can be an essential reservoir of life and hope to aid in recovery, but herein lies a major destructive aspect of disaster. The very traditions, beliefs, and rituals that stood like a canopy of protection and trust over the community prove useless. In disasters, faith collapses along with everything else.

Loss of Faith

Disasters mortally wound faith and trust. Confidence in God, the world, and other people often dissolve in the wake of trauma, and such profound distrust can persist indefinitely. By itself, suffering does not bring an increase in love or meaning. Radical suffering corrodes trust, traditions, and institutions that anchored life firmly before the catastrophe. The once solid terrain of faith shatters, traditions collapse, and belief frays.[36] Kai Erikson puts it this way: survivors of disaster "can be said to experience not only a *changed sense of self* and a *changed way of relating to others* but a changed *worldview*."[37] Ways of thinking and acting that held people together with taken-for-granted certainty in the pre-disaster world dissolve or are so sorely threatened as to no longer support the world.

After disasters, doubt of even the most elemental sense of safety takes over, leaving people God-forsaken and alienated from their beliefs.[38] Like a solar eclipse blotting out the sun, calamity blots out God because death and destruction obscure any sense of God's protective and faithful presence. Inevitably disasters cause people to question the divine: "Is God involved in this mess?" "Is God implicated or indifferent?" "Is there any God at all?" In the wake of disaster, God's own survival is in grave doubt.

In an essay on torture during the Holocaust, Jean Améry tells about the shriveling of his faith.[39] With the first torturous blow, he says, the victim "loses trust in the world." Trust in the world includes many things: "belief in absolute causality perhaps" and belief in "the written or unwritten social contract that the other person will spare me."[40] Faith's demise extends even further for Zachary Braiterman as he reflects on major catastrophes of the twentieth century.[41] Even beyond two world wars, the last century was host to "mass murder and mass death" that form a long list, including the Holocaust, Cambodia, Bosnia and Rwanda, along with the "specters of nuclear apocalypse, global environmental disaster." This "litany" of disasters dwells as a ghostly presence in western imagination, and for Braiterman, undermines "the value of the human person, the meaning of history and modernity and the significance of human cultural practice and social organization" and, he adds in parentheses, "(belief in God)."[42]

While Améry and Braiterman attend particularly to the breakdown of faith among Jews after the Holocaust, others describe similar loss of faith as a typical response to traumatic violence. Psychiatrists Alexander McFarlane and Bessel van der Kolk, for example, observe that most victims of trauma believe "that their pain, betrayal and loss are meaningless." Rather than renewing meaning, suffering causes "disintegration of belief."[43] When disaster destroys the fabric of faith and trust in a society, people are left adrift, powerless, and foundering in a sea of uncertainty.

Bearing Burdens

Haunting memories, broken language, benumbed souls, and impenetrable grief, compounded by the collapse of faith—these common effects of disaster and trauma coalesce into heavy burdens that victims can carry for decades and even for generations. As less visible aspects of disaster, they often hide behind the more obvious harm of physical destruction. They cling to victims mercilessly and hinder survival with palpable force. In our time, many people are hungry for ways to understand and respond to such suffering, yet challenges both to victims and to people who care about the suffering of the world are enormous.

How is it possible to respond to such suffering and understand its nature, without eliminating the force and truth of the reality that trauma survivors face? How can others respond and speak about traumatic violence without weakening its impact or reducing it to banal truisms? And how is it possible for caregivers and friends to avoid being traumatized themselves in our global village, pock-marked as it is with relentless natural and human-made disasters?

These questions lack simple answers. Wounds of such destructive depth do not arrive with roadmaps, blueprints, or disaster dictionaries to lead victims through the morass that faces them. But trauma and disaster studies help name the injuries, point to processes of survival, and set societies onto some new form of life. They place a spotlight on healing measures found in the book of Jeremiah. They show how, in its many facets, this potent literature contributes to the survival of Judah and its God. They bring to the fore the creative, imaginative words that reveal wounds that refuse to be healed. They show how Jeremiah opens the sluice gates of grief and revives Judah's radically disrupted relationship with God.

Studies of trauma and disaster pry open the book of Jeremiah to deeper reflection. They release it from constricting interpretations concerned only with the book's composition or the prophet's true words or from unquestioning interpretations of disaster as God's punishment for sin. They explain Jeremiah's massive attention to collapse as well as the book's preservation as sacred literature. They show how the words ascribed to the prophet contribute to the moral rebuilding of the shattered community. The book of Jeremiah is a story of disaster, love, and rebirth. Hidden beneath its harsh turbulence, indeed, because of its very turbulence, Jeremiah offers readers a process both for coping and for building hope.

Larger understandings of the effects of violence can also expand our compassion for the dead and for the living who today abide in the midst of disastrous events. As Felman puts it, trauma and disaster studies can keep historians from lessening "the impact of events," from turning them "into pious cliché," or from emptying history "of its horror."[44] To survive a disaster physically, or in Jeremiah's words, to "escape with your life as booty of war," is merely to begin the long and difficult process of recovery (Jer 39:18; 45:5). It is into this abyss that the book of Jeremiah accompanies victims, as if with a lantern to light the way.

3

A Relentless Quest for Meaning

The Book of Jeremiah

When I was writing my dissertation on Jeremiah, my mother decided to read the biblical book so she could understand what I was doing. She had the common experience of being thwarted by the effort. "How can anyone read this book?" she wanted to know. Jeremiah's interpreters have long tried to make sense of the book's complicated structure. The long, complex book resembles a collage constructed of a motley collection of materials like paper, fabric, paint, photographs, newspaper clippings, feathers, found objects—all glued together by some not entirely clear connections to the prophet Jeremiah.

I am not overstating the problem. To read the book named after the prophet is to encounter many forms of prophetic literature in rapid succession. There are poems uttered by Jeremiah on behalf of God called "prophetic oracles." There are prayers, liturgies, and stories about Jeremiah's deeds and his captivities. There are sermons, laments, oracles of hope, proverbs, and many other types of literature. To complicate matters further, the book switches abruptly from speaker to speaker and image to image. Metaphors appear, disappear, and reappear as themes of warning, suffering, and hope circulate across the book and interrupt one another. And perhaps most perplexing of all, the book has little chronological or narrative order. The result of this literary profusion is a glorious mish-mash, a book judged to be "unreadable" even by its loving interpreters.

How the Book Became Unreadable

Most biblical interpreters believe the source of Jeremiah's puzzling shape lies in its long process of composition. An earlier group of scholars known as source critics proposed that Jeremiah came to its present shape due to a long process of writing and collecting by many groups of people. First, according to this theory, the book began with Jeremiah's own words, his poetry, collected and written down from early oral performances. Second, his scribe Baruch wrote biographical stories about Jeremiah and added them to the prophet's words. Next prose sermons, written in the style of the book of Deuteronomy, were added to this growing anthology. Then all these written sources or documents gathered over a long period of time were brought together by the same deuteronomists or other editors who also added material of their own. The result is an unwieldy book created by a somewhat incompetent committee.[1]

To Old Testament scholar William McKane, the book's composition appears even more chaotic than that. McKane dispenses with the idea of written sources and proposes, instead, that the book came together in a more or less random gathering of literary pieces from various authors and times.[2] In the world of Jeremiah scholarship, his image describing the book's formation is famous. The process resembles that of a snowball rolling down a hill. The core of the snowball is Jeremiah's words that gathered other words to it in a random fashion.

Interpreters today realize how difficult it is to know how the book came to be. We know with confidence only that it came together from many hands over a long period of time.[3] But these sources critics and McKane after them were excellent readers. They took seriously the book's confusing shape and so tried to understand it. That effort is what endures about their work.

But I am not trying to figure out how the book came to be. I am trying to gain a glimpse of what the book might have meant for its early readers, survivors of the Babylonian disaster and their offspring, the ones who did not know if they would ever again be God's chosen people. Using trauma and disaster studies, I want to ask how the book helps them survive. Its literary confusion contributes to that survival.

Why Leave the Book Like This?

But the question remains: Why would the book's final editors not smooth over the many ruptures in the text, or give it a complete story line, or at least put things in chronological order to overcome some of its literary turmoil? Is something more involved in Jeremiah's bewildering shape beyond its unwieldy composition at the hands of many groups of people over many decades? It is certainly true that many prophetic books also exhibit similar literary disarray, but Jeremiah exceeds them all.

A Moral Act

Trauma and disaster studies suggest that Jeremiah's chaotic over-abundance, its "too-muchness," its very disorder itself turns the book into a helpful text for survivors of disaster. The book's competing images, themes, and voices not only mirror the chaos left in the disaster's wake, they also invite readers themselves to become interpreters of their own reality. In this way, the book is a moral act, a literary work that turns disaster victims into people who must make sense of the literature. I am convinced that rather than being a hindrance to its purposes, the book's lack of order itself works as a mode of recovery. It not only reflects the interpretive chaos that follows disasters, when meaning collapses and formerly reliable beliefs turn to dust. Jeremiah's literary turmoil is also an invitation to the audience to become meaning-makers, transforming them from being passive victims of disaster into active interpreters of their world.[4]

A Search for Meaning

The book of Jeremiah is a quest for meaning, for words, images, metaphors, stories—interpretations of every kind to help the people of Judah survive and rebuild as a people. It tries and tries again to find meaning in a world where meaning has evaporated. This is why I can think it is a "history of love and disaster." Not only is love a recurring theme of the book, but also the whole corpus expresses love, human and divine, a love that emerges in the consuming fires of disaster. This love of Judean identity and of the God who formed them as a people finds expression even in the most abrasive of Jeremiah's words, even in his many images of an avenging, punishing, warrior God. With poetic brutality and with quiet tenderness, the book names their wretched world and gives it meaning. It provides words for wounds beyond speaking, and offers hope for the rebuilding of the community of Judah. Such is the power of this prophetic book. But this interpretation of Jeremiah's confounding literary shape as a quest for meaning will make more sense after we investigate some of its parts. I consider its structure across the book and more fully in my last chapter when I think it will make more sense.

Order and Structure within the Chaos

I begin, instead, by asserting that Jeremiah is not completely unreadable or it would not have survived unto this day. The title of Louis Stulman's study *Order amid Chaos* aptly describes the book's shape, for in the midst of Jeremiah's literary chaos, many orderly elements appear.[5] First, the book divides into two distinguishable parts: Part One: Anticipating and Meeting Disaster (chaps. 1–25) and Part Two: Living beyond Disaster (chaps. 26–52). Here is a very brief outline of major sections of the book:

Part One, Anticipating and Meeting Disaster, deals predominantly with God's plan "to pluck up and pull down, to destroy and to overthrow" (1:10). Part Two, Living beyond Disaster, mostly concerns the second divine intention "to build and to plant" (1:10). This two-pronged motif, set out in the story of Jeremiah's call (chap. 1), acts as a refrain across the book (1:10; 12:14-16; 18:7, 9; 24:6; 31:28, 38-40; 42:10; 45:4)[6] and establishes its larger purposes. Prophecies of destruction predominate, whereas building and planting receive less explicit attention. Yet the two parts of the refrain, destroying and building, and the two parts of the book actually work together to rebuild and to plant anew.

For the book's audiences, God's plucking up and pulling down have already occurred. Even when prophecies tell of the future destruction of Judah, they now tell of events that have already come to pass. They portray the immediate past history of the readers and name the reality in which they live. The prophecies of future catastrophe look backward and name the plethora of losses that have befallen the nation. In this way, the two parts of the book form a loose unity of purpose. They both contribute to the process of recovery, as if language about destroying and language about building were working to arrive at the end, the survival of Judah and its faith in God. Language of breaking down helps to build up.

Beyond the minimal division of the book into two parts, other literary features create a limited poetic and narrative order within the book. The metaphor of God's broken family, for example, unites both poetry and prose into a dramatic story of a failed marriage (2:1—4:2); poems about kings form a subsection (21:11—23:4); oracles against the nations are a collection of similar poems concerned with Judah's neighbors and enemies (chaps. 46–52); stories about Jeremiah follow a common pattern involving captivity, threats to life, suffering, and survival. And as Stulman points out, Jeremiah's sermons organize and tame the poems in which they are embedded, simplifying causes of the disaster.[7] And there are other collections and orderly units across the book. But the wonder of this book is that it does not ever settle on one way to speak about the disaster. It searches relentlessly for language to move through the abyss, to give it shape, meaning, and to make life possible again.

Search for Language

To bring the cataclysm to speech, the book of Jeremiah wanders down many literary avenues. Its tumbling, competing parts search for words to expose the nation's wounds to light and healing. The book searches for language, images, and metaphors to tell how Judah collapsed, how the ancient traditions failed, and how to endure through chaos and pain.

Disasters inflict wounds without words, or at least without words adequate to express the harm that has been done.[8] Although victims' bodies may be fine—they may even be comfortable and safe—the inability to speak about what happened can isolate them and leave them in a world filled with what Jeremiah might call "terror all around" (Jer 20:3, 10).

Contemporary Israeli writer David Grossmann describes how the devastating effects on language around the war between Israelis and Palestinians helps us understand Jeremiah.[9] Ongoing violence "shrinks the 'surface area' of the soul," he writes, and narrows both the world and "the language that describes it." Extreme and continuing violence makes people "unwilling to identify, even a little, with the pain of others," causes them to suspend "moral judgment," and diminishes speech so it becomes "shallow, riddled with clichés and slogans." Without suitable words to tell about terror and loss, sufferers face an ever-deepening abyss, and communal bonds evaporate. The human cost of such shriveled speech is beyond measure.

Telling Truth "at a Slant"

Perhaps this is why the book of Jeremiah is a boiling pot of language. It spills worlds of words into the ruptures of communal life. And its multiple language worlds have the potential to reinvigorate the nation because they are poetic and symbolic. The book largely avoids giving literal accounts of the terror. To find passages that even approximate an "historical" or factual version of invasions of the disaster, readers of Jeremiah have to wait until they reach chapter 39 and then wait again until chapter 52. More surprising still, the book does not even name the aggressing nation of Babylon until chapter 20.

Rather than confronting matters head on, Jeremiah tells and retells the catastrophe indirectly, metaphorically, in unforgettable poetic ways. In the process, the book tells the truth. But to quote Emily Dickinson's words about poetry, it "tells it slant," places it in other dimensions, in symbolic realms of art. Because the book is a work of art, it can provide language to enable Judean victims to speak of the disaster, and because it is art, it can reach through the ages to touch people who have known many kinds of suffering.

Overview

In the chapters that follow, I try to show how various parts of the book of Jeremiah invent language to contribute to the healing process. It is my conviction that the whole book works to lead the community through death to new life, but never in a systematic way. I begin with texts relating to the metaphor of God's broken family as a highly metaphorical retelling of the disaster. Then I consider the poems gathered about the theme of warfare and find there a mythic retelling of terrifying events of the invasions. These poems borrow from the marriage and family poems to provide a kind of musical undertone. From there, I consider the weeping poems as instruments that encourage the expression of grief and make communal space for the renewal of faith.

Jeremiah is a prominent presence in the book, and two chapters address his "biography." He is a complex figure who stands both against his people as God's spokesperson and with them as a symbolic figure whose prayers and captivities gather up their sufferings. His prayers complicate the book's theology by offering an alternative understanding of God's involvement in the nation's fall, and they show the people how to survive though the catastrophe. The many captivity stories about him show him to be a complex literary presence who again represents his people and stands against them, but he escapes his captives every time, suggesting they too will have a surprising future.

His sermons, written in the style of Deuteronomy, show a narrowing and simplifying interpretation of the disaster. They probably come from a later period than the previous material, because one sign of recovery is that explanations become more uniform, narrow, and simplified. The Little Book of Comfort or Consolation, with its explicit poetry of hope, new life, and reprise of family life, comes next and contains the most beautiful and explicitly hopeful poetry of renewal. Then, borrowing insights from Walter Brueggemann, I consider the fact that the book does not come to a satisfactory conclusion. It has three endings "that do not end," because disasters do not end or resolve or come to satisfactory conclusions. Their consequences haunt victims and survivors for generations. Finally, I return to the fact that the book itself is so turbulent and how that turbulence helps.

When I refer to Jeremiah in this book, I try to make clear when I am referring to the person of the prophet rather than to the book named after him. Usually it is to the book, since we can say very little with certainty about the historical person. What we have is a literary character who presides over the book and is credited with words and deeds that enable the nation to endure, to live, and to face a possible future covenanted with God anew. Judah does not perish because of this book, along with other biblical books that address the Babylonian disaster.

A Family Comes Undone

The Metaphor of a Broken Family

JEREMIAH 2:1—4:4

mong Jeremiah's more effective language worlds to name and interpret the disaster is its drama of the broken family (2:1—4:4).[1] The pain, anger, and yearning among members of this disturbed household convey the nation's story on a narrowed stage, in a pared-down version of unspeakable loss. Whether or not these loosely joined chapters deserve to be called a drama is open to question for a number of reasons.[2] The chapters mix prose and poetry to create an implied story rather than a clearly plotted one. Scenes jump episodically from event to event without telling readers how they relate to one another. We have to "connect the dots," make associations, and do the work of interpretation ourselves.[3] But these demands that the literature makes on us are part of the recovery of language, of the quest to make sense of the disaster.

Jeremiah's family drama uses an old story to tell a new one. A borrowed plot from the prophet Hosea (Hos 1–3) unfolds differently in Jeremiah, as God's family splits apart because of divine fury at his[4] adulterous wife.[5] With dismay and shock God accuses his wife of rampant perversion and sexual betrayal. The wife, identified as Judah or Jerusalem, stands for both the nation and the capital city, blended into one female literary figure.

The family in this book is a metaphor. A metaphor compares two unlike things and omits the word "like" in the process. Rather than saying the nation's historical relationship with God is *like* relationships in a broken family, Jeremiah says it *is* a broken family. Metaphors spin off associations, feelings, and ideas that lure us into the imagery and show us what we had not seen before. This extended metaphor of the family turns readers into voyeurs who watch a messed-up couple and their children interact and fail to connect with each other.

But the family drama is actually showing Jeremiah's audience their own world, interpreting how their relationship with God teeters on the edge of extinction. It sets their overwhelmingly painful lives into a domestic realm, onto a small stage. In this family feud, they can see their reality and recover language to talk indirectly about what happened to them. The drama tells the truth "slant" in the symbolic world of poetry, without rehearsing the literal horrors of their past and traumatizing them anew. As Emily Dickinson declares, "tell all the truth but tell it slant . . . the truth must dazzle gradually or every man be blind." Perhaps the children of my fictional families could see their own catastrophes in this one and not be blinded by the horrors.

Domestic Disaster (2:1—4:4)

Jeremiah's family drama unfolds in two acts: Betrayal and Divorce (2:1—3:5) and Aftermath of Divorce (3:6—4:2),[6] and each act contains several scenes.

Act One: Betrayal and Divorce (2:1—3:5)

The first act seems so diffuse as to suggest that I am imagining a drama where it does not exist because of its many characters and layers. As if in a split-screen video, poetic scenes switch back and forth between a female figure, God's wife, and a third party, Israel (a male figure), who seems to have nothing to do with the family.[7] The alternation between scenes about male Israel (2:4-16; 2:26-32) and about wife Judah (2:17-25; 2:33—3:5) are not evident in English translations because English does not distinguish between gender in forms of second person address (you) as does the original Hebrew. Male Israel is the whole nation and, more specifically, the Northern Kingdom that fell to the Assyrians centuries earlier. Yet this much is clear in any language: God is the main character in the family, the principal speaker and interpreter of events. Everything we learn about this family happens from God's point of view. God is the central character because the people strongly doubt God's motives and power in the wake of the disaster.

Love's Good Old Days (2:1-3)

The first poem dares to imagine God's inner life in first person speech:

> "I remember the loving kindness of your youth, your love as a bride,
> how you followed me in the wilderness, in a land not sown" (2:2).[8]

With nostalgic longing, God remembers the honeymoon with his young bride. He yearns for bygone days when his wife followed him lovingly in the wilderness, like the Hebrew slaves when they escaped into the dessert. But in an abrupt switch of attention and with similar nostalgia, God also remembers a golden time when male Israel was "holy to the Lord, the first fruits of the harvest" (2:3).

Right at the beginning, then, the opening poem gives us a key for reading what follows. Wife Judah and male Israel are one national entity, the same people spoken about as male and female characters, both greatly beloved by God and set aside for God alone. By placing the two figures next to one another, the poem invites us to blend them into one reality, a point God confirms later in the drama (3:20). Surely, the poem asserts, God has loved this whole people from of old the way a husband loves his wife, even if disaster now eclipses that love. For victims of the nation's collapse, God's desire for relationships of the past sets out the pressing dilemma of their existence: What happened to that relationship? Is it over? Is God's family to disappear?

Male Israel Gone Wrong (2:4-16)

Divine longing turns into accusation. "What injustice did your ancestors find in me that they went far away from me?" (2:5). Despite happy beginnings, this family has betrayed God for a long time. Israel abandoned God to pursue "worthless things and become worthless themselves." No matter how much good God did for him—freeing him from slavery in Egypt, leading him through the wilderness, bringing him to the promised land—he still turns away and follows other gods, called *ba'als*, an ancient Semitic term that means lords or husbands (2:6-7).

With confused hurt, God laments Israel's infidelity: "They have forsaken me, fountain of living waters . . . and substituted for me cracked cisterns . . . that cannot hold water" (2:13). Water—living non-stagnant water—is essential for life in a desert land like Israel.[9] To preserve it, people dug cisterns, but suicidal Israel abandons life-sustaining water for leaky, useless holes in the ground, that is, the ba'als.

Wife Judah Gone Wrong (2:17-25)

When God turns attention back to his wife, the charges are familiar (2:17-25). Like male Israel, she too has forsaken God and turned to others, but now allegations explode in heightened acrimony. Rather than abandoning living water for empty cisterns, she abandons him for other lovers and for acting lewdly, deviantly: "On every high hill and under every green tree, you sprawled and played the whore" (2:20).

Wife Judah's sins resemble the sins of male Israel. Both characters abandon life for death, but she has betrayed her husband, her most intimate companion, violated the sacred bond of marriage, and acted against taboos and laws of the society. Like a perverted, sex-crazed female, like a camel or "wild ass in heat sniffing the wind" (2:23-24),[10] she has turned everything upside down. And considering all God has done for her, her betrayal is unimaginable (2:21).

Why? (2:26-32)

The third scene returns to male Israel, but now specific groups of people come under attack to remind us that relations in this family are about national realities. God blames rulers, kings, officials, priests, and prophets for idolatry. Like a wounded lover in a country western song, God asks "Why do you complain about me?" (2:29). "Have I been a wilderness to Israel or a land of thick darkness? (2:31). No, this mess is not God's fault, he insists because, "My people have forgotten me" (2:32).

The Divorce (2:33—3:5)

This first act of the family drama closes with the stinging pain of divorce. God's wife has compounded her sins by denying them and thinks of nothing but finding lovers. Then, in the decisive moment for this dysfunctional family, God divorces her, quoting a law that forbids reunion by a divorced couple. "If a man divorces his wife and she goes from him and becomes the wife of another, will he return to her?" (Jer 3:1; cf. Deut 24:1-4). Whatever the law's purpose may have been,[11] God cannot take his wife back after she plays "the whore with many lovers." Yet her furious husband vacillates, uncertain about what to do. Would she "return to him"? he wonders. Their relationship hangs on a thread, but she does not reply.

Divorce proves a telling way to speak of disaster; God cut Judah out of his household because of national infidelity. This is why Babylon was able to triumph, and that triumph must have seemed like a mighty severing of divine-human relationship. But in another complication of the literature, God quotes one who calls him "father," suggesting that the voice belongs to a daughter. I think this quote belongs to his wife, because she speaks nostalgically of their former life together. "My father, you are the husband (or "intimate") of my youth" (3:4).[12]

Poetry need not follow the logic of family relations, and in a patriarchal household, language may slide around among terms of affection and subordination. Here even the gender of nations is fluid.[13] Often cities are called daughter in the ancient world, and Jerusalem is named the Daughter of Zion. Whatever family relationships are implied here, though, the woman begs God to relent, but it is too late. Judah is a cast-off woman.

Making Language

By now, it may be obvious that Jeremiah's drama requires reading on several levels at once. The household drama avoids factual description of Judah's shattered world and instead lifts historical events into the life of one family whose plight interprets the disaster. Although the drama's plot elements are simple and recognizable—betrayed spouse, adulterous spouse, and, soon, bereft children—the text is about a nation's turbulent present, as perilous as that of a disposable wife. God is brokenhearted about it, but the disaster happened because the people have brought disaster upon themselves.

Act Two: Aftermath of Divorce (3:6-25)

The second act shifts the spotlight from the estranged couple to the divorce's consequences for the whole family.[14] Across three scenes, God complains to his friend Jeremiah (3:6-10), sends the prophet to invite wife and children back to him (3:11-20), and the children plead to rejoin their father (3:21-25).

The Husband and His Confidant (3:6-10)

The distraught husband unburdens himself to his confidant Jeremiah and reveals startling news. God once had a previous wife, Israel. He divorced her, too, because she also became an adulterer! In this metaphoric world, female Israel stands for the northern kingdom, Judah's sister nation, conquered by Assyria one hundred and fifty years earlier. She has not returned to her husband either, but God announces that wife Judah is even worse because she learned nothing from the nation's past.

God's complaints about his wives weave Judah's present cataclysm into its larger national story and the history of the northern kingdom. This means that the fall of Judah appears no longer as a complete anomaly. It is not a set of events separate from the larger life of the nation nor unique among destructive events. The two devastating historical disasters become one continuous narrative in an interpretive reframing of events and part of the story of the whole people of Israel. When survivors are able to reframe disaster in such a way, they usually have moved deeply into the process of recovery.[15] But the family story is not over.

Invitations to Wife and Children (3:10-13)

" 'Return, faithless Israel,' says the Lord, 'I will not look on you in anger for I am merciful, I will not be angry forever' " (3:12). The Hebrew word for "return" (*šûb*) also means to "repent," to "turn around," to return to God. To reunite with her husband, God's wife must undergo a "conversion" from her faithless ways. But God's invitation flies in the face of cultural expectations.[16] What kind of husband in the ancient world would be willing to violate the law and take her back?

The invitation itself is the main surprise, the moment of disclosure in the drama, not because it contains new information about God, but because it opens a distant horizon toward a future that rests in divine mercy. I will not look in anger, I will not be angry forever for I am merciful. If there is hope for this broken family, it rests here.

But no wife replies to this invitation. The wives' silence enacts the circumstances of Jeremiah's audience. The northern kingdom has disappeared from history and Judah, too, is on its deathbed. The wives are no longer able to respond.

When God sends Jeremiah to persuade his first wife to return, he divulges another surprise. There are children in this family. They signify the next generation, survivors of the disaster, Jeremiah's readers written into the book, and they are invited to resume life with God. Of God's family, only children remain, the next generation, the book's audience, the remnant of the disaster who must deal with its consequences. The drama sets before them a tentative, precarious future.[17]

The Father Invites the Children to Return (3:14-25)

Despite the betrayal in this household, God still desires a future with the children, a future that requires only that they, too, take responsibility for the rupture. In the community-oriented culture of ancient Judah, no one in the extended family is exempt; no one is innocent. God repeats the invitation: "Return, faithless children" (3:14).[18] For the family to survive, they must enact their return to the father.

To lure the children home, God promises to renew the world. There will be a new government by shepherds (kings) who will follow God's "own heart" and feed them "with knowledge and understanding" (3:15). But before the children accept this invitation, God utters an aside to readers that brings threads of the drama together (3:19-20). One last time, God reminds his wife of his love and how he wanted to give her everything, but she ruined it. "As a faithless wife leaves her husband, so you have been faithless to me, O house of Israel" (3:20). Male and female figures are one people. All along, the text has been telling the nation, and especially the men, that they are just like a whoring wife.[19] God is not the initiator of the troubles. Responsibility for the catastrophe falls upon them.

A Reunion Ceremony (3:21—4:4)

The children accept the invitation, and for the first time in the family drama, someone other than God speaks. In stylized language of liturgy, the children announce their desire to return and model behavior readers should follow to restore right relationship with God.[20] The liturgy:

They march home in procession:

"Here we come to you; for you are the Lord our God" (3:22b).

They confess their idolatry:

"Truly the hills are a delusion, the orgies on the mountains."

They declare their praise:

"Truly in the Lord our God is the salvation of Israel" (3:23).

They lament their losses in the disaster:

This "shameful thing has devoured all for which our ancestors had labored, their flocks and their herds, their sons and their daughters" (3:24).

They prostrate themselves and confess their guilt:

"We have not obeyed the voice of God" (3:25).

The children's liturgy shows the audience, descendants of the first victims, how to enact their return to God. They must return to God with their whole hearts, repent together in public worship. They are to assemble, speak together words of praise and sorrow, enact with their bodies, and sing with their voices their homecoming to God.

Dramatic Language

Action Language

Liturgical language is action language. It coaxes people reduced to passivity by traumatic disruptions to move back together in a common effort.[21] Liturgies are public events that require people to gather, to use gestures and speech in an embodied enactment of a new relationship with God. They provide patterned forms of praying and create a sense of order. They offer language to heal "ruptures in the cultural system of knowing" and promote cultural continuity by evoking prayers of the past.[22] "They piece together the traditions," retrieving, reclaiming, reassembling them to make meaning in the present.[23]

Rituals draw people back to one another from isolating pain and severed bonds that follow disaster. They stir people to life, require exertion and participation, and serve as an antidote to victimhood and helplessness. Yet in these chapters, the children's ritual language does not enact reconciliation because God fails to respond. The invitation remains only a possibility, a hope, an introductory appeal of the book to its readers.

Conditions

For victims of this disaster, the call to enact a renewed relationship with God is premature. There are too many wounds still to heal, explanations to be found, God to be rediscovered and trusted again. But the liturgy opens the possibility of family renewal and national survival. The drama anticipates reunion, but God first sets out conditions echoing the children's liturgy, as if it had not yet happened (4:1-4). The people must take an oath of loyalty, "remove abominations," and acknowledge that "nations shall be blessed by him and by him they shall boast" (4:1-2). And they must "remove the foreskins of their heart" (4:4), that is, perform a symbolic circumcision upon their hearts.[24]

These conditions for reunion add up to one thing—that victims of disaster pledge absolute loyalty to God in public worship. Only all-consuming dedication will secure their future. The choice to live or to die is theirs.

How the Family Drama Helps

God's broken household helps because it finds words for the disaster, simplifies its causes, creates a miniature version of a monstrous reality, and thins it down to approachable segments of pain. Jeremiah's family tells the truth sideways, at a slant, and conveys the nation's suffering more fully than any straight historical report could possibly do. Attending to it, readers can find shadows of their own broken lives in a poetic world that is both alike and different from their experiences.

God Language

The household drama is looking for a way to speak of God when God has utterly failed them, when divine protection has disappeared. Through it survivors of disaster learn what they cannot see. They cannot see that God has been with them all along, sad and disturbed, angry and frustrated through the entire ordeal. They cannot see that God is hurt and longs for them with the love of a husband who yearns for his beloved spouse and wants to be a father to the children. They cannot see that God is wrenched apart by this breakup and burns with loving desire for them. And they learn in this drama that God is not a powerless, defeated deity but the governor of the world and in control of the overwhelming events of history.

Keeping God Alive

The work of this drama, above all else, is to defend God, to insist that God is active in the universe and has been active throughout the disaster and is so even now in the destruction. The drama pushes aside every matter of survival except for the one at the core of Judah's identity, its relationship with the divine. With its emotional, intimate language, it tries to reawaken the community's willingness to trust God again.

Interpreters call the theology of these chapters a "theodicy," a defense of the justice of God. Because disasters nearly always destroy faith, God surely needs defense. This is why the household drama insists that God is not powerless and not absent, that God neither wanted the divorce nor wished to follow through with it. Only with immense regret and anger did God cast Judah out. In accord with the law, God proceeded with the divorce and behaved as might any cuckolded spouse in the ancient world, although with more restraint, since adultery could be punished by execution.[25] God does not take his wife's life or stone her. God wants her back and the children as well. From the beginning God loved them, continues to love them, and wants them back.

Language of Human Responsibility

But when the drama defends God, it places responsibility for the disaster upon victims. For many modern western readers, this is a big problem on two counts, as my former students rightly insisted. First, the husband is domineering, the wife a nymphomaniac, and relations between them miserable.[26] No one today who views women as people with dignity equal to men can embrace its gender views, as abundant feminist criticism has made transparently clear.[27] And when some readers fail to grasp the poetic nature of the text and treat it and others like it as models of the moral life, the same readers reinforce notions of male supremacy, rooted in an angry male deity. But because Jeremiah is a product of its culture, it would be a surpassing marvel were it to have escaped limitations regarding relations between men and women.

A second problem of this theology and no less important is its assignment of sole responsibility for the disaster upon its victims. The claim that Judah's sin caused the disaster heaps more wounds upon the already downtrodden survivors, and it oversimplifies causes of historical cataclysm. Because this theology of human responsibility is present in many texts of Jeremiah, I will return to it often, but here I want to defend it as a brilliant survival strategy.

Traumatic Language

Rhetoric of Responsibility and Survival

Trauma and disaster studies make clear that when lives have been chopped down by sudden and devastating violence, victims have to find an explanation. To resume life, they need to know why. "Why did this happen to us? Who is to blame?" These are ever-present questions for survivors of disastrous events from the tsunami in Southeast Asia, Darfur, the Gulf Coast oil spill, Iraq, Afghanistan, Israel/Palestine, 9/11, Haiti, and many other recent communal and personal catastrophes. If the world is ever again to be trustworthy, victims need interpretation. For their lives to rest on the most minimal order, they must have meaning, interpretation, explanation, even if the explanation is ephemeral, inadequate, partial, or outright wrong. Explanation puts order back in the world.

When Jeremiah places responsibility upon the people of Judah for the nation's collapse, he helps them survive because he finds cause and effect in a world that has come unhinged. When he says God is not to blame but you are, he makes God a victim and puts readers on God's side for God is broken-hearted and feels bereft. He claims without qualification that God is still in charge of the world; God controls events and governs justly. But perhaps even more important and more surprising, when he places responsibility upon the people, he gives people a sense of control.[28] If they caused the catastrophe, if they know what they did to bring it about, that means they may be able to get out of it and perhaps even prevent similar catastrophes from happening in the future. They gain a sense of control.

Yet Jeremiah's rhetoric of human responsibility is not satisfactory to me. It explains the disaster only partially, questionably, and unsteadily. Human sinfulness and betrayal surely contribute to and amplify disasters, but rarely do they fully explain them for modern western readers. Charges by outsiders that sinful people caused the tragedies in New Orleans and New York and Haiti, for example, do not satisfy as historical explanation because they overlook so many other factors. Jeremiah's household drama overlooks the aggrandizing greed of Babylon, the economic weakening of Judah, the failure of Judah's leadership, the failure of allies to come to their aid, and many other matters. Fortunately, this "rhetoric of responsibility," as I call the book's blaming speech, is only one of many explanations of the disaster in Jeremiah, each of which is a provisional interpretation, an effort to make meaning.

Despite its misogyny and blaming rhetoric, Jeremiah's household helps keep faith alive. To reject it because it does not fit modern western sensibilities seems to me a failure of historical imagination. A world that appears utterly meaningless here receives provisional meaning, some semblance of order in a universe gone amuck.

Dead Language Reborn

Jeremiah does not invent this disturbed household. If he did, his words would probably not have survived. Instead, the book revives the broken family of Hosea (Hos 1–3). It revitalizes Hosea's wrecked household as a way to speak about the nation's collapse. The familiarity of the story of this discordant family is critical for survivors of disaster in search of a lost identity. Interpretations must necessarily retain key elements of the past while they also create something new from them. Studying resilience among refugee women, Elzbieta M. Gozdziak calls this process "a dynamic relationship of custom and innovation."[29] This means

Jeremiah cannot start from scratch and enable the people to remain Judeans. Only a vision rooted in their old traditions yet also making them new can maintain continuity with their past and direct them toward the future. This process is the work of art and why spiritual recovery is the work of poets, artists, preachers, musicians, and storytellers.[30]

Introductory Language

Jeremiah's family drama looks to the future tentatively, conditionally. The readers themselves have to decide whether or not to resume family life with God. If they do not return wholeheartedly, divine wrath will go forth like unquenchable fire (4:4). But for the book's audience, the wrath of God has already burned up the world; disaster has already befallen them. The question now is whether that destruction will become total.

Before they can begin to imagine life in the future, they have a long, arduous process ahead of them. Recovery, of course, does not occur in chronological order nor in any order at all. Victims have to come to terms over and over again with catastrophe, to find language for the terrors, to re-enter and face fragmented memories, to overcome numbness, to grieve deeply, to find stories to guide them through the void. Jeremiah's poetry is not predictive of future calamity nor is it simply an historical record of past calamity. It is a potent agent of change. It acts upon the world by creating vital, explosive speech that both reveals and heals wounds.

Fragmented Memories of Trauma

The War Poems

JEREMIAH 4:5—6:30; 8:16-17; 10:17-22; 13:20-27

Memories of violence have a life of their own. They overtake people's minds, uproot former securities, and leave them anchorless. Because violent memories splinter into frozen moments of horror, they can cause what theologian Serene Jones refers to as a "cognitive breakdown."[1] Merely bringing to mind past violence does not heal traumatic memories. Recalling the violence is more likely to revivify memories as if the violence were still happening.[2] Nor can a literal depiction of frightful memories automatically remove their poison. To reduce terrors, victims of traumatic violence have to extract their toxic power slowly and indirectly. Then they have to assimilate violent events into the larger flow of their lives.

According to psychologists Paul Antze and Michael Lambek, trauma sufferers are condemned to reenact their memories of violence until they begin the work of interpretation.[3] Jeremiah is a work of interpretation from beginning to end. It is art more than history, or better, art intervening in history.

Interpreting to Survive

To interpret disaster means to generate new ways of seeing the past and to create language to speak about the unspeakable. Interpreters have to search for ways to assimilate overwhelming experience into a comprehensive narrative, into a story that brings the violence into the stream of life rather than leaving it as an unassimilated anomaly, as an incomprehensible disruption. Survivors of disaster can detoxify fractured memories of violence when they integrate them into a larger world of meaning, when they reframe them.

Although such interpretive processes may not destroy raging ghosts of the past, they can gradually deprive them of their power. Interpretation can begin to heal horrible memories when it expresses them in terms similar enough to the violence to activate the past yet incompatible enough to change it. This means approaching violent memories in tolerable doses and as if at a slant.[4]

Pastoral counselor Debora Samuelson illustrates this process of interpreting and integrating traumatic memories in her own work.[5] Samuelson might ask her clients to tell about disturbing events by imagining them from far away, as if from a helicopter looking down at the scene, or she may invite them to tell the events in pieces, such as recalling only the moments that led up to the trauma, or to think about how to tell it as if they witnessed only a small part of it. These and other counseling strategies honor memories by entering them from a different angle, cutting them into more manageable pieces, and revisiting them in piecemeal fashion or at a slight distance to reduce their overwhelming power. But ultimately, the sign that fractured memories of violence are beginning to heal is that people are integrating them into their life stories or religious frameworks. The symbolic world of Jeremiah's war poems works upon readers in a similar fashion.

War Poems as Memory-Makers

We do not know if many people in Jeremiah's audience were individually traumatized, nor if they carried haunting memories of the disaster, nor for how many generations the disaster remained an unassimilated disruption of their world. But viewed through the prism of trauma and disaster studies, the book itself testifies to colossal violence inflicted on the nation.[6] With few exceptions, however, modern interpreters of Jeremiah have accepted poetry of battle as predictions of future disaster from the prophet's mouth, preserved because they came true.[7] I am skeptical that we can know which words were Jeremiah's or when he proclaimed them, but for readers of the book the disaster has happened. His poems about warfare remember, express, and reframe the nation's collective, violent past.

Fractured Memories of War (Jer 4:5—6:30)

I call the cluster of poems found primarily in Jer 4:5—6:30 (and also in 8:16-17; 10:17-22; 13:20-27) "war poems," because war imagery dominates them. Other kinds of imagery interrupt the war in 4:5—6:30, but when they do they comment on the war, blame someone for it, or explain why it happened. War in these passages is no ordinary battle. It is a cosmic event in which an ethereal enemy, called "the foe from the north" (or sometimes "evil from the north"),[8] comes closer and closer to invading the nation, portrayed as a woman. Language of siege gives the poems a loose, arcing coherence in a steady heightening of terror that culminates in the woman's rape (13:20-27). Jeremiah's war poems do not merely recall war memories; they create them afresh in a symbolic universe.

Mythic Warfare

The war poems are dramatic theater in which scenes switch around abruptly like fragmented memories of violence.[9] In them, battles come to life momentarily only to be interrupted by a family dispute. Characters take center stage, recede to the background, then reappear. The war is mythic because it does not occur on a human plane.[10] Its combatants are not historical nations but symbolic ones, metaphorical warriors engaged in a cosmic battle.[11] The "foe from the north," who originates in ancient Near Eastern mythology, is an archetypal enemy and a code name for the Babylonian army.[12] He is an alien, invading force—superhuman, unstoppable, and beyond resistance—who attacks and subdues a city-woman, Judah/Jerusalem. The battle between them is gravely uneven.[13]

The woman, known variously as "Daughter of Zion" or "Daughter of Judah,"[14] is God's beloved wife whom we have already met in the drama of the broken household (2:1—4:4). Interspersed with military attacks, that sad family story continues here (4:18, 30-31; 5:7-10; 6:1-8; 13:20-27).[15] Warfare and marriage—two metaphoric arenas—tell about the same disaster on a cosmic scale and a domestic one. Going back and forth between battle and family helps reduce the terrors of memory, breaks the war into small glimpses, and creates two symbolic language worlds to express the catastrophe.

The War Begins (4:5-8)

The first war poem announces impending attack. Jeremiah commands the people to run for shelter because an unnamed invader is about to pounce like a lion upon its prey.

> Declare in Judah and proclaim in Jerusalem and say:
> Blow the trumpet through the land;
> Shout aloud and say,
> "Gather together, and let us go
> Into the fortified cities!"
> Raise a standard toward Zion,
> Flee for safety, do not delay,
> For I am bringing disaster[16] from the north,
> And a great breaking.

A lion has gone up from its thicket,
A destroyer of nations has set out;
He has gone from his place
To make your land a waste;
Your cities will be ruins
Without inhabitant. (4:5-7)

Using only a few details of sight and sound, the poem carries readers into the terrifying moments before assault by means of a poetic device known as "synecdoche," small glimpses of battle that evoke the whole thing and bring memories to the fore. The audience knows that the trumpet blast musters troops and that the raising of standards gathers horses and riders to strike.

Who Caused the Catastrophe? (4:9-11)

Responsibility for the disaster changes hands frequently in Jeremiah. "Why did this happen to us? "Whose fault is it?" Holding someone accountable for disaster is an interpretive task, a necessary effort to find explanation, to discover cause and effect, and to enable understanding of the catastrophe to emerge.

The war poems place responsibility on the Daughter of Zion, her children, and on all the people, but prose verses also single out community leaders for blame (4:9-10). "Courage shall fail the king" and officials, priests, and prophets (4:9). "Astounded" and probably inept, political and religious leaders face the realization that their secure world is faltering.[17] But Jeremiah shifts the spotlight of blame again, this time onto God. "Then I said, 'Ah, Lord God, how you have utterly deceived this people, saying, "It will be well with you," even while the sword is at the throat'" (4:10).[18] Immediately, God deflects responsibility back to the community; the disaster is a judgment against them (4:11).

Typical of interpretations after disaster, conflicts emerge here full-throttle. Leaders failed; God failed. It is God's fault; it is our fault; it is everybody's fault. There is no resolution, no single cause, only complex distribution of responsibility.[19] These verses complicate cause and effect the way the ruinous floods in New Orleans and Hurricane Katrina along the coast produced multiple causes and culprits. The very act of seeking out responsible parties for disaster is an inevitable human activity, a necessary strategy of survival. It gives reasons for events, reins them into palatable size, and finds cause and effect in a quagmire of fear and chaos. Blaming is a search for justice and order in the universe when all signs of justice and order have vanished from view.

Two Wars (4:13-22)

Jeremiah's war poems are really about two wars, cosmic and familial. The next poem plunges readers back into battle, transposed again to a mythic world. As the foe and his vast military machine approach on the horizon, the people cry out in fright, "Look, he comes up like clouds," advancing with chariots "like the whirlwind," with horses "swifter than eagles." In despair, the people cry, "Woe to us for we are ruined!" (4:13).

But with increasing restlessness, the poetry changes gears yet again, shifting attention away from the enemy to a conversation between God and his divorced wife (4:18).[20] The effect of this jump into family quarrels is to lessen the terrors of battle momentarily and to set events in what should be, but is not, a less terrifying place. We can imagine the divine husband shouting at his wife to "wash her heart clean" because disaster may still be averted. "How long will your evil schemes lodge within you?" (4:14), he demands. "Your ways and your doings have brought this upon you!" (4:18). Her evil is so pervasive, it has taken up residence in her being.

Born from historical events, domains of family and battle illuminate each other in the intermingling languages of the war poems (4:19-20). The family scenes do not insulate from war; they enact it. As the army advances, the wife collapses: "My anguish, my anguish! I writhe in pain!" (4:17). She hears the trumpet, watching powerlessly as "disaster overtakes disaster" and her "tents are destroyed." Often the Bible depicts Judah and Zion living in a tent, the fragile and defenseless dwelling of a desert people.[21] From this precarious lodging she cries, "How long must I see the standard and hear the sound of the trumpet?" (4:21). Her scolding husband "explains" why this is happening: my people "do not know me" (4:22).[22] They have refused intimacy with God.

Creation Undone (4:23-28)

The subject appears to change again in the next poem, but instead, language of creation revisits memories of war (4:23-28). The poem "uncreates" the world[23] as it reverses the work of God completed during the seven days of creation (Gen 1:1—2:4a). In the first chapter of Genesis, God says, "Let there be light," let there be birds and beasts, let there be humans, and that divine word turns "waste and void" (*tohu wabohu*, Gen 1:2) into light and life.

In Jeremiah's poem, the opposite happens. Like a film played in reverse, elements of the world disappear one by one until chaos returns:

> I looked to the earth and, behold, waste and void and to the heavens and there was no light.
> I looked to the mountains and, behold, quaking and all the hills were shaking.
> I looked and, behold, there was no human and all the birds of the heavens had fled.

> I looked and, behold, the fruited plain of the wilderness and all the cities
> were in ruins before YHWH, before his hot anger (Jer 4:23-26, my
> translation).

Jeremiah's looking creates a staccato rhythm of shock. He "looked" and looked and looked, stunned and powerless, and "behold" the earth returned to "waste and void" (4:23; see Gen 1:2). Jeremiah himself is a helpless witness of disaster, a horrified onlooker, powerless and traumatized before the unfolding cataclysm as the earth turned into a lunar surface and a bombed-out landscape. And God's word is still the active agent, but now it "uncreates" the world, "for I have spoken" (4:28).

Even as Jeremiah's poem unravels the first story of creation, it manufactures a strange continuity with it by translating violent memories into the familiar terms of Judah's sacred story. It reverses Genesis' steady march toward lush abundance and harmonious goodness and turns it into a nightmare of terror. The world empties of creatures, cities, and human culture. Birds flee, desert returns, life disappears in the deathly stillness after battle. Old language, reappropriated, now expresses shock at the destruction wrought by Babylon and reconnects survivors with their larger life.

Attack and Its Causes

Scenes of war return to the foreground in the next poem as people frantically scatter before horsemen and archers (4:29-31). Waves of refugees escape the city, and the unlucky search for safety among thickets and rocks. But the poetry turns abruptly from the cosmic to the microcosmic as husband again berates wife:

> What do you mean, O desolate one,
> What do you mean that you dress in crimson,
> That you deck yourself with ornaments of gold
> and enlarge your eyes with paint? (4:30).

Still a flamboyant whore, God's wife cries out like "woman in labor," but her pains announce death, not new life.

Dizzying Imagery (5:1-13)

Jeremiah's war poems make acrobatic leaps from scenes of cosmic battle to family battle, to the destruction of a vineyard (5:10; 6:9) to the scouring of the city in search of one innocent person (5:1-7). The literary term for this metaphoric mixing is "parataxis," that is, the setting of different materials next to each other without clues as to how they fit together. This literary device requires readers to engage actively to make sense of the literature. As frightening as these poems of invasion are, the frequent scene switches benefit readers by placing them in the thick of battle only briefly and intermittently. Exposure to violence occurs in small doses. Family disputes, the uncreation of the world, and interrupting prose comments are unsettling and confusing, yet they reduce contact with memories of war itself, even as they mimic war's randomness. And they create multiple ways to speak of violent memories at a slant.

The Foe Devours (5:15-17)

The prophet announces the foe's approach "from far away." He is terrifying and enduring, ancient and unintelligible (5:15). Although "all of them are mighty warriors," the attacking hordes form a single monster who consumes everything in its path.

> He will devour your harvest and your bread;
> he will devour[24] your sons and daughters;
> he will devour your sheep and cattle;
> he will devour your vines and your fig trees;
> he will shatter with a sword
> your fortified cities that you trust (5:17, my translation).

The devourer gobbles up children, sources of food, and strong, defended cities. With a giant maw, he ingests everything that sustains human life.

God's War against a Woman (6:1-30)

Cosmic and domestic realms merge again explicitly in chapter 6. As God longs for his once lovely wife (6:2-3), trumpet blasts and warning signals threaten from the north (6:1). Enemy voices shout commands in preparation for attack, and the shouts engulf the people's words like an army surrounding a city:

The Foe:	"Prepare war against her; up, and let us attack at noon!"
The People:	"Woe to us for the day declines and the shadows of evening lengthen!"
The Foe:	"Up, and let us attack by night, and destroy her palaces!" (6:4-5).

But this army is not self-directed; it acts under orders of the "Lord of Hosts,"[25] who designs the military strategy and even pumps up the troops with motivations for the attack.

> "Cut down her trees; cast up a siege ramp against Jerusalem."
> This is the city that must be punished;
> there is nothing but oppression within her (6:6).

The angry commander husband pours his wrath over the land, destroying everything: "the children in the street," young men, husbands and wives, the old and the elderly, houses, fields, and wives (6:11-12). Husband and foe together sweep away Judah's future.

> See, a people is coming from the land of the north,
> a great nation is stirring from the farthest parts of the earth.
> They grasp the bow and the javelin,
> They are cruel and have no mercy,
> and their sound is like the roaring of the sea;
> against you, O Daughter of Zion (6:22-23).

Warriors with fierce weapons and merciless cruelty, ferocious as wild seas, have one target; she is the one whom God loves.

The Rape (13:20-27)

Love turns to horror in a further blending of battlefield and household. God commands the Daughter of Zion: "Lift up your eyes and see those who come from the north" (13:20). When she wants to know why, the answer is clear. "It is for the greatness of your iniquity that your skirts are lifted up and you are violated" (13:22). The "lifting of skirts" is probably euphemistic speech for rape, but the parallel clause, "you are violated," makes rape certain.[26] The poem leaves the violator unnamed in verse 22 but reveals his identity later: "I myself will strip off your skirts over your face" (13:25-26, my translation).[27] God rapes her; Judah is destroyed.

The Language of Rape

God's rape of Zion in Jeremiah's war poem is appalling and unbearable speech. Female rape is a familiar metaphor for war in the Old Testament and a common weapon of war throughout history. Rape brutalizes in the most intimate of ways. A stronger one subdues a weaker one, hurts her, shames and humiliates her,[28] and turns her into a bleeding victim, gasping for life.[29] Jeremiah's rape language is horrendous because it translates military attack into the violation of a woman and because it portrays God as the rapist.

Appalling Language

Some interpreters think language of rape is an utterly outrageous way to speak about God, and for good reasons. Jeremiah's poems make women scapegoats for the nation's fall, sees sexual assault as suitable punishment by a husband, and locates hideous violence within God's own being. But trauma and disaster studies suggest a different way to understand the poetry. The fact that God's rape of Zion is outrageous, unbearable, and unspeakable is surely the point of the imagery. To be invaded by another country, to be victims of attack, occupation, and dislocation *is* outrageous, unbearable, and unspeakable. God's rape of Wife Judah tells the people's story and brings to speech the horror and harm of Babylonian assaults. Rape is a language for telling Judah's memories and its experience of God.

Rape as Language of Horror

Rape makes an apt language for invasion because it "reproduce(s) the difficulty of the world itself."[30] War is rape on a national scale. Rape conveys life-threatening violence, intrusive and painful physical penetration, traumatic powerlessness, and shameful humiliation of women, husbands, brothers, and sons.[31] God's rape of Jerusalem expresses the horrors Judah experienced as a society. It reveals aspects of the nation's destruction, now reduced to an attack on one vulnerable figure who embraces the whole. Rape is what happened to them. It is their collective history rendered symbolically, their fractured memories drawn into a narrative, into new speech for a speech-destroying disaster. Jeremiah's rape poem restores capacity to speak what cannot be spoken.

Violent God as Survival Strategy

Still, for many of us imagery in which God inflicts sexual violence seems beyond the theological pale, beyond the possibility of redemption as God-talk. To speak of God as a rapist says God is violent and condones male violence against women. Because this is true, the biblical text must be treated critically and condemned for its dangerous reinforcement of male supremacy and female victimhood today. But the reality that God's rape of Zion is a "text of terror"[32] is central to its purpose and, paradoxically, to its capacity to defend God. Defeat by Babylon meant for Judah, among other things, that God lost the war to superior deities, to the more powerful Marduk and his pantheon. Defeat meant that Judah's God is ineffectual and disappeared.

To portray God as Zion's rapist reverses the divine diminishment that follows in disaster's aftermath. It says that Judah's God is powerful, active, and present, lord of the world and not a defeated lesser being. To make God the active agent of Judah's humiliation is to insist that Babylonian deities have not triumphed, nor has ungoverned Fate propelled events. The language gives the invasions predictable causes that extend beyond the visible world. But of deeper importance, the language of rape describes and makes vivid the suffering of the community. To eradicate the language would be to deny the profound physical, emotional, and theological disruption and humiliation at the center of Judah's experience in this historical period.

Jeremiah's portrait of a punishing, raping God is a culturally potent conception that begins the work of interpretation, of uttering the unutterable, of making sense of the senseless. It is, like all portraits of the divine, a partial, provisional effort. It offers one way, among many in Jeremiah, to integrate the disaster into the long stream of the nation's existence.[33]

Provisional Thinking about God

Perhaps Jeremiah's poetry of a violent God is, as Robert Frost said about poetry, "a momentary stay against confusion."[34] The theological confusion the war poems attempt to "stay" is the confusion about God that usually follows disasters. The poems defend God from charges of arbitrary injustice and strive to persuade readers that God is innocent of cruelty, reluctant to punish, and required to do so because of Judah's sin. Jeremiah's violent, raping God is "momentary" because it is not Jeremiah's only word about God but one of many, none of which are final. The war poetry, like the rest of the book, characterizes God in complex, conflicting ways as both fierce military commander and troubled husband, as innocent of injustice and as a deceiver of the people (4:10). Perhaps Frost's description of how poetry functions suits all theological words about God. They are momentary glimpses, provisional, partial attempts to say what cannot ever be fully said but which stave off chaos for the moment.

Provisional Thinking about Human Responsibility

The character of God is not the only theological difficulty raised by the war poems. The other side of Jeremiah's defense of God is that responsibility for causing the cataclysm again falls upon Judah, whose sinfulness prompted God to act in first place. But simplistic theology does not explain disasters. Both national and personal catastrophes usually result from complex webs of cause and effect. Even when rulers are corrupt, leaders fail, and people contribute to their own downfall in any number of foolish, sinful ways, other historical forces contribute to disasters. Other historical causes of Judah's destruction, such as Babylonian greed and its brutal acquisition of smaller nations, do not appear in these passages because the war poems are concerned with only one thing: restoring Judah's relationship with God. Babylonian crimes appear only at the end of the book in the poems called Oracles against Babylon (chaps. 50–51).

Jeremiah's rhetoric of human responsibility is a survival strategy, another way to try to make sense of incoherent, inexplicable events. When the poetry lays responsibility for toppling Judah upon the people, it moves victims out of despairing passivity, erects an arbor of safety over them, and shows them how to avoid similar perils in the future.[35] Psychologists insist that taking responsibility for experiences of trauma and disaster can be helpful even when the analysis is inaccurate or wrong. Finding responsible parties projects order onto the universe and claims that behavior has predictable results.[36] This is, of course, far different than being blamed for disaster by outsiders.[37]

No matter how inadequate an explanation of historical events the war poems present to western sensibilities, they proclaim that life is not utterly random, God is not powerless, and survivors have some control over their world. They are still God's people, their pre-disaster traditions still name them as God's people, and the system itself has meaning.

Language of Memory

Jeremiah's war poems struggle with pain and march into its center. Rather than stripping away disaster's horrors, they translate them into symbolic dramas. Paradoxically, these poetic worlds of war and marriage depict horror and mute it at the same time. By reconstructing memories of invasion in imaginative space, they invent other ways to speak of it. They revise a vocabulary of experience and build common language to name what has happened, to give it shape, and to revisit it emotionally and spiritually. The literary creativity of the war poems brings the community into its own fragmented memories of a world unhinged and makes collective experience conscious and public. In them, survivors can recognize both what they have lost and what they have endured and survived. Perhaps they can begin to face their suffering.

Memory-Making as Moral Act

Jeremiah's war poetry not only evokes traumatic memories and brings them to the surface, it also builds memory. Memory is anything but a photographic record of experience. It is not a set of snapshots nor videos of the past, not a film-like recall of events, not an object of the past brought into the present.[38] It is, rather, a collection of conversations about the past like an "ever changing river or a roadway full of potholes, badly in need of repair and worked on day and night by revisionist crews in the mind."[39] Or in a poem by Alan Williamson, memories are "like a wave, that doesn't know it is at every moment different water."[40]

If memory is not a literal recounting nor even an actual retelling, then memory depends upon the words put to the memory itself.[41] To remember is to tell stories, to build identity, to get through life; it is a moral practice that reconstitutes reality. This means that rather than a careless collection of poetic pieces representing Jeremiah's earliest spoken words, the war poems are highly interpreted portrayals of events. It is this poetic world itself that creates continuity in Israel's narrative memory, its traditional story, and gives language to people whose memories have made them mute.[42]

The war poems give little hope for a reconstituted life. Instead, they enact the breakdown of the culture and offer language to tell it. They guide victims into the dark terrors of their fractured memories of violence, requiring them to process the war in bits and pieces, slowly, in small exposures. They relive Babylonian assaults in a controlled fashion, in a world apart from their own, in cosmic space. And even the poetry's assertions that Jeremiah predicted the cataclysm in advance, that he saw it coming, affirms a hidden order in the universe, an order governed by God for whom he speaks, an order that belies the mad randomness threatening the nation. The war poems retell the war as a cosmic battle so that it will one day no longer be the fire-breathing horror that engulfs everything.

6

If Only Tears Were Possible

The Weeping Poems

JEREMIAH 8:22—9:11

In the midst of disasters, victims need food, shelter, and physical safety before any other form of comfort. Only later, when life has regained some semblance of stability, do less physical needs come to the fore for attention.[1] Among these is a common response to trauma known as "psychic numbing." Robert Jay Lifton, who coined the term, says it "has to do with exclusion, the exclusion feeling."[2] In the face of terrible violence, people become insensitive to death. "If I feel nothing, then death is not taking place."[3]

Numbed Spirits

Traumatic suffering turns off feeling, depletes the body, and deadens the spirit. A state of shock automatically locks up mind and emotion, knowing and affect. This numbing is an automatic protective measure that isolates and protects people during attack. Observed among survivors of violent events, such as abuse, rape, torture, warfare, and child abuse,[4] the turning off of feelings is a healthy adaptive strategy, an involuntary defense mechanism that allows people to live through unbearable pain. In another study, Lifton and Kai Erickson report that in "even minor disasters the mind becomes immobilized, if only for a moment."[5] Survivors emerge from the debris "of every catastrophe for which we have records" with the sense that they are "naked and alone . . . in a terrifying wilderness of ruins." Under some drastic situations, "immobilization may reach the point where the psyche is no longer connected to its own past."[6]

Perhaps more familiar experiences of depression or, theologically speaking, of despair, can offer a pale connection to numbness following trauma.[7] Lack of interest in life, exhaustion, and deadening hopelessness can inhabit one's spirit indefinitely, and death appears to be a permanent companion.

Becoming Human Again

Psychic numbing afflicts Jeremiah's audience.[8] How else to explain the tears and laments that move through the book, the abundance of which distinguishes it from other prophetic literature? If disasters turn people's hearts to stone, if trauma drains away emotions and creates a "dam of silence,"[9] then acts of grieving have the potential to reverse the dehumanizing process. Grieving practices can help restore people's humanity by opening them up to a whole range of emotions.[10] They can begin to melt the icy despair that cuts them off from their own spirits and from knowledge of divine presence. Under such circumstances, grieving is not simply something to be desired; it is necessary for human flourishing.

To become thinking, feeling humans again requires the capacity to confront pain and to mourn loss. Grieving is not an activity for the faint-hearted but a fearsome enterprise that may take generations to complete. Yet to look into the heart of overwhelming loss and to mourn them are the very things psychic numbing inhibits. To be able to grieve requires access to emotion, but disasters bury feeling.[11]

Weeping Poems

It is not by accident, then, that Jeremiah is often called "the weeping prophet." Tears saturate the book and cascades of sorrow envelop the prophet, the people, God, the land and even the animals. A cluster of poems that I call the "weeping poems" gives forceful and eloquent expression to grief in the long process of recovery (8:22—9:11, Eng., and 6:26).[12] In these passages, lamenting, grieving voices heard earlier in the book (3:21; 4:19; 6:26; 7:29) erupt full-throttle. Within the book's narrative world, the grief in these poems is anticipatory, stirred up before the disaster to dramatize its coming destructiveness. But for the book's readers, the weeping poems work to bring on sorrow and loss, as if the poems themselves were mourning women, come to awaken the grief of the bereaved.

Traditional Mourning Customs

To encourage mourning, Jeremiah draws on customs from the cultural world of Israel and its neighbors.[13] In traditional societies, mourning rites can give structure to sorrow and become a "poultice for . . . sores."[14] Perhaps they are the "balm of Gilead" that is supposed to heal the nation (8:22).

By contrast to ancient Israel, modern western culture is "ritually adrift, bereft of custom, symbol, metaphor, and meaningful liturgy or language," according to funeral director and writer Thomas Lynch. Whether Lynch is correct about us or not, he gives us a glimpse of the power of traditional rituals around death. The "ritual wheel . . . worked the space between the living and the dead . . . [and] made room for the good laugh, the good cry, and the power of faith brought to bear on the mystery of mortality."[15]

Israel's own mourning customs help people face death, express grief, and then begin to come back to life. They include earthy gestures, such as putting on sackcloth, rolling in ashes, tearing the hair, and throwing dust in the air. According to biblical scholar Saul Olyan, these practices cause pain and discomfort for mourners and this releases grief over much larger life disturbances.[16] The bereaved participate in death symbolically, lying in ashes and dressed in sackcloth for burial, as if they are dwelling among the community of the dead, temporarily joining their loved ones. It is precisely these customs that Jeremiah urges upon the Daughter of Zion in the first weeping poem.

Mourning for an Only Child (6:26)

When Jeremiah commands Zion to perform mourning rituals, he gives grieving the status of other prophetic commands, like "repent," "obey," and "do justice."

> O Daughter of my people, gird on sackcloth and roll in ashes.
> Make mourning as for an only child, most bitter wailing,
> for suddenly the destroyer will come upon us (6:26, my translation).

Jerusalem, "the daughter of my people," should perform mourning rites and wail bitterly (see 7:29 and Job 2:12-13). Her grieving should be volatile, dramatic, and extreme. The loss of a child, of an only child, or of any child, is a grief beyond bearing, so intimate a devastation that it hardly can be taken in for its shock and loss. And that is exactly how Zion should grieve. But in this poem, the deceased is not a child; it is the Daughter of Zion herself for whom the destroyer comes. In the imaginative world of the poem, the loss lies in the future but mourning must begin now. Yet for the book's readers, death has already arrived.

A Benumbed God (8:18-9:3, Eng.)[17]

"The daughter of my people" is not the only one to grieve in the book. Resuming the role of broken-hearted husband, God also mourns in this poetic dialogue among sad and frightened voices as they express abandonment and despair.[18]

> 8:18   My cheerfulness is gone, grief is upon me,
>   my heart is sick.

8:19	Listen, the cry of the daughter of my people from far and wide in the land:	
	[Zion and people]	Is YHWH not in Zion? Is her king not in her?

Why have they provoked me to anger with images and with their foreign idols?

8:20	[People of Zion]	"The harvest has past, the summer is ended and we are not saved!"

8:21 For the shattering of the daughter of my people I am shattered, and I grow leaden in spirit, and dismay has seized me.

8:22 Is there no balm in Gilead?
Is there no physician there?
Why then has the health of the daughter of my people not been restored?

9:1 Who will make my head waters and my eyes a fountain of tears, that I might weep day and night for the slain of the daughter of my people?

9:2 Who will make me a traveler's lodge in the wilderness that I might abandon my people and go away from them?
For they are all adulterers, a band of traitors.

9:3 They bend their tongues like bows:
they have grown strong in the land for falsehood and not for truth; for they go from evil to evil and do not know me, says YHWH (my translation).[19]

Interpreters generally underplay the daring imaginative leaps of these verses, but I think it is God who wants to weep in this poem. And even more audaciously, the poem portrays God, like the people, as numb at one moment and deeply disturbed and angry the next. It is as if God has become unhinged like survivors of disaster. For some interpreters, a poem about a wounded God is too much of a challenge to ideas about the Almighty, but this is poetry making a way through disaster, not a definitive statement about God's being.

The speaker's identity is far from clear, and only a few scholars think God is the main voice in this beautiful poem.[20] A prominent feature of Jeremiah's poetry is its mix of voices, gliding in and out without announcing who they are.[21] This weeping poem contains several speakers. The main voice quotes both the daughter of my people and the people themselves. Those who prefer to understand Jeremiah's voice to be Jeremiah may be right.[22] The reason the decision matters, though, is that if it is God, then God exhibits the effects of trauma, just like the people. But even if it is Jeremiah, the prophet speaks on God's behalf.[23]

The reasons I think God is the implied speaker here are several. The primary user of the phrase "my people" is God in the book,[24] and the speaker of the phrase "the Daughter of my people"[25] also seems to be God.[26] And since God is clearly the one who asks, "Why have they provoked me to anger?" in the very next verse (v. 19), and because God laments, weeps, and grieves elsewhere, I think God wants to weep here too. J. J. M. Roberts adds strength to my argument by providing a long list of ancient Near Eastern deities who weep over the fall of their cities.[27] This means the poetic convention of a weeping god that had a place in the literature of Israel's neighbors influences the poem.[28]

Make My Eyes Water

The poem opens with the divine speaker comparing past cheerfulness, or in some translations, "joy," with its absence.[29] Overwhelming grief has extinguished cheerfulness, for it is "upon" the speaker like a sickness. A cry heard "far and wide in the land" (8:19) provokes God's grief because the one crying out is God's unfaithful wife, "the daughter of my people," the capital city, the daughter of Zion herself.[30] She asks in disbelief if God and king have disappeared. Are they not in Zion? Do they not protect the people from enemies? But God repeats the earlier charge that she abandoned him and broke up the family in the first place (2:1—4:2).

The people shout in frenzied fear: "The summer is over and we are not saved!" (8:20). Perhaps they are referring to Judah's failed hope that Egypt would save them from Babylon, but the poem's focal point extends beyond international politics. God's inner life is its subject. "For the shattering of the daughter of my people I am shattered" (v. 21). God and people suffer equivalent pain and inhabit a similarly benumbed emotional world.

How utterly remarkable of Jeremiah to echo in a poem about God's inner being the people's own stunned, blunted condition. God's spirit is "leaden," dismay takes possession, as if God were in a state of stress, beyond recovery.

"My heart is sick within me."[31] Inner sickness and psychic numbing mirror the people's reality, set it outside them, and summon them to face it.

Wanting to Weep

Like a doctor seeking a cure, God cries out, "Is there no balm in Gilead?" Is there no healing ointment, no physician, no way for the "daughter of my people" to be become healthy again? The answer is, "Yes! There is a balm in Gilead," that place famous for healing unguents, but the medicine is useless.[32] There is no way to repair this unspeakable shattering. The only thing left to do is weep. And in one of the more moving poetic lines of the book, God longs to do so:

> Who will make my head waters and my eyes a fountain of tears,
> that I might weep day and night for the slain of the
> Daughter of my people? (8:22, Eng.)

Yet no one actually weeps in this poem. I have translated the first words of the verse literally—"who will make?"—but the Hebrew expresses a wish, a situation contrary to fact: "would that there were," or "O that my head were waters."[33] So grief-stricken, God wishes to have a fountain for eyes, a never ending source of water, [34] to weep "day and night for the slain of the Daughter of my people." Desire to grieve is so strong, according to Else Holt, God wishes to become water.[35] Only such a source would provide sufficient tears to grieve what has been lost and broken. Who can provide such a fountain, who can help God release tears? No one can.

In this startlingly vulnerable depiction of the deity, the people of Judah receive an invitation to weep. That God wants to weep is an enticement, a permission, and a beckoning to awaken Judah's grief. Caroline Moorehead, writing about refugees and Holocaust survivors, suggests why an invitation to grieve is helpful. "Because they are in limbo, and because all their concentration and energy have to go into surviving and helping their children survive, they feel they have no permission to mourn and grieve."[36] God's own desire calls them to weep for the mountain of losses too immense to imagine.

Tears are the body's automatic response to sadness and reveal that the soul is alive, that feelings are emerging, affectivity recovering, and humanity reappearing. They are a sign that healing might come. Yet God seeks help in opening the sluice gates of weeping because God's own tears are blocked like theirs. "Who will make my head waters and my eyes a fountain of tears?" No one can.

Quickly the vulnerable interlude passes, and anger replaces empathy. God or the speaker wants to "go away," to abandon the people in a kind of reverse pilgrimage to the wilderness of the past.[37] Again God accuses them of their familiar sin: "They are all adulterers," a "band of traitors" who "do not know me" (9:2-3). Divine rage and grief are two aspects of the same broken relationship.[38]

In an act of theological license, Jeremiah's poem imagines numbness and seething anger in God's being, if I am right about the identity of the speaker. Distraught and unstable, God is like victims of traumatic violence. And even if the people have no feeling and cannot yet grieve, they can find their condition reflected here and know in some poetic way that God, or whoever the speaker might be, shares their plight. The portrait of the weeping God is another of Jeremiah's efforts to defend God, but it does so much more.

Although identifying speakers in these weeping poems is tenuous at best, I am suspicious of commentators who do not want a weeping God, a poetic character with human-like emotions. Perhaps such a God may not appear godly or macho enough. Perhaps a weeping deity is too vulnerable. But a weeping God, like an angry one, arises from human experience to name the One beyond every name. Half a century ago, Rabbi Abraham Heschel rightly insisted that the God of Israel is not a Greek deity of stoic power and unchangeableness but a fluid being filled with pathos and emotionally engaged in the life of the people.[39]

Weep for the Earth (9:10-11, Eng.)

If God is not yet able to weep for the shattered people, in the next lament God does weep for the ecological catastrophe afflicting the land in the war's aftermath.[40]

> For the mountains, I take up weeping and lamenting,[41]
> For the pastures of the wilderness, a dirge
> Because they are desolate and no one passes through
> And the sound of cattle is not heard.
> The birds of the heavens and the beasts
> Have fled and gone.
> And I will make Jerusalem a rubble, a den of jackals,
> And I will make the cities of Judah a waste without inhabitant
> (9:10-11, Eng., my translation).

God weeps over a terrain emptied of living creatures and devoid of sound like the ruined landscape in the poem of "uncreation" (4:23-27). Once a living world of humans, birds, and animals, the land no longer can support life. Cities are piles of rubble, places for jackals to roam (see Lam 5:18). God's world is undone and God weeps on its behalf to call forth grief and open the door to the long, arduous process of mourning.

Mourning Women (9:17-22)

Mute shock and benumbed emotions are not the final word in this poetic world. Instead, mourning women come forth to weep and wail a funeral dirge for Zion. Mourning women in the ancient world had the task of "kick starting" the grieving process by performing lamentation for the dead.[42] Their very arrival declares death's triumph, makes its reality undeniable and something to be mourned. Their keening and lamenting creates an environment of sorrow and expresses the grief of the bereaved, even if the bereaved are too shut down to do so.

The poem divides into two stanzas: Call for the Women to Come (9:17-19) and Instructions for Mourning (9:20-22). With gruesome imagery, it also conjures up memories of the ruin and death that follow disasters everywhere.

Call for the Women Come (9:17-19)

> Thus says the Lord of Hosts:
> Consider and call for the mourning women to come
> And to the skilled women send and let them come.
> Let them hurry and raise a lament over us
> So that our eyes may run down with tears
> And our eyelids flow with water.
> For the voice of lament is heard from Zion:
> [People of Zion] "How we are devastated and deeply shamed
>> Because we have abandoned the land
>> Because they have thrown down our dwellings" (9:17-19, Eng.).

Instructions for Mourning (9:20-22)

> For hear, O Women, the word of YHWH
> And let your ears receive the word of his mouth
> And teach your daughters a lament
> And each to her neighbor a dirge.
> For death has climbed into our windows,
> It has come into our palaces
> To cut off the infant outside,
> Young men in the streets.
> Speak, thus says YHWH,
> Human corpses fall like dung upon the face of the field,
> Like cut grain after the reaper
> And there is no one to gather them. (9:20-22, Eng.)

Because I think the weeping poems address what trauma and disaster studies call "psychic numbing," I notice that God does not simply order people to call in the mourning women but more gently asks them to "consider and call" (9:17). The first verb really means to "consider diligently" or to give careful thought to something. The matter requiring deliberate consideration is whether or not to send for these women, a decision emphasized by being repeated in a parallel clause:

"Consider and call for the mourning women to come
And to the skilled women send and let them come."

But why should the people have to think so hard about this and who is being told to do so? Lundbom proposes that the need to "consider" implies communal hesitation to mourn, so the people have to be persuaded to "let them come."[43] Grieving demands enormous energy and courage that victims of catastrophe may not have, so it seems better not to do it, better to remain leaden and blunted, safer than revisiting memories that haunt survivors with terrifying power.

But God insists multiple times: "call for the mourning women to come," "send," "let them come," "listen," "speak." The call is urgent; the women must hurry. Let them make "our eyes . . . run down with tears and our eyelids . . . flow with waters." But it is not simply the people who must weep. God too is among those who need to weep; "our eyes" and "our eyelids" must run down with tears.

When the women arrive, they find a world devastated by war. Their instructions are so serious that the poem twice insists that they come from God as the "word of YHWH" and "the word of his mouth" (9:20). Grieving is so pressing a need that God must authorize it. And grieving is so enormous a task that the women must mobilize neighbors and teach daughters their skills. Only then might dormant grief be awakened from bereaved spirits, for death, that terrifying intruder, climbs in the windows.

Death climbs into homes and the king's palace, into private and public life. Death cuts down infants and young men in the streets. Corpses fall as freely as animal dung and with as little value. Bodies lie where they fall with no proper burial and no one to gather them.

The command to grieve in these verses is neither gentle prodding nor sentimental manipulation. It is a frightening call to face the blanket of death that has befallen the nation, covering them with lethal power. Death is a force, a mythic person, who leaves behind humans who can feel nothing and are half-dead themselves. The call to mourn is a demand for brute courage.

Grieving and Recovery

Writing about literature produced after the Holocaust, Sidra Koven Ezrahi claims "It is not the recounting of atrocities which produces terror . . . but the reflection of a world which has lost its center, a world abandoned by God and filled with the corpses of His worshippers."[44] Ezrahi may as easily have been writing about the book of Jeremiah. The weeping poems offer up a landscape strewn with corpses, an awful place where the center of life has collapsed and meaning has been withdrawn. This disaster in its many dimensions must be grieved. It is time to weep day and night, with heads turned to water and eyes flooded with tears. But if the people cannot yet do it, if God only wishes to do so, then the mourning women will weep for them until they can begin to confront their paralyzing grief.

Whether disaster afflicts an individual or an entire community, the numbing that begins as a protective response can quickly become a dehumanized, passionless condition. In this situation, grieving is a moral act. It involves living in the present with knowledge of the self and of the world as they are. It engages present reality, the only place from which the communal rebuilding can begin. When mourning occurs, life in communion with other people can become possible again.

Judith Herman, who writes about psychotherapy following trauma, offers insights that, by extension, illuminate Jeremiah's weeping poems. She identifies two stages of recovery from trauma.[45] The first is when survivors begin to tell what happened to them and find language to name the disaster. The book of Jeremiah provides such language in its war poetry and other accounts of the original events.

A second stage of recovery, according to Herman, involves the work of the witness, one who receives the grief hidden in the haphazard narratives recalled by the victim. By receiving grief, the witness validates the suffering, connects with victims on a human scale, and so restores them to community. Jeremiah's weeping poems are one more way the book witnesses to all that Judah has lost, to the chaos, death, and deadened spirits. In the "vivid imaginative space" of the poems, readers "can experience, without negative judgment, the outrage and grief that emerge as they remember and name the traumatic harm they have suffered."[46]

When I ask what experiences these poems seek to create among readers, the answer is clear. Their purpose is to rouse up grief like mourning women whose wailing and weeping makes space for tears, awakens sorrows, and releases buried feelings from benumbed spirits. In them, God calls the people back to knowing, feeling, and living. And for a brief poetic moment, God suffers with them in their losses.

7
Telling a Life

Biographical Stories

**JEREMIAH 1; 16:1-9; 20:1-6; 26; 32;
37:11—38:13; 40-43**

E ven as a bold and persistent spokesperson for God, the prophet Jeremiah is
not a hero of epic proportions. He is an anguished man, a kind of anti-hero,
wounded, isolated, and broken like the people of Judah in the grip of catastrophe.[1] Pain and suffering dominate his life according to stories and poems about
him that form major components of the book named after him. This rare biblical portrait of a prophet's life tells about both his public ministry and his inner
life of prayer, the former in biographical narratives often attributed to his scribe
Baruch, and the latter in prayers of laments often called the "confessions."

It is true that snippets from lives of other prophets appear in the Bible.
Hosea, for example, marries a prostitute and has a dysfunctional family (Hos
1–3). Isaiah and his wife give their children symbolic names, and he runs naked
around Jerusalem (Isa 7:1-25, 37-39). And Ezekiel performs symbolic acts that
seem at first glance to reveal a psychologically disturbed character.[2] But the
stories and prayers from Jeremiah's life are different in scope from those of
the other prophets because they spread across a ministerial lifetime from birth
(chap. 1) to an ignominious deportation to Egypt at the end of his ministry
(chaps. 40–43).

Contemporary western readers may find accounts of Jeremiah's life to be an
expected feature of a book containing his words, but from the vantage point of
interpreters, the prophet's "biography" is hard to explain. Why would ancient
writers tell a prophet's life at all? Ancient Israel did not celebrate individuality
and personality the way we do, nor was there, in the world before Freud, a great
deal of interest in people's inner struggles for their own sake. Yet both are present here.

Historian and biographer Dana Greene observes that biographical writing flourishes in times when systems of meaning collapse and fray.[3] In such a context, life stories provide a form of coherence missing elsewhere. "They ferret out cause and effect and create explanation and meaning in terms ordinary people can understand."[4] Reading stories of others forces an encounter with realities that can lead to deeper reflection about one's own reality. In this way, language of a single life can tell the story of many lives and provide metaphors for understanding collective experience.[5] Something similar is happening here. Jeremiah's life both expresses the sufferings of his people and augurs hope for their survival.

Scenes from a Life

Episodes from a life such as we have for Jeremiah do not make a full-fledged biography in any modern sense. For one thing, readers have to create the prophet's life from separate strands of material scattered across the book without chronological order. Confusing matters further, Jeremiah's life appears in different kinds of writing. Besides the prophetic oracles and sermons ascribed to him, there are two types of prose narratives (stories about his prophetic actions and stories about his captivities), and there are his personal prayers in the form of poetic laments. These different types of literature give us sporadic moments in a life without the benefit of a unifying plot.

An Iconic Figure

Some interpreters view Jeremiah's biography as an historical record of what actually happened to him.[6] Others, among whom I count myself, recognize in his life a prophetic "persona," that is, a literary portrait with theological intentions.[7] Trauma and disaster studies offer still further ways to think about the prophet's life. No matter how he actually lived and preached, he is a symbolic figure whose life embodies the sufferings of his people and the long-term effects of the disaster.[8] His prophetic actions, captivities, as well as his prayers (see next chapter) convey the nation's anguish and hold out hope that they too may escape captivity.

A Life Replete with Meaning

Things are not really that simple, of course, because Jeremiah is more than someone who suffers with his community; he suffers on account of them. He is a prophetic adversary of his people, rejected by the very ones to whom God has sent him. His prophetic role is "the incontestable starting point for interpreting his life,"[9] and his personal suffering is its consequence. Everybody is out to get Jeremiah for his dread-filled preaching, including kings, other prophets, priests, the people, and even his family and friends. Viewed from this angle, the people of Judah are his enemy, especially in the first half of the book where he is a singular, isolated figure (chaps. 1–25). But seeing his suffering only as the result of his preaching flattens this literary portrait and misses how his life interprets with the disaster afflicting his community. As I search for a more nuanced interpretation of Jeremiah's biography, I do not mean to blur his prophetic identity but to expand it.

Trauma and disaster studies bring to the surface other dimensions of the prophet's biography. His life illuminates the disaster, embodies it, and signifies survival beyond it. His sufferings as a rejected prophet help "explain" the disaster and contribute to the book's rhetoric of responsibility. Because the people reject him and his word, Judah falls to Babylon. Despite the by-now-familiar harmful side-effects of this rhetoric, its effect is to provide order and meaning, cause and effect to a world gone awry. But beyond that, the particular afflictions heaped upon Jeremiah by his people are not solely about him; they are a mosaic of the cataclysm. They incorporate the sufferings of the very people who reject him.[10] In complex ways, Jeremiah's biography is a work of social repair for rebuilding the community. His prophetic call, prophetic sign acts, and stories of his captivities create a prism through which to see the disaster, explain it, and survive it.

The Call to Prophesy (Jer 1)

The story of Jeremiah's call to be a prophet opens the book by hammering the prophetic stakes into the ground. Vivid details introduce a character profoundly alienated from the people to whom he is to preach. Every detail of Jeremiah's call separates him from the people.

> Before I formed you in the womb I knew you,
> and before you were born I consecrated you.
> I appointed you prophet to the nations (1:3).

Before Jeremiah can even agree to it, God chooses him to be prophet in his mother's womb. That means his vocation is not his own doing but God's.[11] To provide speech for the task, God touches his mouth. A God-touched figure, Jeremiah speaks directly with God and, like Moses, resists his assignment: "Ah Lord, truly I do not know how to speak, for I am only a boy" (Jer 1:6; cf. Exod 3:11; 4:10-11).[12] But he must go anyway "to uproot and pull down, to destroy and to overthrow, to build and to plant" (Jer 1:10). His commission alienates him and isolates him from his people.

The call narrative makes many contributions to the book, but for my purposes, it establishes in advance that Jeremiah will suffer because the people will reject him and his words about the disaster that will "break loose upon all the inhabitants of the land" (1:14). Although people will resist him, God promises to strengthen, be with him (1:8), and make him a "bronze wall," "an iron pillar," "a fortified city" (1:19).

Rhetoric of Responsibility

By separating the prophet from the people and identifying him with God, the call story is the first to articulate the book's rhetoric of human responsibility for the disaster. When it announces that the nation will reject the prophet, it asserts at the book's beginning that the cataclysm was not a reckless unloosing of pandemonium upon Judah. It was divine punishment for the people's refusal to hear the prophet's word. Cause and effect are clear. And with all its inadequacies as explanation of disaster, this interpretation helps disaster victims by pulling into focus the inchoate forces that have ruptured the world. It reduces fear and makes space for recovery to begin.

Signs and Wonders

After his call, Jeremiah's biography takes narrative form in a series of stories, first in chapter 16 and then in a scattered collection of stories about his captivities that begin in chapter 20 and appear mostly in the book's second half (chaps. 26–45). In each of them his suffering is emblematic of the suffering of the very people who refuse to listen to this message. The first of these concerns "prophetic sign acts" he is to perform, and it helps illustrate my claims about the many levels of meaning in Jeremiah's biography.

Sometimes called "symbolic acts," prophetic sign acts proclaim the prophet's word through actions, physical deeds that are often interpreted in the same passage.[13] Most of Jeremiah's sign acts perform the disaster symbolically, as if in street theater. In them, everything collapses or comes to nothing. He buries a loin cloth near the Euphrates River and it disintegrates (13:1-11); he breaks a jug in front of witnesses (19:1-15); he wears an iron yoke of captivity about his neck (chaps. 27–28); and in a more hopeful direction, he buys a field while invasion is occurring (32:1-25). These and other symbolic actions portray overwhelming destruction in simple images that encapsulate the disaster and provide vivid images to speak about it. They are aspects of the book's unceasing quest for language to express and name the disaster, to narrow down the many dimensions of destruction into one expressive symbolic event.

Living in Isolation (Jer 16:1-9)

But in chapter 16, Jeremiah's personal life itself becomes the sign. Rather than performing acts, God commands that he refrain from them. He may not "marry

[nor] have sons and daughters in this place" (16:1-4, v.2), and he may not attend social gatherings in the "house of mourning" (16:5-8). Houses of mourning were probably funeral societies, social gatherings, and mutual aid societies for men who feasted together at times of bereavement[14] and perhaps for weddings.[15] Whatever they were, Jeremiah cannot participate. In a culture built around community, he must remain alone without a wife, family, or friends, a situation he laments bitterly: "I have not sat in the circles of merry makers. . . . I have sat alone because of your hand upon me" (15:17, my translation).

From this prophet, God demands everything. He is to live without people, bereft of love and of human companionship, but these demands are very odd in the Old Testament because they overturn biblical confidence in the blessings of family and community. To avoid marriage is to fail to keep the first biblical commandment to "be fruitful and multiply" (Gen 1:28). Such is the high cost of a prophetic vocation where life and message become indistinguishable, where, as Fretheim puts it, Jeremiah's life "is an embodied word of God."[16]

But disaster studies point to further dimensions of Jeremiah's isolation. Inevitably war, exile, and military occupation rupture domestic life and undermine community. Deaths of husbands, children, and the elderly, the destruction of homes, land, and livelihoods—these mortal imprints of war splinter families, shred relationships, and isolate victims from their communities. Disasters damage the very "tissues of life that hold people together."[17]

In this light, Jeremiah's celibacy and social isolation enact the social destruction that is central to the disaster. His prophetic signs perform social isolation, show it in a living picture, and give it words. He neither marries nor begets children because, as God explains, the children of Judah will die of disease, perish by sword and famine, and their bodies will become food for birds and animals (16:1-4). The prophet's lonely condition dramatizes God's banishment of the "voice of mirth and the voice of gladness, the voice of the bridegroom or the voice of the bride" (16:9).[18] In his most intimate life, Jeremiah personifies social rupture and communal erosion that consumes Judah. One life expresses many. Jeremiah lives in social isolation just like other disaster victims. His own alienated body is an icon of the community's alienation.

Stories of Captivities

Jeremiah's multiple roles as rejected prophet, figure of suffering, as well as agent of survival and hope come together in stories of his captivities. He is like an action figure who escapes one catastrophe only to fall into another and survive every time. The captivity stories follow a common pattern: enemies capture him, beat him, and attack him (11:18-19, 21-23; 20:1-6; 26:1-24); they threaten his life (20:1-6; 26:1-24; 32:1-25; 37:11-21; 38:1-6), they deport him (chaps. 42–43), and every time he mysteriously escapes death. The cause of each arrest is his prophecy, but the suffering also embodies Judah's suffering under Babylonian domination.

Jeremiah Survives the Stocks (Jer 20:1-6)

The story of Jeremiah's first imprisonment takes place in the temple, the one place where the prophetic word should be eagerly heard and the high priest its ready recipient. But the opposite happens. High Priest Pashur rejects the prophet and tries to silence God's word by striking him and locking him in the stocks.[19] Jeremiah, in turn, uses the occasion of his imprisonment to announce Judah's imprisonment in Babylon:

> And I will give all Judah into the hand of the king of Babylon:
> he shall carry them captive to Babylon,
> and shall kill them with a sword (20:4).

Jeremiah's capture blends into Judah's because Jeremiah connects the two. He announces the disaster and specifies Babylon's role in it for the very first time in the book. He brings the "foe from the north" out of the realm of myth into the glaring light of the literal. It is Babylon who will take away wealth, riches, treasures, and possessions of the city and carry off Pashur and "his friends to terror" (v. 4, twice, and vv. 5, 6). And as in other stories of Jeremiah's capture, this one names responsible parties. Here, it is not all the people who are at fault but the high priest and friends who bear responsibility because they have refused to listen to the prophet.

Escaping with Your Life

Perhaps for the Judean audience of the book, the most important feature of Jeremiah's episode in the stocks is its ending. With no explanation, Pashur releases him the next day (20:2-3). Painful though it surely is, Jeremiah's captivity is neither permanent nor death-dealing. It ends, as do all stories about his incarcerations, with his surprising survival. His multiple miraculous escapes act out a promise sprinkled in various forms across the book's second half: "You will gain your life as booty of war" (38:2; 21:9; 39:18; 45:5). The promise of life as booty made to several characters is ironic. To gain your life as "booty of war" means that your life is all you have at war's end. You acquire neither treasure, slaves, women for your harem, nor honor and glory in battle. You live. You survive. That is it. After every catastrophe, people, stunned by their losses, express their dismay in similar terms: "All we have is our lives!" Yet having one's life is no small thing; it is the first requirement for a future, any future at all.

Jeremiah Survives the Trial (Jer 26)[20]

In the next captivity story, Jeremiah goes on trial for his sermon prophesying the temple's destruction, a sermon reported earlier in the book (7:1—8:3) and a destruction that has already occurred for the book's readers.[21] Before the trial, an outraged mob threatens Jeremiah with death for his words. Leaders and people together seize him and shout, "You shall die!" (26:8). Priests and prophets threaten him: "The death penalty to this man because he has prophesied against this city" (26:11). It is easy to read this turbulent response to the sermon with a single interpretive eye, noticing only the community-wide outrage over Jeremiah's prophecy. But the prophet's fate signifies the fate of the people.

In the ensuing trial, Jeremiah warns that putting him to death will bring a curse upon his captors. His calm response to threats against him splits up the community so that some supporters oppose the use of the death penalty. After all, Jeremiah spoke "in the name of the Lord our God" (26:16). To resolve the dispute, two prior cases about prophets serve as competing precedents. One concerns the prophet Micah who also prophesied Jerusalem's destruction, and former king named Hezekiah accepted the word. The second concerns the prophet Uriah, whom the current King Jehoiakim rejected and had tracked down, kidnapped, and killed. After these reports, Jeremiah's own life teeters on a knife edge between life and death. Like Judah in the wake of disaster, he could fall either way.

Jeremiah suffers in this biographical story because he is a rejected prophet, and that rejection furthers the book's rhetoric of responsibility. At first everyone rejects him, but then only the king and royal leaders insist on rejecting Jeremiah.[22] But like the story of capture in the stocks, the trial story ends with his escape. Out of nowhere, a previously unknown official shows up and rescues him.[23] "The hand of Ahikam son of Shaphan was with Jeremiah, so they would not put him into the hand of the people for execution" (26:24). The literary abruptness of the rescue makes it seem like an afterthought to the story, but this surprising turn of events changes the narrative from tragic to hopeful.[24] It breaks open possibility, implies that life is open-ended, able to be penetrated by a reality beyond the obvious, beyond the despair of the present.

And, in the highly dangerous circumstances of the trial, Jeremiah shows curious restraint and submits to his captors. "Look, I am in your hands, do to me what is good and right in your eyes" (26:14). Such calm endurance shows the people of Judah how to survive captivity until the time of their own rescue. The ideal survivor, Jeremiah accepts, digs in, and lives day to day (cf. 29:1-14). The people of Judah, too, may yet gain their lives as booty of war.[25]

The Land Survives (Jer 32)[26]

The next story begins with another imprisonment because Jeremiah's prophecy enrages King Zedekiah. The timing is rich with symbolic import because the captivity coincides with the Babylonian invasion of Jerusalem. Brueggemann calls the time the *"Nullpunkt,"* the point of death in its many forms.[27] Just as the army invades, Jeremiah buys land from his prison cell. A cousin visits him, so Jeremiah can "redeem" family property according to the law (32:6-8) that provides for the next of kin to buy back property in danger of being lost to debt (Lev 25:25-28). Jeremiah is that next of kin. With the help of Baruch, he prepares a deed, gathers witnesses, pays for the land, and meticulously follows rules of a legal land transaction.

At the worst moment in Judah's life, Jeremiah's land deal signifies a hopeful future. His purchase is a promissory note, a statement of obdurate, bare-bones hope in the face of the impossible. It proclaims in the thick of captivity that there will be life again in the land of Judah. Not only does Jeremiah survive but the land too will be redeemed from the hands of the enemy.

Jeremiah Survives the Pit (37:11-21; 38:1-13)

Like a proverbial cat with nine lives, Jeremiah suffers captivity twice more during Babylonian attacks on Jerusalem (37:11-21; 38:1-13).[28] Plot, vocabulary, location, and setting unite these two stories.[29] In both, the king confines Jeremiah to a prison where he faces death because he is a prophet, yet he escapes again with his life.

In the first story, Jeremiah is leaving Jerusalem to go to Benjamin to acquire his property, but a Judean soldier stops him, accuses him of defecting to Babylon, and arrests him (37:11-21).[30] Officials beat him and imprison him in a pit (*bôr*), where he "remained: a long time" (v.16). The two Hebrew words translated "prison" and "remained" connect Jeremiah's sufferings to the nation's predicament. The word for "prison" (*bôr*) also means "cistern" or "pit." It is a place of death, akin to the empty cisterns that God accuses Israel of digging for their stagnant water (2:13), or like the pit in which Joseph's brothers put him to die (Gen 37:24, 28).[31] The same word appears again in 38:6 making a frame around these two captivity stories (chaps. 37 and 38).

Jeremiah "remained" (from the Hebrew root *yāšab*) in this prison-pit a long time (37:16). The verb joins Jeremiah with the people who "remain" in the land under Babylonian occupation. Like them, he remains in the pit there a long time. The verb for "remain" carries a sense of duration, of "dwelling," "abiding," or "settling into" something. And this same verb appears as a refrain across several chapters, referring either to Jeremiah or to the people who remain in the land (Jer 37:16, 21; 38:2, 13, 28; cf. 40:6, 9-10). The teller of the story does not want us to miss the point that, like the people left in the land, Jeremiah "remained" in the pit of suffering a long time.

Suffering with the Ones Remaining

These repeated Hebrew words portray Jeremiah as a participant in the sufferings of one group of Judeans.[32] Because other stories place him clearly on the side of the exiles (for example, 24:1-10), some interpreters argue that the book makes Jeremiah an advocate for the exiles alone.[33] The stories where he sides with the exiles in Babylon authorize their return to power when they return to Judah.

But the prophet's biography is both more complicated and more inclusive. His captivities in the prison pit unite him with the ones left in the land after the invasions. And again he escapes with his life. He pleads with the king not to be sent back to the jailhouse to die (37:17-20). Against expectation, the king complies with Jeremiah's request and even provides him with daily bread until all the bread is gone (v. 21).[34]

The Pit Again

Themes of capture and survival continue in the second story of the prophet abandoned to die in the pit. The cause this time is his demand for the people to surrender to the Babylonians, also known as Chaldeans (38:1-13).

> Whoever remains ($y\bar{a}\check{s}ab$)[35] in this city shall die by the sword, by famine, and by pestilence, but whoever surrenders to the Chaldeans shall live; he shall gain his life as booty of war and live. (38:2)

These instructions are patently treasonous to the king's officials. The wishy-washy king who saved Jeremiah's life in the previous chapter now hands him over to officials who use ropes to lower him into the pit ($b\hat{o}r$, 38:6-13). "There was no water in the pit, only mud, and Jeremiah sank in the mud" (38:6).

Gerhard von Rad calls this a story of "grim realism," but it is also clearly symbolic as the prophet sinks into the mud of hopelessness, a place of abandonment and death.[36] Threatened, impotent, and humiliated in the pit, his portrait gathers up the hopelessness of those who remain in the land after the Babylonian siege. They, too, are mired in mud, deprived of food and hope. They too face extinction.

But then another "out-of-the-blue" rescue by a previously unknown character concludes the story. As famine sweeps the city (v. 9; see also Lam 4), an African from Cush named Ebed-Melech[37] sees Jeremiah's peril and convinces the king to allow him to rescue Jeremiah "from the pit before he dies" (38:10). Rescuers use rags from the king's treasury—strips of cloth as tattered as the monarchy—to lift Jeremiah to safety. And God rewards Ebed-Melek with his life.

> I will save you on that day. . . . I will rescue you, and you shall not fall by the sword. You shall escape with your life as the booty of war because you trusted me. (39:18)

Jeremiah suffers in the prison-pit because he is a prophet rejected by the king. But his life is larger than that of a singular prophet. He suffers with the remnant in the land; he knows their pain and the sucking mud of hopelessness; he is one of them. The next story solidifies their mutual identification.

Jeremiah Escapes Fetters (40:1-6)

Like a character in a bad novel with too many mind-boggling escapes, Jeremiah again avoids death as Jerusalem falls. This time the Babylonians release him from captivity, commanded to do so by Babylon's emperor Nebuchadnezzar. Although the Babylonians may simply recognize Jeremiah as an ally, symbolic elements of the rescue are hard to miss. At the war's most desperate hour, Jeremiah gains his freedom. "I have just released you today from the fetters on your hands," says the Babylonian captain of the guard (40:4). Then the captain makes Jeremiah choose where to go. "See the whole land is before you; go wherever you think it is right to go" (40:4). Jeremiah can choose to go to Babylon or remain in the land, and he adamantly chooses to joins the remnant "left in the land" under the Babylonian-appointed governor, Gedeliah (40:6). He chose them, and they can claim him as their own. But the final story we have about his life sets him among a different group of survivors, deportees.

Jeremiah Survives Exile (chaps. 41–44)

Jeremiah's last captivity follows the outline of the previous stories. He suffers because he is a prophet and escapes with his life, but there are other complicating elements here. Judean insurgents assassinate Gedeliah and his followers and throw their bodies into another pit or cistern (*bôr*, 41:9). In response, Jeremiah urges survivors of this massacre not to flee Judah out of fear, but the leaders refuse to listen and depart for Egypt. For Jeremiah, Egypt is a cursed land, a place without a future, a place of idolatry and death, a place he does not want to go. But despite his fierce resistance, insurgents force him, Baruch, and others to go with them to Egypt (chap. 42). His own people deport him.

This story portrays Jeremiah as an exile not to Babylon but to Egypt. His own people rudely and forcibly deport him against his will to a land he curses with pestilence, captivity, and the sword (43:11). Like the deportees dragged to Babylon, others drag him away to a place he finds hateful, inhospitable both to him and to his God. Again his life is like that of some of his people, exiles in Babylon. His captivities mirror Judah's various captivities and sufferings.

Judah's Fate in Jeremiah's Body

Jeremiah's biography portrays in his body the pain and loss of the people. It identifies him with those who stay in the land and with those forced to leave against their will. It presents him as a man familiar with sorrow—their sorrows—whose life embodies every major consequence of the Babylonian disaster—deprivation of family, social isolation, captivity, abandonment, assault, threats of death, imprisonment in the land, and finally deportation. Each painful event comes from his prophetic calling, but all of them also symbolize sufferings of Judah.

Jeremiah Does Not Die

The prophet's biography ends with exile. His life trails off and his fate is unknown. Jeremiah does not die in this book or anywhere on record. Although we learn about his life from before his birth, about his forty years of ministry, there is no report of his death. At every turn, he escapes death and survives in the most hopeless conditions, even in Egypt where his story disappears yet does not formally end. I think this, too, is symbolic. Jeremiah must survive because the Judean people must survive, even up to seventy years (29:10). The silence surrounding his death leaves his life story open, filled with possibility for the unknown future.

Perhaps these strange stories about a life steadied the book's readers in their immense sorrow, displacement, and frayed existence. They may have helped Judean survivors reimagine life as they blended Jeremiah's life with their own.[38] Perhaps these stories helped survivors find their "bearings in the world"[39] or unlocked the future for them, gave them energy to endure, and showed them a way forward in their life together with God, mysteriously obscured from view in these captivity stories.

8

Survive by Praying

The Confessions

JEREMIAH 11:18—12:6; 15:10-21; 17:14-18; 18:18-23; 20:7-13, 14-18

J eremiah's prayers, often called "confessions" (11:18—12:6; 15:10-21; 17:14-18; 18:18-23; 20:7-13, 14-18[1]) are an important component of his "biography" and the reason I was attracted to the study of Jeremiah in the first place. A unique feature of prophetic literature, the prayers provide him with a rich spiritual and psychological life and distinguish him from other prophets.[2] They offer vivid glimpses of inner turbulence and outrgage and contradict God's promise at the beginning of his ministry that he would become a "bronze wall" and a "fortified city" (1:18). Jeremiah speaks to God in his own voice in the confessions, as an "I" besieged by doubt and desperate in the face of all he is suffering. It is that inwardness that makes him into a more rounded literary character.

Jeremiah's confessions are laments, that is, prayers of complaint to God similar to laments in the book of Psalms. In them, his relationship with God balances on the breaking point. But ultimately, his prayers—in all their bitterness and anguish—keep that relationship alive and teach readers how to move through the frightening spiritual wreckage left by disaster. By clinging to God in their own thick jungles of pain, God and they might together survive the cataclysm. And like the biographical stories, Jeremiah's confessions expand his prophetic role from that of adversary to his people. They serve as instruments of communal survival.

What Are the Confessions?

Terrence Fretheim thinks the term "confessions" is not suitable for Jeremiah's laments because the prayers confess neither sin nor faith.[3] It is true that Jeremiah does not admit to being a sinner in these texts; rather, he insists on the opposite. He is innocent. But the very purpose of prayers of lament is to *confess faith* in the midst of fear, anger, and doubt. Even as Jeremiah speaks to God accusingly, even as they verge toward hopelessness, they adhere to God with fierce insistence.

Without complaint there are no prayers of lament. Laments argue, protest, whine, and mewl; they berate God even as the one praying holds fast to God like a lover in a life-altering quarrel.[4] Laments compose a poetic forum in which to express fury at the deep fissures of the world and the ways God fails to care for it. These qualities make laments ready-made prayers for victims of trauma and disaster.

The Prayer Form

Laments are "ready-made" because they are a part of Judah's prayer traditions, composing more than one third of the Psalter—Israel's prayer book.[5] They follow a traditional pattern or format that, to quote Walter Brueggemann's famous phrase, gives "formfulness to grief."[6] In a typical prayer of lament, the ones praying

> call out to God,
> complain to God,
> petition God for help.

Sometimes laments contain an additional voice that assures the complainers that they are heard. Sometimes the ones praying also praise God in confident hope that their petitions will be answered. Between the complaint and the expression of hope lies a gap, an abrupt switch as the ones speaking seem to reverse completely their grasp of reality, as if voicing the complaint makes room for something new to break in.

Jeremiah's confessions use the lament form creatively, choosing some parts and ignoring or rarely using others.[7] But the beating heart of this prayer, that without which there is no lament, is complaining.[8] Perhaps this is why I like them so much. They convey in the most vulnerable terms a grasping for faith and a desperate clutching toward God despite massive discontent with God's treatment of the world.[9] And because in them Jeremiah insists on his innocence and refuses to see himself as the cause of his suffering,[10] they too participate in the book's rhetoric of responsibility, ultimately turning blame onto God.

Faithful Prophet

Since Jeremiah's confessions focus on his vocational meltdown, they seem to belong to him alone, but they do not. Like other components of his biography, his prayers embrace the pain of anyone mired in anger and loss. And since his laments resist the rhetoric of human responsibility so prominent elsewhere in the book, they destabilize Jeremiah's fire and brimstone to further muddy interpretation of the disaster. By the rhetoric of responsibility, I refer to the book's efforts to explain the causes of the disaster as the result of the behavior of someone or some group. Mostly the book of Jeremiah places blame on the general sins of the people, the adulterous idolatry of wife Judah, or on the failures of the kingly, prophetic, or priestly leadership. But the confessions blame God. God has failed, betrayed, turned away, left the prophet to suffer. In these prayers God is responsible.

Suffering Prophet

Like the captivity stories, Jeremiah's confessions arise from his prophetic vocation. Prophecy is their starting point and the subject of his complaints, and prophecy is my first lens for interpreting the prophet's biography. In all five confessions, he starts from the fact that he should not suffer because he is wedded body and spirit to the prophetic word. Like Job, another expressive complainer, Jeremiah claims to be innocent of anything that might be a self-induced cause of his misery. He should not suffer because he has been a most obedient prophet:

> Your words were found and I devoured them,
> your words became a joy to me and the delight of my heart
> because I am called by your name, Yahweh of Hosts. (15:16)[11]

So faithful has Jeremiah been that he understands God's word as his food, part of his body, inseparable from his being.[12] Even his enemies know this, so they mock him, asking: "Where is the word of YHWH? Let it come" (17:15). And in case God should forget how dedicated he is, Jeremiah has the effrontery to remind God of his efforts to intercede for the people: "Remember how I stood before you to speak good on their behalf, to turn your anger from them?" (18:20).

And when he has suffered so much that he wants to quit his onerous mission, an internal force, a spiritual compulsion, a fire burning within, compels him to keep prophesying on God's behalf:[13]

> Whenever I think, 'I will not remember him,
> I will speak no longer in his name,'
> then it is like a fire consuming my heart and shut up in my bones.
> I become weary and cannot hold it in. (20:9)

Try though Jeremiah might to escape his prophetic calling, he shows himself to be a true prophet, consumed by the power of the divine word. He insists that he has been God's faithful spokesperson, one with God's word, suffering insult and shame for his fidelity, calling faithfully upon God, and refraining from merry-making because God's hand rests upon him (15:10-21).[14] Although his prophetic calling has made him truly miserable, he has never wavered.

Rejected Prophet

And it is precisely this fidelity to his vocation that causes Jeremiah's hopeless anguish. It is fidelity to that word that creates enemies who want to "cut him off from the land of the living" (11:19). His adversaries taunt him and scheme against him to silence him. They persecute him "like a lamb led to the slaughter" (11:19). They want to kill him and cut him down like a young tree, to leave a hole in the world as if he never existed:

> "Let us destroy the tree with its fruit
> And let us cut him off from the land of the living
> That his name may be remembered no more." (11:19)

His enemies are everywhere, even among his kinfolk. The people in his hometown of Anathoth and even his family "have dealt treacherously" with him (11:23 and 12:6). Crowds mock him, asking "Where is the word of the Lord?" (17:15). Enemies call him "a laughingstock every day" (20:7-8). They dig a pit "to capture" him and hide "a trap" for his feet (18:22).

Forlornly, the prophet stands alone, isolated and threatened at every turn by his own community. He complains that his spiritual wounds are chronic, and again like Job, he demands to know why. "Why has my pain become endless, my wound incurable, refusing to be healed?" (15:17). In the midst of this overwhelming suffering, his prophetic fidelity turns out to be useless; God has abandoned him anyway.

Laments of the Suffering Community

Jeremiah's confessions emerge from his painful vocation, but these prayers simultaneously bring into their orbit the wretchedness of the suffering nation. For readers who live in the hungry maw of disaster, Jeremiah's prayers express their desolation, misery, and doubt. Although the confessions appear on the surface to be purely personal, they actually enact in the life of one person Judah's shattered faith. They dramatize the shutting down of trust among disaster victims and put it into the public sphere.

Only the last verses of the last lament give a glimmer of faith's resurgence (20:7-13), a resurgence quickly drowned in despondency and hopelessness (20:14-18). When Jeremiah treads the pathways of distrust and anger, he articulates common experiences that follow trauma and disaster. Principal among these is the frightening awareness of divine absence, what contemplatives might call a collective "dark night of the soul," that place of impasse where God is among the disappeared and the future is tightly shuttered against hope. Jeremiah's confessions depict his people's psychological, spiritual, and theological reality.

Ruptured Relationship

At one level, the confessions sing the same old God-defending, people-blaming song that courses through the book. Jeremiah complains that the people persecute and reject him as God's spokesman.[15] Yet complaints against human enemies are but a thin veneer in the confessions, barely covering the rupture in his relationship with the God who sent him. His prayers move quickly past charges against his people to biting accusations against God whose treachery causes his present anguish. And because the prophet's life is larger than his own, his sense of abject betrayal by God conveys the people's abandonment as well.

Jeremiah's confessions ultimately resist the God-defending theology of much of the book. They provide another voice, another claim about the disaster. To the implied question, "Why did this happen?" the confessions reply: God is at fault. Whatever else his laments do, they challenge the book's theodicy and its twin, the rhetoric of human responsibility.

Who Is Innocent?

I imagine readers thinking, "Wait a minute! As God's prophet, Jeremiah really was innocent and the Judean people were not!" But the book's rhetoric of human responsibility is not a definitive interpretation of the disaster but one among many interpretations. Does human sin alone explain historical catastrophe? Not everyone thinks so, not even in biblical times. Jeremiah's search for responsible parties is a theological survival strategy, a partial, provisional explanation, another "momentary stay against confusion."[16]

I often wonder why we believers and interpreters accept the Bible's rhetoric of human responsibility at face value as the single most authoritative interpretation of Judah's fall, as if one static set of meanings explains everything. Is it because self-blaming has been an unconscious survival strategy for us that it is doubly hard to recognize its theological limitations in the authoritative biblical word?[17] Biblical language about human sin and divine punishment is, after all, as culturally-conditioned as ancient biblical practices of slavery and the subjugation of women. Like all speech about God, biblical words are products of their culture; they are provisional, partial, and incomplete. They stutter and stammer to say that which cannot be fully said. In the confessions, Jeremiah turns from an adamant God-defender to a passionate God-resister.

Jeremiah, the God-Resister

The prophet bemoans God's complicity with his enemies' treachery. The responsible party behind them, feuling and encouraging them, is God who is not just and not on the side of the good. Jeremiah imagines himself in a courtroom, submitting his case before God who serves as both Judge and Defendant. The prophet demands a balancing of the scales, a fair and just decision (11:18—12:6). Like a skilled attorney, he begins his case by honoring God. The Judge, he says, is righteous, trustworthy, one who will bring justice against enemies:

> Yahweh, Righteous Judge, Tester of heart and mind,
> Let me see your vengeance upon them
> For unto you I have revealed my case. (11:20, my translation)

But this gentle approach is a setup, an ironic tease that Jeremiah contradicts immediately. No matter what he says, no matter what evidence he brings forward, God will claim to be in the right, beyond human questioning.

> Innocent are you, O YHWH,
> when I lay charges against you.
> Yet I want to present charges against you. (12:1)

The divine Judge with whom he pleads is beyond reach, unassailable. God claims to be innocent, but Jeremiah thinks God is indifferent to charges even from himself, God's ally and chosen prophet. He begs for explanation: "Why does the way of the wicked prosper and all those who commit treachery flourish?" (12:1). The question "why" has one indisputable answer:

> You have planted them and they have taken root.
> They grow.
> They bear fruit. (12:2)

The wicked prosper because God favors them; they flourish because God nourishes them; they do evil because God enables them. God may claim to be just, and ancient tradition may claim that God is just, but the facts speak to the contrary. Jeremiah demands proof of divine justice in his own wretched life, and that proof will appear only when God separates the wicked from the innocent "like sheep for the slaughter" (12:3).

God Betrays

When he prays, Jeremiah accuses God of outright injustice. But here is his most fundamental complaint: God is a traitor and false friend who has forsaken him. "Truly, you are to me like a deceitful spring, like waters that fail" (15:18). The "deceitful spring" and failing waters may refer to a river bed in the desert that evaporates in torrid heat and then floods in drowning torrents during rainy seasons, sweeping away everything in its path. A God who is like a dried-up spring is worse than an enemy because divine pretenses disguise divine infidelity. A deceitful spring of a God cannot be trusted. A dried up river bed of a God is dangerous to life and not a "fountain of living waters" (4:13). An evaporated life-source of a God is a deceit, a treachery, and a death-blow.

Jeremiah believes he is a failed prophet, but it is not his fault. God delayed in fulfilling the prophetic word, and this delay makes Jeremiah a sitting duck, an object of scorn from his enemies, friends, and family who simply do not believe him. "Where is the word of the Lord?" (17:15).

In his last confession (20:7-13), Jeremiah's accusations against God reach a pinnacle of abrasive speech. "O YHWH you have seduced me and I was seduced. You have raped me and you have prevailed" (20:7).[18] Interpreters often shrink from the brutality of Jeremiah's sexual language, and translators often translate the verse more mildly: "O Lord you have enticed me and I was enticed; you have overpowered me and you have prevailed." I prefer the harsher translation because it conveys intimate violation and rupture of faith that accompany disaster, and it connects Jeremiah's outrage with the fate of Daughter of Zion, raped by her divine husband (13:20-27). Sexual assault again expresses the horror and desecration that constitute trauma and disaster. Jeremiah's prayers do not shrink from the truth of his predicament, nor do they hesitate to say how trustless his relationship with God has become.

Emblematic Sufferer

Jeremiah's harsh attacks on God appear to be his alone, not only because they arise from his prophetic calling but also because they take the form of individual laments. Individual laments use a first person singular voice (I, me, my), as does Jeremiah, and not the plural voice of the communal lament (we, us, our). But against other interpreters,[19] I do not think the distinction between the personal and communal laments matters very much in a community-oriented culture like ancient Judah. Some psalms even mix language of the individual and the community, so that the single voice stands in for everyone and everyone for the individual.[20] Whether they are the words of one or many, laments are liturgical prayers that carry the weight of the community's life in worship.[21]

So it is in the confessions. Jeremiah's first-person speech concerns more than himself. His faltering faith in God brings to the foreground Judah's crisis of faith created by the Babylonian disaster. His personal prayers represent the spiritual predicament of deep distrust in God that follows the smashing of life in its many dimensions.[22] They name this experience obliquely, indirectly, through the life of one person, and in the process they show the people how to place it all before God. They refuse to let God off the hook and they simultaneiously hold onto God, no matter what.

Like the biographical stories about Jeremiah, his confessions trace the contours of open wounds of his people, draw the shapes of their suffering, and center on the invisible loss of faith and meaning. Jeremiah's assault on the divine Judge looms over a nation that has watched Babylon flourish and wonders why.

Language to Voice Pain

The confessions provide language for disaster victims to complain about all that is unendurable. Attacked, defenseless, and mortally threatened, Jeremiah is "a lamb led to the slaughter," his enemies try to "cut off his life from the land of the living, to destroy the tree with its fruit" (11:19). He is isolated and alone; even his family and kinfolk turn against him (11:21-23; 12:6). His wound is incurable, refusing to be healed (15:18; 8:22, Eng.; 10:19; 14:20). And like his people, he too needs to be saved and healed (17:14-16; 18:20b).

Jeremiah's prayers make him an iconic character as much as do stories of his captivities. People can identify with him because he suffers from the same festering wounds that afflict them. His profound misgivings about God portray a kindred soul who mirrors their suspicion, skepticism, and outrage. And because the confessions take the traditional form of lament, they have the capacity to bring the people together in communal worship and gather them again as a praying people. Although we have no evidence the confessions were actually used liturgically, their form suits them for such use.[23] They provide a way to pray that gathers in the afflicted, draws them back from social isolation, articulates doubt, and shows how it is possible to cling relentlessly to God in the wreckage of their world.

Endure and Repent

Jeremiah's complex identity in the confessions as both prophet and symbol of the people converges again in words of divine assurance that come at the end of the first two confessions (12:5-6; 15:20-21). Twice God responds to Jeremiah's prayers. But God's words of assurance are not very reassuring. After Jeremiah complains about divine injustice in his first confession (11:18—12:3), God announces that worsening conditions lie ahead (12:4-6). "If you run with footmen and they weary you, how will you compete with horses," and if you fall down in a peaceful land, "how will you fare in the thickets of the Jordan?" (12:5). Brace yourself for what is to come. God's response to Jeremiah signals a long road to recovery. Survival will require mental strength, steadfast courage, and enduring patience. The vast and persistent suffering created by the nation's collapse will not end quickly. Endure, persist, be strong.

The other word of divine "assurance" from God after the second confession is equally puzzling:

> If you turn to me, I will turn to you.
> I will make you a wall of bronze,
> they will not prevail over you.
> I will deliver you from the hand of the wicked.
> I will redeem you from the grasp of the violent. (15:20-21)

But Jeremiah has turned to God. The Hebrew word translated "turn"[24] can mean to "repent," but nowhere does the book identify Jeremiah among those who need to repent. Yet the people of Judah—its kings, priests, prophets, and ordinary people—are repeatedly called to repentance, to turn back to God, the source of their life and their only hope for renewal. When God replies to Jeremiah by urging him to "return" so God may turn to him, Jeremiah stands in for the whole people. If they turn to God now, they will survive and their relationship with God will live.

Faith Revives

Although Jeremiah traverses dark regions of doubt and grief in his prayers, the confessions do not submerge under the weight of total despair; they reach toward life partially, slowly. Even if only for a moment, he does turn to God with renewed trust and confidence. The final confession (20:7-13) concludes with a startling change in outlook that seems utterly contradictory of his previous discontents. "Sing to YHWH, praise YHWH, for he has rescued the life of the needy from the hands of evildoers," Jeremiah urges (20:13). After all his churning spiritual turmoil, he asserts without explanation, without preparation, that the "Lord is with me as a Mighty Warrior." Perhaps it is the capacity of laments to bring unspeakable suffering into the light that expands the heart and makes room for hope to emerge across the gap of emptiness.

Survival

Like the stories of his captivity, the trajectory of Jeremiah's confessions is toward survival. Following the form of lament, his accusations against God are, for the moment, absorbed in praise, and relationship with God again seems sure. So it might be for Judah. Yet Jeremiah's confidence recedes quickly. He brings readers abruptly back to reality by cursing his birth (20:14-18, cf. Job 3). He would rather have been aborted in the womb than to have lived through this destruction. "Why did I come forth to see trouble and grief to end my days in shame?" (20:18). The reality surrounding Jeremiah and his readers remains a world of cursing, where life is filled with "toil and sorrow" and days are spent "in shame" (20:18). Jeremiah's quick reversal from confidence in God to cursing reflects how fragile and elusive faith can be on the other side of catastrophe.

How to Survive

Jeremiah's confessions compel readers to exercise critical judgment. He refuses to assent to a monopoly of opinion, to a settled interpretation of the disaster by one overriding, human-blaming explanation. The dramatic poetry acts upon readers to undermine the dominant rhetoric of human responsiblilty and to open other ways of interpreting what has happened to Judah. The confessions draw us into a complex ethical and theological world, not a simple place of good and bad, of justice and injustice, but a place that demands interpretive reflection.

To remember that Jeremiah is a symbolic character whose meaning embraces more than his prophetic calling is to hear the voices of survivors of the Babylonian disaster in his prayers. And if that is so, the confessions model how relationship with God might come back to life after disaster.

Ideal Survivor

Jeremiah's prayers make him a model for other sufferers, an ideal survivor. His words honor suffering in its many bitter dimensions and give voice to the mute pain of destroyed faith. They reflect back to victims their own spiritual and theological quagmire.

The confessions offer words and actions for spiritual survival of the nation by showing them how to pray in the thick of the theological devastation that accompanies disaster. Here is what to do in the pit of hopelessness: cling to God, even when God has slipped away. Yell at the top of your collective lungs. Hold tightly, mercilessly, and with every ounce of strength, shout and scream at the deity. Tell the truth, voice rage and despair right to the face of the "Just Judge." Hold nothing back. Complain, protest, resist. Reclaim experiences of misery and pain, see them and name them before God. "Give God an account" and approach God "like a prince," to return to the words of that other God resister (Job 31:37). Communicate all that is shattered, despair-creating, and spirit-defeating. Lay it out so you can see it yourselves and can see each other in this deep, unending wound. God is hidden there in that space.

Turning to the disappeared God is how to survive disaster. Public, communal worship can revivify life with the God of their past. Jeremiah's confessions give shape and words with which to do this, not by wholesale invention but by reinvention, by retrieving and retooling traditional liturgical prayers of lament.

As the ideal survivor, who suffers every loss yet refuses to be silent before God,[25] Jeremiah navigates the crashing, breaking storms of their lives. It is exactly the laments' bitter assaults on divine justice that paradoxically make them into a perfect vehicle of fidelity. Jeremiah fastens on to God with all his strength in the midst of catastrophe. Because Jeremiah's inner world is branded by doubt rather than simple certainty, his prayers invite readers to look at their own broken faith in God. And if Jeremiah's suffering is unjust, then perhaps theirs is too. Perhaps God has failed. At least for them it is a thinkable interpretation of disaster.

Prayers of Resistance

Following disaster people look everywhere, desperately seeking explanation, understanding, and meaning.[26] The confessions stand as resolute resistance to the rhetoric of human responsibility that dominates the book. By merely putting words to doubts about God's role, they generate questions about causes and complicate interpretation of disaster. They set into the public domain a counterview, a contrary opinion, and perhaps they even voice opinion present among some survivors.

At the least, the confessions turn divine justice into a question that forces readers to wonder about it, to let into their spiritual world the possibility that they may not deserve such overwhelming destruction, that their behavior may not be the chief cause of the disaster, that as Second Isaiah will say, they "have suffered double for all their sins" (Isa 40:2). Here the searchlight of blame settles upon God, but in the process, Jeremiah keeps talking and praying and imploring. He keeps God alive.

9

Encoding
Catastrophe

JEREMIAH 7:1—8:3; 11:1-14; 17:19-27

ecause disasters shatter "the sense of what life deeply means,"[1] and because they destroy the symbolic universe that formerly held up the world, new ways of conceiving identity must emerge for a people to survive as a people. Institutions and traditions that once were basic pillars of Judean life remained an inchoate rubble long after the Babylonian invasions. The burning of the temple, the razing of the king's palace, and the death and displacement of God's people—these demand explanation. A group of passages that specifically address temple, monarchy, and worship contain sermons ascribed to Jeremiah. These sermons take the form of prose passages of different lengths, scattered across the book.[2] In them, the prophet addresses the audience directly, sounds something like Moses in his sermons in the book of Deuteronomy, and offers a strongly authoritative interpretation of the disaster.

Until recently, Jeremiah's sermons have been the least interesting part of the book to me because they threaten the audience and firmly advocate the book's rhetoric of human responsibility for the nation's fall. But trauma and disaster studies suggest that it is these very features that make the sermons into works of resilience and recovery. They too are part of the book's relentless pursuit of language to speak of the disaster, part of the interpretive diversity that flows through the book, part of the "crucible of art" that is Jeremiah.[3]

Why Sermons?

The benefit of using the sermon form is the license it gives the preacher to speak to the community directly as "you" (second person plural forms in Hebrew). This manner of address reduces the space between speaker and readers and brushes aside the possibility that readers will miss the authoritative demands being made upon them. Sermons create an interpretive arena that permits certitude, even encourages it, at least in the book of Jeremiah. The prophet's sermons are not dialogical; they contain no weasel words, no conflicting opinions. Instead, they explain the nation's fall with confidence, teach lessons aggressively, and restrict their content to a few basic themes.

Simplifying Interpretation

Many interpreters think that Jeremiah's sermons are among the last materials to be added in the book's long process of composition. I agree that they come late because they offer the least nuanced explanations of events. As Stulman puts it, they "tame and codify" the wild poetry in which they are embedded.[4]

Trauma experts Robin Fivush and Beth Seelig describe an interpretive process akin to the one I see taking place in the sermons: "When experienced events cannot be understood, the human mind returns again and again to the event to try to make sense of it in a repetitive and compulsive way."[5] Adults try to create sense out of senseless experience. They "look for causal links and explanation for how and why events occurred the way they did."[6] Repetitive retelling of the catastrophe helps survivors "gain control over what happened," and eventually "reduce(s) the traumatic events to a set of standardized narratives."[7] Aspects of the narrative change in the retelling; interpretation does this. But the more coherent and better organized explanations become, the more they aid survivors. By simplifying explanations, narrative helps "turn frightening chaos into a contained and predictable event."[8]

Jeremiah's sermons simplify the causes of disaster. In his temple sermon (7:1—8:3), for example, there is only one reason for the nation's collapse—liturgical malfeasance. No other lens comes to bear on the situation. In the process, the sermon funnels the whole disaster into a narrow liturgical rant.

Yet despite the ways the sermons simplify and uncomplicate causes of the disaster, they also exhibit a subtlety of expression that may help survivors plunge more deeply into memories of war's terrors. Jeremiah encodes the fall of Judah within another set of disasters.

To show how Jeremiah's sermons use these processes of interpretation, I reflect on three of them: the temple sermon (7:1—8:3), the covenant sermon (11:1-14), and the Sabbath Sermon (17:19-25).

Sermon about the Temple (7:1—8:3)

Jeremiah's most famous prose sermon drops into the poetry of chapters 1–10, conspicuous against its surroundings. Set next to war poems, the sermons are jarring, but Stulman explains how they relate to the poetry. The poetry "depicts the coming judgment in thick, mythic terms, whereas the temple sermon gives concrete shape to the coming destruction."[9] The sermon fixates on one subject like a dog with a bone: sinful worship is the cause of the nation's fall. It simplifies causes that take multiple shapes in the poetry.

The temple sermon divides into two parts: Sinful Practices within the Temple (7:1-15) and Sinful Worship in Jerusalem (7:16—8:3).

Why the Temple Matters

The Jerusalem temple was a major symbol of Judean identity before its destruction. In some sense, the temple *is* the nation, and its ruin signifies the collapse of the whole society. It represents a shorthand way to speak of Judah's life and faith.[10] From the time of King Solomon centuries earlier, Israel believed that God dwelled with them in the temple and from there protected them in a precarious world. The temple's existence marked them as God's chosen people, and its destruction crushed all the beliefs associated with it, along with economic and leadership systems that supported it.[11] The temple's ruin transformed the world from a solid place to a liquid one.

Sinful Practices in the Temple (7:1-15)

The temple fell, according to Jeremiah, because of sins committed there. Period. Injustice, oppression, the shedding of innocent blood, and the failure to obey brought the disaster upon the people. These terrible things do not involve explicit idolatry; they are immoral behaviors that make a sham of worship, turn it into a lie. The prophet accuses everyone: "all you people of Judah, you that enter these gates to worship the Lord" (7:2). The accusation assumes that the people share an identity as worshippers (7:2). Worship of God is what constitutes them as one people, but false worship will destroy or, for readers, has already destroyed the temple and caused their expulsion from the land (7:14-15).

Like Shiloh

Jeremiah does not say outright, "The temple will be destroyed." He encodes the destruction by reminding them, instead, of another temple, a house of God also "called by my name," the temple at Shiloh north of Jerusalem.[12]

> "Go now to my place that it was in Shiloh where I made my name to dwell at first, and see what I did to it for the wickedness of my people Israel." (Jer 7:12)

When the sermon commands the people to "look at" the Shiloh ruin, it forces them to see a threat looming ahead of them. To look at Shiloh is to see how God will treat their temple if they do not repent (7:12, 14).

But the Shiloh temple is a substitute for the Jerusalem temple in this sermon, for the Jerusalem temple has already fallen. Its loss marks the vacuum of meaning in which they live. The reference to Shiloh helps them see what has happened to them without explicitly dredging up their own horrifying experiences of destruction. Shiloh encodes the traumatic violence of the razed Jerusalem temple by conjuring in the mind's eye a catastrophe similar to it. When they look at Shiloh, they see the burned ruins of the Jerusalem temple from a distance, set in a parallel world drawn from the past. That reference brings into public conversation memories of their own destroyed temple, obliquely as if from afar.

Such a sermonic tactic places the disaster slightly outside the people's immediate experience, as if they were watching a film clip about another event that ushers in their partly suppressed memories of terror. The veiled reference is a healing practice, a way of helping people assimilate the whole of the disaster through one symbol, touching one element that evokes the whole of their lost world. And of no little importance, the reminder of the Shiloh ruins reconnects them to the long story of the whole people of Israel before the kingdom divided into two. It joins their loss with the larger memory of their national past and moves a step closer to assimilating the disaster into their lives.

The sermon also links the temple to the exiles, calling up memories of the invasions and the splintering of the community (7:15; 8:3). But again Jeremiah speaks about the disaster indirectly. He draws another analogy with an historic dispersion in the North. "I will cast you out of my sight, just as I cast out your kinfolk, all the offspring of Ephraim" (7:15). Ephraim, another name for the northern kingdom of Israel, was destroyed by the Assyrians more than a century earlier (721 B.C.E.). The sermon's comparison of Judean deportations with the dispersion of their northern kinfolk lifts the Babylonian exile into a parallel past, into a universe that both belongs to their story yet is removed from it by time and geography. Ephraim's deportations work in the sermon to reveal Judah's own shattered life and potential disappearance from history.[13] The historical distance created by the comparison helps disaster victims to approach their situation without being retraumatized and reminds them of their larger history.

Sinful Worship in Jerusalem (7:16—8:3)

The second part of the temple sermon moves through a catalogue of increasingly heinous liturgical sins. These sins and their consequences call forth memories of the disaster directly (7:16—8:3). The sins are idolatrous but they are not necessarily committed in the temple. Biblical scholars have given a great deal of attention to the sins, but from the perspective of trauma and disaster studies, the punishments are equally important. They depict the hideous consequences of war and bring before the people their memories of war's hideous aftermath.

Punishments in this sermon expose experiences that can haunt people for generations. Here are the sins and punishments:

1. Worshipping the Queen of Heaven (7:18-19) will yield ecological disaster that accompanies every war. God will pour wrath "on human beings and animals, on the trees of the field and the fruit of the ground" (7:20).
2. Making sacrifices that God did not desire and refusing to listen to the prophets (7:21-28) will cast the community into profound mourning for "they themselves will die" (7:29).
3. Defiling the temple, worshipping idols, and burning "their sons and daughters in the fire" of child sacrifice (7:30—8:3) will turn the land into a place of slaughter with no room to bury hordes of the dead. Corpses will be food for the birds and animals. Bones of the king, bones of the priests, bones of the prophets, and bones of all the inhabitants of Jerusalem will be desecrated, scattered, and left unburied "like dung on the surface of the ground." Death shall be preferred to life (7:32—8:3).

Like freeze frames from a battlefield, the sermon's punishments portray a land strewn with the residue of unthinkable violence. Although set in the future, these scenes rekindle memories of the past. The temple sermon reminds the community of its many traumas, but these elements of the disaster are only part of the calamity. The sermon cares most about the invisible world of faith obliterated by disaster, the shared loss of confidence in the temple, the prophet, and in God.

Breakdown of Faith and Trust

The temple sermon tells the surviving community what it already knows. Their belief that the temple would protect them is not true. At the heart of the matter is the conviction common in the ancient world that the deity's presence in the temple kept city and land safe from attack. If the temple has fallen, was trust in it always false? To this question, the sermon proclaims a simple answer: the temple fell because God punished Judah for its faithless, violent idolatry. That means that divine capriciousness is not the driving force behind the disaster no matter how it seems. Nor was the temple itself the problem. It was the people's infidelity inside and outside the temple that explains the disaster.

God Tried

The temple sermon never says directly that the people no longer trusted God, but because the entire sermon tries to rehabilitate God's reputation, it is clear that faith has failed. Like so much of the book, the sermon is a theodicy, that is, it defends the justice of God, puts God in the right. The sermon does this by telling readers all the things God did to prevent disaster: God sent all "my servants the prophets . . . yet they did not listen" (7:25-26). God reminded them of their covenant relationship (7:22, 25). God tried to win them back, to persuade them to listen, but they refused.

God tried so hard to warn them. God has been the constant one, still reliable, still powerful, still seeking them, but anger was the only suitable response to their false worship. The sermon is a public defense of God, a work of healing ministry, and another way to begin to incorporate this disaster into the larger, pre-disaster narrative. It insists that the whole disaster was not a random event but an utterly predictable one.

Anthropologist Kai Erikson and others note that traumatized people often feel they have lost an important measure of control over circumstances of their own lives and so they are very vulnerable.[14] When Jeremiah says the disaster is the consequence of human sin, he gives them both a predicted and predictable world. He stabilizes the universe. He does not merely say, "If you had repented sooner, this terrible suffering might have been avoided." The sermon demands something much stronger. Obey my voice now! Live justly now! Turn from idolatry now! Prompting readers to act, the sermon presses them to break out of torpor and numbed shock. Perhaps God will relent and take you back. Perhaps you still have a future.

Like an artist who uses a visual frame to obliterate from view everything that might distract from the essence of her drawing, the sermon's thinned-down focus on liturgical infractions revisits physical and theological dimensions of the whole calamity in veiled fashion. It speaks about the temple's destruction, deportations, and the memories of corpses, and it attempts to revive faith in God. Its violent fire and brimstone is an expression of the violence of their history. By abbreviating the disaster's causes to false worship, it encodes the disaster into one liturgical frame of reference. The next two sermons do something similar as they focus on other foundational traditions: covenant and Sabbath keeping.

Sermon about the Covenant (11:1-14)

The ancient covenant God made at Mount Sinai, after rescuing Israel from slavery in Egypt, is the root of Israel's identity, the deep ground from which they have become God's chosen people. The covenant, too, collapsed in the disaster, and covenant encapsulates the whole being of the nation. On Mount Sinai, God promised, "You shall be my treasured possession out of all the peoples (Exod 19:5). In grateful response to their rescue from slavery, they, in turn, are obliged to keep the covenant. It formalized their relationship, gave it structure, and laid out the terms of mutual obligation. "So shall you be my people, and I will be your God" (Jer 11:4).

To explain the disaster, Jeremiah's covenant sermon narrows attention differently than the temple sermon. Rather than committing liturgical sins, the people broke "the covenant that I made with their ancestors" (11:10). They did this continuously, ever since the time God brought them out of the "iron smelter" of slavery in Egypt (11:4). And since that time, everyone has "walked in the stubbornness of their evil heart" (11:8), turning "their backs on the sins of their ancestors" and going "after other gods to serve them" (11:9-10, 12, 13, 17). "Therefore . . . I am going to bring disaster upon them they cannot escape" (11:11).

What strikes me about the covenant sermon is its abstraction. Compared to the temple sermon, it offers no specific details either about the people's offenses or about the disaster itself. The people turned to "the iniquities of their ancestors," following other gods, making offerings to them, and setting up altars to Ba'al (Jer 11:12-13). These accusations are similar to the ones made against Wife Israel and Wife Judah (2:1—4:2), but they are no more specific. They are generalities, perhaps sinful dispositions, an orientation away from God expressed in conventional language. Lack of specificity may mean that everyone knew what covenant-breaking sins were, so there was no need to explain. Or it may mean, as I think, that in explaining the disaster as a result of covenant-breaking, the sermon is again simplifying interpretation to one cause and effect chain from among an infinite possibility of causes.

Like the temple sermon, the covenant sermon lets God off the hook. God is not to blame for the disaster; the people are. Just as they desecrated the temple, they also broke covenant and ruptured their relationship with God. The people are the obstructers, and Jeremiah could not prevent it because God closed off prayer as an avenue of prophetic intercession (11:14).

Many interpreters notice how the covenant sermon draws upon Moses' sermon in the book of Deuteronomy (Deut 28). There, God promises the people covenant blessings as well as curses. But Jeremiah mentions only curses. "Cursed be the one who does not heed the words of this covenant," is the sermon's topic sentence (11:3). There are no blessings in Jeremiah's sermon, as if "covenant-breakers" renames the community. I used to think this sermonic narrowing reflected no more than the narrative arc of the book toward the inexorable fall of the nation, enacted symbolically in chapters 18–20. The covenant sermon may omit the expected covenant blessings simply because the curse approaches in the book like an arrow, zinging inexorably toward its target.

But there is another important difference between this sermon and Moses' sermon in Deuteronomy 28. Moses promises a deluge of curses upon those who do not keep the covenant (Deut 28:16-68).[15] Jeremiah limits curses to one, incorporating all of them into the "disaster" they cannot escape (11:11). "I brought upon them all the words of this covenant, which I commanded them to do but they did not" (Jer 11:8). I think Jeremiah leaves out promises of covenant blessings because disaster has already befallen them. The curses have been enacted. When Jeremiah speaks of the curse as a single event, he simplifies the disaster, explains it, and makes it more manageable.

Such simplified thinking reduces the disaster to a predictable event. From the time of their ancestors, the people were warned to keep the covenant, but they failed. They followed other gods. They turned away. Their life in the "land flowing with milk and honey" depended solely upon their fidelity, and predictably they failed. Predictability means that traumatic events are not evidence of overwhelming chaos afoot in the world, and it means that right behavior can prevent a reoccurrence of the violence in the future. They can have a future.

The covenant sermon, like the temple sermon, defends God. The covenant has not failed, but its curses have been executed as promised. Although this sermon does not call for repentance, it implies that "fixing" their life depends upon total loyalty to God. The sermon invites reconsideration of the shredded covenant tradition.

Sermon about the Sabbath (17:19-27)

The Sabbath sermon focuses on still another crushing dimension of the disaster, the collapse of the monarchy. The monarchy, too, is a stand-in for the nation. When the head of a nation is brought down, the whole nation is greatly wounded. Judah's kings are not only the head of the government; they are the institution divinely ordained to be God's regent on earth, and David's offspring are to sit on the throne forever (2 Sam 7). Consequently, the capture of the king, death of princes, and deportation of King Jehoiachin to Babylon meant that Judah's monarchy was reduced to ashes in the fires of invasion and occupation. According to the Sabbath sermon, kingship has ended in Judah because kings and people failed to keep Sabbath. The sermon (Jer 17:19-20) "explains" how and why the monarchy was destroyed.

Like the previous sermons, this one joins in the quest for meaning in the aftermath of disaster. Across the book of Jeremiah, leadership groups—prophets, priests and kings—come under severe censure for moral bankruptcy and infractions that cause the nation's downfall. This is not surprising since, according to

Erickson, "People whose worldview has been tempered by exposure to trauma easily lose faith not only in good *will* but in the good *sense* of those in charge of a dangerous universe."[16]

The Sabbath sermon encodes the disaster as the consequence of divine anger at the royal leaders for failure to keep the Sabbath. Keeping the Sabbath is an ancient command, part of the torah given on Sinai (Exod 20:8-11; Deut 5:12-28). Jeremiah preaches this sermon urging the people to keep the Sabbath "for the sake of your lives" (17:21-23). If they observe Sabbath, they will survive. Jeremiah shaves down Sabbath-keeping to a few prohibitions: do not carry a burden or do any work,[17] and "keep the Sabbath day holy" (v. 22).

The first part of the sermon declares that the ancestors violated the holiness of the day (17:19-23), but the second part is open-ended.[18] If the people keep the Sabbath, kingship will be restored (17:24-27).

> Then there shall enter by the gates of this city kings who sit on the throne of David, riding in chariots and on horses, they and their officials, the people of Judah, and the inhabitants of Jerusalem . . . bringing thank offerings to the house of the Lord. (17:26)

Sabbath-keeping offers a structure of action and responsibility. It brings people together and makes them again a community of worshippers. Refraining from work on the Sabbath is the condition by which rulers and people will live in the city of Jerusalem forever, a center of worship for all the people (17:24-26). But:

> If you do not listen to me to keep the Sabbath day holy and to carry no burden through the gates of Jerusalem on the Sabbath day, then I will kindle a fire in its gates; it shall devour the palaces of Jerusalem and it shall not be quenched. (17:27)

Failing to keep the Sabbath will bring the fires of destruction.

Jeremiah's Sabbath sermon crams the massive impact of disaster inside the boundaries of limited topic: the kingship does not rule in Jerusalem and the world is burned down because of failure to keep Sabbath. But note the strangeness of the explanation. Devastation of kings and city occur not because the kings made inappropriate political decisions, wrongheaded alliances, governed with arrogance and corruption, or lacked wisdom. The kings' failures are not directly related to their capacity to govern at all. They failed because they and the people carried burdens that interfered with Sabbath rest. They violated the divine law given at Sinai.

The Sabbath prohibition of burden-carrying here may seem legalistic, but it is not. It refers to the need for workers to rest, for commerce to cease, and for time to be devoted to worship of God.[19] For a skeptic like me, it makes me laugh to think that people and kings carrying something, say a sack of money, or a bale of grain, or engaging in business, would put God out so much, would make God so furious that burning the world down would be a suitable response. But the point of the sermon is that Sabbath-breaking behavior reveals profoundly distorted relationships.

Sabbath practice is rooted in the Ten Commandments and its observance is part of the ancient covenant (Exod 20:8-11; Deut 5:12-15).[20] Stulman proposes that Sabbath observance "is essential to the maintenance of the cosmos. As long as the Sabbath is sanctified, the community maintains some measure of blessing, protection, and order. Violation jeopardizes the social symbolic order of the world."[21] The sermon narrows interpretation of the disaster, explains the collapse of government, and urges the people to live in accord with their ancient tradition. They are to be a people who practice Torah.[22]

Sermons as Survival Strategies

These three sermons offer three separate sets of reasons for the nation's fall. They "provide causal links and explanation of how and why events occurred the way they did, and they help to integrate raw emotion into an explanatory framework."[23] They simplify explanation and contribute to the book's quest for meaning in terms that defend both God and ancient faith traditions. They call the people back to their most basic identity as a worshipping people. When the sermons narrow their lines of sight, focusing on simplified causes and culprits, they make overwhelming catastrophe more graspable and perhaps more endurable. This is how they build resilience and encourage recovery.

The destructive swath of disasters includes the less visible world of meaning. They destroy faith and trust. They unravel the tapestry of beauty and sense that secured the world. Chaos prevails. Jeremiah's sermons narrow and temper the scope of chaos by encoding it in stories of the nation's past, in institutions that mark them as a people, and in urging the people to united action of repentance and worship. The sermons are pastoral interventions to rebuild the broken community of faith, part of the process that Stulman calls "sculpting words out of the rubble of devastation."[24]

10 Rekindling Hope

The Little Book
of Consolation

JEREMIAH 30-31

I t is a profound paradox that when there is no way forward, when the future is cut off and death is winning, hope can appear unexpectedly, and the universe expands in unthinkable ways.[1] After disaster, hope emerges slowly, if at all. First, it needs space in which to take root, a fallowing of the land, a turning of the soil to aerate and open it. Before hope can appear, survivors of disaster have to find language to tell of it; they have to grieve accumulations of loss and begin to place the catastrophe into larger frames of meaning. Hope arrives in stops and starts, risings and fallings, in painful switchbacks between despair and trust. Hope in Jeremiah is not optimism but unbidden, unexpected revelation of divine love.

Within the larger book of Jeremiah, words of explicit hope appear sporadically, as if to keep readers going and inoculate them against utterly succumbing to despair. But even so, readers are simply not prepared for the explosive beauty of the "little book of consolation." These brief chapters of hope are a tour de force that sweeps aside the general bleakness of most of the book.

The Little Scroll of Consolation (Jer 30–31)

The little book or "scroll" of consolation (30:2), refers to Jeremiah's lyrical vision of hope and love in chapters 30–31 (33).[2] These chapters contain poetry and prose of radiant power. Their location just after the middle of the book rather than at the end suggests that an intuitive sensibility guided the book's arrangement, as if its editors understood how unsteady is the process of recovery, how no straight lines exist along the path to hope.[3] Jeremiah's words of comfort in these chapters disrupt the harsh, clamped-down life of people who live in the persistent grip of trauma and disaster. Hope's abrupt appearance wakes them up to visions of an alternative world.[4] That world is utopian; it exists only as a promise, as a call to bring the people back to life.

The Disaster Again

Before forcefully challenging the status quo,[5] Jeremiah's scroll opens with stark reminders of the terrors and violence of the disaster. It speaks directly to "survivors of the sword" (31:12) who "have heard a cry of panic, of terror, of no peace" (30:3-4), who live with incurable hurt, grievous wounds, who lack someone to execute justice, and have neither medicine nor healing (30:13). Upon them, God's wrath has gone forth in a fierce storm (30:23-24). By beginning with the searing pain of terrifying memories, the scroll honors the suffering of survivors, neither whitewashing nor trivializing their losses. This starting point gives the scroll a chance to be heard by its audience because it witnesses first to their reality. As Fretheim suggests, "the great distress endured by the people has entered the divine life."[6]

Then, without explanation, the scroll reverses the world wrought by the disaster. God directly addresses female Zion, noticing that she is abandoned, wounded, unloved, filled with pain (30:12-14). "I will restore you to health," God promises. She has been punished for her guilt, but God will now punish her foes (30:15-16). God will restore the fortunes of the "tents of Jacob" (30:18), rebuild the city, bring back the displaced, and reunite the broken family.[7] The transformed world imagined in the scroll does not restore what was; it builds new life from threads of the old. That new world will be born from God's love for the displaced, the broken, and the comfortless.

The scroll, like the rest of the book, is a survival strategy, another interpretation of the past, but in these chapters more than survival is at stake. The scroll promises a reconstituted community and the flourishing of all the people of Israel.

The Rebuilt City

After disaster, the first requirement of survivors is without question physical safety for themselves and their loved ones. Against historical probability, Jeremiah's scroll imagines the rebuilding of Jerusalem as a protective citadel arising from the ruins.

> I am going to restore the fortunes of the tents of Jacob,
> and have compassion on his dwelling:
> The city shall be rebuilt upon its mount
> and the citadel set on its rightful site. (30:18)

God will rebuild the city, Judah's traditional holy place, as a safe habitat and shielding fortress for its inhabitants. Called "Zion" (30:17; 31:6, 12), the hallowed and mythic name of "ancestral traditions,"[8] the city will shelter the homeless and fulfill the yearnings of the displaced and the broken. On Zion they will live together in safety. Yet the rebuilt city of shelter and safety is only the beginning of Jeremiah's vision (30:18-20). The transformed community that will return there may be even more important. Survivors of the sword will again be a worshipping people who live in right relationships with God and one another.[9]

A Renewed Identity

The unifying mark of the returnees that forms them into a community, is their unique identity as a gathering of worshippers who will sing together in gratitude and praise:

> Out of them shall come thanksgiving and the sound of merrymakers,
> and I will make them many and not few,
> and I will make them honored and they shall not be disdained. (30:19)

In the promised future that lies just over the horizon, they will recognize God's care of them and know that God has brought them home. God will claim them for "their congregation shall be established before me; and I will punish all who oppress them" (30:20).

Social Renewal

Flowing from their worshipping life will come a new society of economic and spiritual justice. By contrast to their past life together, the new community will live according to radically altered, egalitarian social expectations. Those usually judged least suited for leadership—the feeble and the vulnerable, the lowly and the wounded—will become the center of new life.[10] The ones whom God calls home in this poetry are the same ones who cried out in panic, had no peace, lived in distress, and endured terrors (30:5-7). They are the ones freed from bondage, whose hurt is incurable. They are without medicine, without healing; plundered and preyed upon, they cry out in endless pain (30:12-17). They are the victims of disaster.

> See, I am going to bring them from the land of the north,
> And gather them from the farthest parts of the earth,
> Among them the blind and the lame, those with child and those in labor,
>   together,
> a great company they shall come. (31:8)

The survivors returning to Zion will form a procession of the forgotten, the disabled, and the vulnerable. Although they are the lowest in the society, they will be the beating heart of the restored community. The blind and the lame are physically different, weak, deemed deficient in the ancient world, stigmatized, and perhaps despised.[11] Pregnant women are of low public stature and holders of little political power, but together these people have the astonishing capacity to give birth to new life. For a nation seemingly doomed to extinction at the hands of Babylon, the vulnerable and broken themselves will become the promised bearers of its future, a future of unimaginable reversals. The whole people, once afflicted, despised, and broken, will live together in safety, merriment, and thanksgiving (30:18-20). Grace and joy, prosperity and fertility will overtake the turbulence of their present lives.

Economic Well-Being Reinvented (31:10-14)

The new community exists to live in right relationship with God. This is their root identity, the bedrock from which their society arises. From that identity follows a vision of a society where mutual respect and honor prevail, where they are thankful for life together, for any life at all, for survival from the ashes. Reconstituted as a people, they will establish a community of well-being for everyone.

> They shall come and sing aloud on the heights of Zion,
> And they shall be radiant over the goodness of the Lord.
> over the grain, the wine, and the oil, over the young of the flock and the herd.
> Their life shall become like a watered garden . . .
> Then the young women shall rejoice in the dance,
> and the young men and the old shall be merry . . .
> I will give the priests their fill of fatness,
> and my people shall be satisfied with my bounty. (31:11-14)

Survivors of disaster will live in a watered garden, an oasis of abundance. The new Eden will yield enough food and fatness for the priests and their sacrifices, enough joy for both old and young, enough beauty to satisfy everyone bountifully. More than simple survival awaits them in this new paradise. There they will thrive, grow, and be satisfied with the physical and spiritual gifts of a new creation.

But like the rebuilt city, the garden of delights also serves as the backdrop for God's revived family, so dramatically severed at the book's beginning (2:1—4:2) but reunited here in love, mercy, and forgiveness.

Love in the Family Renewed (31:15-34)

When the scroll of consolation reconvenes God's broken family, there are no requirements and no demands placed upon its members,[12] only announcements of divine love: "I have loved you with an everlasting love, therefore I have continued my faithfulness to you (31:3b). But how can the little book of consolation speak of God's everlasting love and faithfulness after the poem in which God rapes the beloved Daughter of Zion (13:20-27)? How can this relationship resume after the infidelity and violence of its past?

One answer to these questions is that the little book of consolation comes from a later and different author than the poetry of the broken family and warfare. From the perspectives of trauma and disaster studies that is probably right. The vision of hope contained in these hopeful chapters would be meaningless for victims immediately upon the heels of disaster. Later in the long processes of survival and recovery, the little book presents a different language about God's relationship with the people, although it draws from earlier parts of the book and reuses imagery and language that appeared there (chaps 1–25). Much of that material struggles with bringing pain, collapse, and grief to the surface and with finding explanations and causes for the disaster. The poems and prose pieces in the little book of consolation work to lead the community past the disaster by imagining an alternative future in continuity with the past but different from it. At the center of that effort is yet another interpretation of the disaster. God never left them; God was with them and seeks to restore them to the divine self and to one another. The broken family split apart in the book's early chapters will regather, revive, and begin anew.

God's Family Reconceived

The scroll depicts God's family members with new names, mother Rachel and child Ephraim. They are members of one of Israel's original families, first seen in the book of Genesis when the whole people were being formed into the family of Jacob. The old family names used here help to retell the disaster within the context of Judah's larger national story.[13] The new family poetry joins victims to their former identity and helps to assimilate the disaster with their larger story.[14] Rachel and Ephraim symbolize the nation revived and living again on Zion. They personify and gather up the generations of the destroyed community.[15] Although these figures also evoke the now defunct northern kingdom of Israel, the scroll uses them to restitch survivors to their past as Jacob's family of old.[16] Such harkening back to pristine beginnings is a sign of healing, an indication that recovery has begun, no matter how tentatively.

Family Reunited (31:15-22)

The poem of family reunion divides into three stanzas: Mother Rachel (31:15-17); Child Ephraim (31:18-20); and A New Thing (31:21-22).

Mother Rachel (31:15-17)

A sound of "lamentation and bitter weeping" dramatically captures readers' attention at the poem's beginning. "Rachel is weeping for her children" (31:15), like the widowed Jerusalem in the book of Lamentations (Lam 1:2). A narrator announces that there is no way to comfort her, for she is beyond recovery.[17] Then abruptly, God contradicts the narrator's assessment of Rachel's condition. God tells her to dry her tears and then adds a heart-stopping, world-overturning promise. Her children whom she believed to be dead are coming "back from the land of the enemy; there is hope for your future" (31:16-17). Her offspring are alive and coming home. A more poignant announcement hardly can be imagined as the poet climbs into the heart of a grieving mother in a moment of emotional earthquake, the moment she learns her children live. She is, of course, Jerusalem—the people of the land, and the land itself—God's wife.

Child Ephraim (31:18-20)

The second stanza shifts from mother Rachel to the child Ephraim. Again there is a voice, this time speaking words of shame, repentance, and pleading (31:18). Rachel weeps, but the child speaks to God directly as in the scenes of the broken family (3:21-25). He uses liturgical language that embellishes the earlier repentance of God's children who admit their shameful youth and appeal to their father in a liturgy of repentance. Ephraim begs to be brought back, "for you are the Lord my God" (31:18-19; 31:6; cf. 3:22). In this poem, he interprets his suffering, not as an end to the family but as the discipline of an unruly son by his father. The disaster was an act of "tough love" to make him better.

But unlike the children's expression of repentance at the book's beginning, this expression brings forth a response from God:

> Is Ephraim my dear son? Is he the child I delight in?
> As often as I speak against him, I still remember him.
> Therefore I am deeply moved for him,
> I will surely have mercy on him. (31:20)

According to this interpretation of the national cataclysm, God never forgot the children even in the middle of the former alienation between them. And again, child Ephraim serves as an example of return and renewal for the audience, the next generations still flattened by the disaster. Ephraim represents them, the children of God and of Judah/Rachel. God calls them back to live in this family. And like Ephraim, they too must repent and express absolute loyalty to God.

A New Thing (31:21-22)[18]

The poem of family renewal ends in mystery. God turns back to a female: "Return, O virgin Israel" (31:21-22). Road makers point the way back home and the way back to her husband/father (cf. 3:12b). "How long will you waver O faithless daughter?" The faithless daughter is Rachel, the Daughter of Zion, the displaced people, and in this poem, Ephraim's mother. And she is also God's wife who has been wavering since the book's beginning (3:1—4:2).[19] The old narrative of marital infidelity is not dead; it has merely grown in new directions. From her comes no response, but God counters her silence with a surprising act of creation: "For the Lord has created a new thing on the earth, "a woman encompasses a man" (31:22).

This is a difficult and astonishing verse. Deciding on the translation of the Hebrew verb to "protect," "encompass," "surround" (sbb) is only part of the difficulty. Another is the problem of understanding what the new thing is that God is creating, followed by uncertainty about the identity of the woman and the man.

In the context of Jeremiah's family metaphor, the woman and man appear to be Rachel and Ephraim, God's wife and repentant child. If so, then God's new thing is that the mother again surrounds, encompasses, and protects her child, Ephraim. The generations that experienced the disaster and the present displaced generation reunite, and God's broken family begins to come together again.

Woman, Man (31:21-30)

But three prose comments follow the poem of the restored family and appear to interpret the puzzles of its last verse simply by being set next to it. Rather than narrowly pinpointing meaning, the comments open the poem out to multiple interpretations.[20]

In the first comment, Jeremiah receives a dream revelation in which God pronounces a blessing upon restored Jerusalem. (31:23-26). The city will be a place of rest and replenishment for the weary who will live there together. If these prose verses are commenting on the poem, then Jerusalem is the woman encompassing the man; she is the Daughter of Zion welcoming and embracing her returning children, all the families of Israel.

The second comment on the family poem promises future fertility to the destroyed nation (31:27-28). "I will sow the house of Israel and the house of Judah with the seed of humans and the seed of animals." Seed imagery suggests that the woman sexually encompasses man to become pregnant, as God builds and plants the nation anew. Rather than disappearing, the destroyed people receive the promise of fertility, offspring, and new generations, as well as livestock to feed them.

The final prose comment shifts to the question of moral responsibility for the disaster by contradicting the proverb, "the parents have eaten sour grapes, and the children's teeth are set on edge." (31:29-30). According to the proverb, the children's suffering results from the infidelity and sinfulness of the previous generation. But God revises that view in these verses, for each generation will die for its own sins. This is not a statement about individual responsibility, as interpreters often claim, but generational or corporate responsibility, or at least it seems so in a community-oriented culture in search of responsible parties in the aftermath of disaster.[21] The post-disaster community can no longer blame its parents' generation—God's unfaithful wife—for its predicament. They, too, are accountable for their behavior and must repent. If these verses comment on the family poem, as I propose, then woman does not encompass a man. Rachel's guilt does not encompass Ephraim's. The present generation is responsible too and must turn back to God in absolute loyalty and repentance to renew their broken relationship.

Whatever a woman encompassing a man (v. 22) may denote, this poem reverses gender imagery from earlier parts of the book. Rachel, weeping mother, virgin daughter, faithless daughter, is invited home again by the God/Husband who had cast her off (3:1-5). She symbolizes the future in some unexplained, yet over-explained, fashion. She is a many-layered symbol, the restored Israel, mother of north and south, rebuilt Jerusalem, soon to be reunited with her children, laughing, not weeping, protecting, surrounding, embracing them, and leading them into a future of flourishing life.

The new thing God creates in the poem of family reunion is unclear, ambiguous, and mysterious, but it is a potent overturning of the present order. The poem of family renewal promises restored intimacy with God and the survival of the reunited people of Judah. They will live together again, and this time their bonds will be firm, loyal, and forgiving. But their repentance is not determinative. It is God who seals this renewal by proclaiming a new covenant, a new way of relating within the family. The new covenant is about new life in God's restored family. It is about the renewal of the broken marriage and family.

The New Covenant (31:31-34)

In the past, God's covenant with Israel was like a marriage that the people destroyed by their adulterous idolatry, even though God was "their husband."[22] But now, God promises to restore them and to recommit to them.

The days are surely coming, says the Lord, when I will make a new covenant with the house of Israel and the house of Judah. It will not be like the old one that I made with their ancestors when I took them by the hand to bring them out of the land of Egypt, a covenant they broke, though I was their husband. (31:31-32)

God's relationship with the people cannot resume the way it was when God rescued them from slavery in Egypt (31:32). Disasters nearly always demolish faith and trust; they tear down the symbolic firmament that protects the world. How could the covenant with Moses have survived through Babylonian invasions, national collapse, and massive displacements of the Judean people? How could the people trust that they are God's chosen ones set free from slavery, when Babylon enslaved them anew? The new covenant and the entire scroll of consolation address the crisis of faith created by the disaster, the cosmic crumbling at the heart of the book.

The promise of the new covenant in Jeremiah seeks to revive trust, make it thinkable, offer a way the people might live again one day in wholeness and peace. But like any good preacher or artist, Jeremiah uses old materials, words from Israel's past, and redesigns the ancient tradition. The new covenant will be different from the old one "when I took them by the hand to bring them out of the land of Egypt," as the prophet reminds them of the past. "This is the covenant I will make with them," a "new covenant," an eruption of something innovative and unexpected in their midst.

But is there anything new about the new covenant that God creates among them? A number of similarities connect the new one with the old one. Again God will rescue them from a cruel empire, this time from Babylon, not Egypt. Again God will give them the law—the "torah," or "instruction"—for daily life that they received at Sinai. And again God promises fidelity to them in the traditional covenant formula: "I will be their God and they shall be my people" (31:33; cf. Exod 19:1-6).

The new covenant is not radically new; it is the old covenant reasserted, reaffirmed, re-inaugurated. What is new about it is the manner of speaking about it as a deeper, more intimate, more egalitarian union. The new covenant resembles a miraculously revivified marriage, begun again after conflict, infidelity, and a long, painful struggle. This time, "I will put my law within them and write it on their hearts." God recommits the divine self to them and announces their transformation in which the law will be part of them, internal to their beings. No longer will the covenant exist only on tablets of stone and require obedience to external rule. The law will be something they live and breathe, it will take up residence within their very beings. They will no longer have to teach one another about God or say to one another, "know the Lord." Soon "they shall know me, from the least of them to the greatest, says the Lord for I will forgive their sins" (31:34). Soon, God will renew their family relationship, forgive their iniquity, and remember their sin no more. The new covenant will be profoundly egalitarian. It will grant no individual or group spiritual superiority in the community; "from the least to the greatest, all shall know me." Members of God's family will share equally in human dignity and in participation in God's life.

The Knowing of Lovers

The throbbing heart of Jeremiah's new covenant is the promise that "They will all know me" (31:34). God promises presence in full, attentive, and loving mutuality. To "know" (*yd'*) God means to relate in intimacy, sexual knowledge, and reciprocity. It is the knowing of lovers. The promise that they all will know God again identifies the people of Judah as God's chosen who will experience God's presence. They will be focused on the divine; they will be breathers of God's life; they will live in union with God. Their lives will be spiritually grounded, centered on God's love within and among them. To have knowledge of God means to participate in God's life, glimpsed provisionally and partially and practiced in community.[23] The promise of the new covenant reaches toward those without hope, reunites them, and grants them rebirth as forgiven people.

Jeremiah declares the covenant to be "new," but it is not new. From the time of Moses onward, the covenant always marked the community as God's chosen people, always set out the law for the practice of just relationships, always named God's life among them. Jeremiah amplifies Judah's theological tradition, intensifies it, and renames it in ways a good spiritual renewal program or a fine sermon or transforming spiritual book attempts to bring the tradition to life again for people broken, wearied, and doubt-ridden.

Ever Ancient, Ever New

The new covenant is a highly conservative theological assertion. Jeremiah's little book of consolation rethinks and reinvents the covenant tradition as a deepening, a reigniting of what once was. Through one of Israel's most hallowed traditions, Jeremiah's new covenant both preserves and re-enlivens Judah's relationship with God, at once ever ancient and ever new. The new covenant is the old one reborn, internalized, intensified to gather in the whole family and reunite them with the God of their past. Through it, the old covenant made at Sinai becomes stronger, deeper, and firmer. Jeremiah's creative innovations save the original covenant from destruction in the disaster. They reframe Judah's present brokenness in light of a nation's whole story. They reset Judah's relationship with God in the most appealing terms.

I need to stress the continuity between the new covenant and the old one because Christians have so often perceived it as an invalidation of God's covenant with the Jews, replaced by the new covenant in Jesus. In the process, I want to celebrate Jeremiah's theological creativity from which springs not only a renewed Judaism but also Christianity itself in a further appropriation of the covenant tradition.

The Gap between Past and Future

Jeremiah's little book of consolation enflames possibility and awakens yearning for a better world. It breaks into the frightful aftermath of disaster by insisting on divine power as the enacting agent of new life. The little book invites a kind of wounded alertness to the new world God is about to bring forth. It defends God yet again and promises intimacy with God, profound, life-altering, and life-sustaining. Such life in God is marked by social justice, physical nourishment, and radical joy that will one day disperse the bitter sorrows of the past.

Although Jeremiah conjures the future in light of the past, the new world does not evolve from what has gone before,[24] nor do the past or the present cause the future.[25] The family of Jacob cannot achieve its promised, incandescent future on its own. Only the God of the ancestors can bring it to birth. Only this God satisfies the weary and nourishes the faint (31:25), ransoms Jacob and redeems him "from hands too strong for him" (31:11). Only God promises fidelity until all the mysteries of the cosmos are revealed (31:35-37). The future is an act of God, beyond the capacity of human beings to bring it forth.

Jeremiah's vision disrupts the inertia of the present time[26] And portrays God as the interrupting energy at heart of the world, the enacting agent of return, and the designer of a society led inexplicably by the weak and vulnerable. In that new world about to break in, old and young, laity and priests eat, rejoice, and dance together in the watered garden of Zion restored.

11

Running Out of Strength

Endings

JEREMIAH 45; 50–51; 52

The book of Jeremiah has no proper ending, no resolution, no summing up of interpretations, and it has no set of agreements about how to go forward. It simply stops. Rather than concluding, Jeremiah has three endings (chaps. 45, 46–51, and 52), none of which resolves or satisfies because disasters refuse to resolve or come to satisfactory ends. The effect is to leave open the questions the book has been raising for fifty-two chapters. Brueggemann describes the book as having an "ending that does not end" precisely because it plunges into "unreadable lived experience."[1] The searing pain it portrays does not end but lingers as turbulent presences for generations. By refusing closure, the three endings continue the work of survival that gave rise to the book in first place.

Shoshana Felman's theories about literature help explain Jeremiah's piled up endings.[2] Felman contrasts effects upon trauma of both legal trials and literature. Trials do not settle matters related to trauma, nor bring redress, nor promote healing. They cannot do these things because trials reenact the violence in the courtroom as they try to reconstruct events in a literal fashion for adjudication. The result is that trials tend to reactivate toxic experiences, retraumatize victims, even while they seek to cauterize the wounds.

Works of literature, by contrast, bear witness to trauma and disaster in a search for ways to speak about violence in its multiple dimensions. Literature finds frames of reference that testify to wounds from both inside and outside the experience. For Felman, literature expresses concrete experiences of pain and loss in "language of infinitude,"[3] that is, symbolically in language that opens out to many horizons of meaning. Perhaps this is another way literature obeys Emily Dickinson's imperative to poets; tell the truth but tell it "slant."

Something like this happens in the book of Jeremiah. Its "language of infinitude"—drawn from myth, drama, metaphor, symbolic actions, oracular poetry, biography, sermons—builds poetic worlds. These poetic worlds leave the disaster open to invention of new meanings even as they profoundly evoke and reframes historical disaster. The book's three endings continue to probe the meanings of disaster and in the process create what Felman might call a form of "literary justice."[4] Jeremiah's lack of resolution and its uncertainty about the future is a form of justice because the meaning of disaster never fully closes. By not settling matters prematurely, by refusing to reduce disaster to one final, settled interpretation, Jeremiah's three endings honor victims of the Babylonian disaster. They acknowledge the difficulties of closing matters, at least not quickly, not clearly, not finally. The endings leave readers with a set of questions about justice, about Judah's relationship with God, and about whether or not the nation will have a future.

First Ending: The Word Lives (45:1-6)

The book's first ending is a short prose scene where God transfers Jeremiah's prophetic vocation to his scribe Baruch (chap. 45). The passage assures readers that Jeremiah's prophetic word will not die but continue through his scribe. That potent word extends beyond the life of the prophet and has a kind of infinitude of its own. It lives into the future, and so it must, because the disaster's effects live into the future. That word is alive and growing and recorded in a scroll (45:1; cf. 36:32). Jeremiah's mysterious disappearance in Egypt does not make his words disappear.

Like Jeremiah, Baruch laments, "weary with . . . groaning" at God's plan to "pluck up" the whole land (v. 3). Like Jeremiah, Baruch will also gain his "life as booty for war in every place in which you may go" (45:5). Like Jeremiah, Baruch will survive to herald the survival of the prophetic word and of the nation. Those victims of disaster and their descendents still trying to make sense of the nation's collapse, to understand the God who eludes their grasp, and to reunite as a people can rely on this word to lead them forward. Jeremiah's words will not only endure; like the disaster to which they bear witness, they have a life that does not end.

Second Ending: Exploding Words (Chapters 50–51)

The second ending of the book comprises a collection of poems known as the "Oracles against the Nations" (chaps. 46–51).[5] This collection about Israel's neighbors comes to a dramatic conclusion with two oracles against Babylon that portray the empire's catastrophic destruction in an unspecified future (chaps. 50–51). Highly theatrical in style, the oracles against Babylon testify to Judah's profound longing for justice, for a leveling of violence that gives back to the oppressors what they have given to Judah. They express yearnings for a future where God will return to Judah's side and vindicate the nation. These desires are momentarily realized and enacted in the world of symbolic poetry; they create a form of literary justice.

The oracles take as their starting point a scene at the end of Part One of the book (25:15-26) where God promises to punish the invading Babylonian empire. In that tense episode, Jeremiah performs a prophetic sign act. God commands Jeremiah to pass a poisonous drinking cup filled with God's wrath among the assembled nations and then force each of them to drink from it. First, Israel drinks, then other nations that Babylon invaded and destroyed must drink, and finally, Sheshack, a code name for Babylon, must drink from the cup (25:26). The cup makes the ones who imbibe from it mortally drunk. They stumble and die as worthless as "dung on the surface of the ground" (25:33). In this symbolic enactment at the end of Part One of the book, the "fierce anger" of God balances the scales of justice in some future time (25:37-38).

A Sword of Destruction

The oracles against Babylon at the end of Part Two reprise the themes from the poisoned cup, dramatize them, and perform them. Like an animated action film pulsating with the energy of destructive violence, the oracles depict invasion. A disembodied sword possessing mythic power flails out against the whole military establishment of Babylon, its advisors, warriors, military equipment, and its treasures (50:35-38). The mythic "foe from the north," previously symbolizing Babylon, now turns against Babylon itself as the Babylonian king collapses in a faint of anguish and hopelessness (50:41).

Once again, in this explosion of bloody violence, God appears as the architect of war and takes full credit for stirring up "a destructive wind," but this time deadly force aims at Babylon, not Judah (51:1). In a stunning set of role reversals, the violence previously heaped upon Judah now comes back to overturn Babylon. A future attack will not "spare" but will "utterly destroy," because "Israel and Judah have not been forsaken by their God the Lord of Hosts" (51:3-5). And the role of antagonist held by Babylon in previous poems now falls to Israel: "You are my war club, my weapon in battle" (51:20), the "destroying mountain . . . that destroys the whole earth" (51:25).

Proof

To build confidence that God will create justice in a future different from the present, Jeremiah seals the oracles against Babylon with a prophetic sign act, but the prophet does not actually perform it. He instead commissions his emissary in Babylon named Seraiah. Jeremiah commands Seraiah to tie a stone to the oracles against Babylon that the prophet has written on a scroll. Then Seraiah must drop the scroll and the stone into the middle of the Euphrates River in the heart of Babylon. They sink to the bottom. "Glub, glub, glub, down they go to the bottom of the river." So pronounced Walter Brueggemann in one of my classes as he enacted the scene like Seraiah himself, watching the scroll submerge, delighting in the justice nearly at hand, performing Seraiah's performance. The prophetic oracles sink into the water, out of sight, yet they remain alive and explosive at the center of the empire, until God will activate them like a bomb with a secret timer to set off the explosion. Readers know what the scroll says—Babylon will collapse in the face of brutal acts of destruction, and so Babylon will "rise no more because of the disasters I am bringing upon her" (51:64).

Jeremiah's sunken scroll enacts literary justice as do the oracles written upon it. The fall of Babylon is certain, but that fall and the destruction accompanying it exist only in the imaginings of the poet, in the world of literature, and in the hearts of the people. The disaster is not over. The prophetic sign is promissory, an event to be hidden at the heart of the empire, sunk in the river, until its future fulfillment in history. The oracles leave justice in God's hands, but they tell the people of Judah that, although they may not see the turning of the tables now, that word has been spoken, performed, and that word is certain.

Changed Relationships

In a surprising turn of events, the oracles against Babylon express an altered perception of Judah's relationship with the enemy. The people of Judah "tried to heal Babylon" but the nation "could not be healed." Because saving the enemy is hopeless, the people say to one another: "Forsake her, and let each of us go to our own country." The poem imagines a humane concern for the oppressor, offered by the people who suffered so much but who finally must escape from the nation's clutches.

And, accompanying this alteration of attitudes toward Babylon, relationship with God appears to be transformed as well. No longer does God attack Judeans or send enemies to quell them. Now God justifies them, for

> The Lord has brought forth our vindication. (51:9-10)
> Come out of her my people! Save your lives each of you . . .

do not be fainthearted or fearful at the rumors heard in the land. (51:45-
46)
Babylon must fall for the slain of Israel,
as the slain of all the earth have fallen because of Babylon. (51:49)

In this ever-so-satisfying ending to take place in the future, God stands at Judah's
side. God alone will vindicate the people, honor the slain, and the Babylonian
Empire will get what it deserves in pain equivalent to the destruction it caused.
God will enact revenge for the sake of the people; God will bring forth justice.

Poetry of Revenge

Many modern readers resist this violent imagery about God and the depiction
of justice as the table-turning equivalence of pain and suffering to be heaped
upon the enemies. Justice in these oracles is retaliation in kind, equality of terror
and brutality, an eye for an eye. The biblical injunction to love our enemies does
receive a nod here when the poems imagine Judah trying to heal Babylon, but
on the whole, the oracles embrace justice as a form of revenge.

The poetry of revenge can heal. It hallows out space for hatred, fury, and
outrage, already born into the world in the monstrous violence against the
Judean nation, its people, and its way of life. Judah lost nearly everything at the
hands of this invading power, but in the oracles against Babylon, they expect
the Creator to right the wrongs. They appeal to the one who made the earth
by divine power, who established the world by divine wisdom and stretched
out the heavens by divine understanding (51:15). To this God they plead for an
equal distribution of suffering, they express their desires for payback, and they
entrust the task of retribution. Hatred and violence live in the oracular world
because they remain alive among survivors, and they will stay alive, grow more
virulent, and become feral until they gain expression, receive a hearing, and
find acceptance. It may be that the literary justice enacted in the oracles makes
it possible to recover, to move through the burning hatred that survives long
after the violence ends, and perhaps to avoid perpetuating that violence against
others. Perhaps.

Theological Amnesia

The oracles against Babylon stand at a disjuncture from other parts of the book,
as if in them the community has forgotten other interpretations of the cataclysm. They do not remember God as the angry dispatcher of the foe from the
north, the divorcing spouse, and the raping attacker, the one who blames them
and abandons them. The rhetoric of responsibility takes yet another turn here.

God names Babylon as the principal aggressor, destroyer of Judah, and primary cause of the disaster. Rather than blaming the people, God laments their shepherdless condition, their plight as lost sheep devoured by enemies (50:4-7). God sides with them, "hunted sheep driven away by lions" (51:17). God sees, takes in, and absorbs their suffering.

Past and present enemies of Judah, both Assyria and Babylon, come under siege from this avenging God. Within the boundaries of the oracles, God no longer employs these aggressors as divine agents but calls them the "plunderers of my heritage" (50:11). And to make matters even more topsy-turvy, the sins of Israel and of Judah receive very little attention in the oracles. In a future search for sin, "there shall be none," "none shall be found" (50:20). Like an x-ray that no longer shows signs of cancer, God cannot find the sin of the remnant spared from extinction.

The book of Jeremiah repeatedly faces readers with contradictory testimonies about causes of the disaster. The oracles against Babylon yet again invite survivors into interpretive confusion and require them to make their way toward a new *terra firma* of understanding. But there is no solid land, no resolution, no ending. There is instead continuing debate about causes, agents, and God's role in the collapse.

Liturgical Performances

Pete Diamond thinks the oracles against Babylon are "bizarre poetic performances in which God, formerly a horror to Judah," now becomes "a horror to the world."[6] But Stulman disagrees and insists that divine violence in these oracles is "language of imagination and rhetoric, not of military hardware."[7] The oracles may even be liturgical pieces, according to Stulman, that is, rituals of public worship designed to assert divine sovereignty and announce divine triumph against the unjust. As rituals, they would act out recovery among survivors as if it were already true.[8] Liturgical rituals create meaning by giving form, substance, and focus to the past and to the future.[9] In shared gesture and speech, in body and emotion, they gather people together, draw them back into community, and provide hope for a different future.

Whether or not Jeremiah's oracles against Babylon are liturgical texts, they do require readers to face fury and rage at the injustice that has overtaken their world and to look again toward God. The worst of the catastrophe may be over, but it has not ended and will not end until there is justice and until there is public, even cosmic, recognition of what they have suffered. In snippets of liturgies across the book, the community is to enact repentance through communal worship, but here they anticipate the overturning of the oppressor in a divine gesture that evens the scales, at least in the potent world of symbolic literature.

The oracles re-narrate and reframe the disaster. They encourage survivors of the cataclysm to trust divine justice, to imagine and enact a balancing out of terrors, to create a space to make vindication and retribution thinkable, achieved not by their own hands but by the bloody hands of God. When they place intolerable destruction and loss into the transcendent realm, they create hope amidst Judah's fractured existence and mobilize energy to rebuild the community.

The oracles against Babylon at the end of Jeremiah do not end the disaster, nor heal it, nor close the doors on it. They do not cleanse it of the ways it leaches into the souls of a people, but they do make room for it, and they prevent its victims from avoiding their deep desires to do unto others what has been done unto them. Yet the oracles do not explicitly invite violence; instead, they set the whole thing in the cosmic realm before the throne of the God of justice.

The Third Ending: Ambiguity

The third ending, the place where the book of Jeremiah actually stops, abandons the cosmic realm and the world of poetry to come back down to earth, to the present, to the place of divine silence. Chapter 52 is often called "an historical appendix." Its history-like narrative of the fall of Judah is nearly identical to the final chapter of the Second Book of Kings (2 Kings 25). In Jeremiah, this last chapter abandons the heightened emotional tone that characterizes the oracles against Babylon with their fierce battles, attitude of expectant triumph over the enemy, and implied glee at Babylon's reversal of fortunes. Jeremiah's final chapter, by contrast, is an emotional letdown, a flat telling of invasion in the historical style of the books of Kings, as if it were simply reporting the facts. The chapter resembles a report told through the eyes of a neutral observer, bereft of emotion, or as Deborah Samuelson suggested in one of my classes, a recovering survivor, at last able to tell the story of the nation's collapse without being emotionally overwhelmed by its horrors yet not fully alive and flourishing.

Whatever the relationship of Jeremiah's final chapter to the final chapter of the book of Kings, its effect here is to end Jeremiah in a thick cloud of ambiguity. An unidentified narrator tells of invasion, destruction, fires, collapsed walls of the city, and the deportations as the Babylonian army captain Nebuzaradan leads away "some of the poorest of the people," "the rest left in the city," the ones who defected to Babylon, and "the rest of the artisans," the treasures taken from the destroyed temple, and also leaders (52:15). The account is grim, emotionless, and hopeless, as if told from the inside of the stream of events.

But then, in the last scene of the chapter and book, the king of Babylon releases the captured Judean King Jehoiachin from prison. Although he does not set the king free of captivity, Babylon's king honors the king of Judah, frees him from his prison garb, and invites him to eat meals at the royal table. Like Jeremiah, Baruch, Ebed-Melech, and others, Judah's king survives in a half-free state. He gains his life as booty for war. His rescue from prison to sit at the table of the king of Babylon is as mysterious as all the other rescue stories in the book. And because I think this is as much a symbolic account as an historical rendering, his survival augurs Judah's own survival as it faces an unknown future.

Whether or not this good treatment of Judah's king in captivity is a sign of hope remains a much disputed point among interpreters. But the scene makes for a realistic cessation of a book about disaster because it, too, leaves the disaster unfinished, the disaster that still inhabits every aspect of Judean life. It is not over. The nation's many wounds cannot be wiped away, nor eradicated by will power, nor suppressed in communal memory.

Absences

God remains conspicuously absent in this final chapter, receiving only cursory mention in the report of the burning of the temple described as "the house of the Lord" (52:13) and in a formulaic characterization of King Zedekiah, typical of the book of Kings: he "did evil in the sight of the Lord" (52:1). In a book where God has been the main character from the beginning, these are the only references to the divine in its last chapter. God's absence is all the more remarkable here. Why is God missing from the book's last chapter? Does telling the story in an historical style, a sort of face value account of events as purely human interactions, express an altered sensibility about the disaster and its causes? Is God's absence an indication of uncertainty about divine involvement in the nation's collapse, yet another perspective on the long history of terror? Or is it a tacit acknowledgment that God has absconded from the mess that is Jerusalem, once God's dwelling place, once a city full of people, lying desolate now with jackals prowling over it (Lam 1:1; 5:18)?

Nor does the second most important character in the book receive any mention in its final chapter. Last heard from in Egypt, Jeremiah does not appear here at all. He does not die, but he has been replaced by his scrolls written by his companion Baruch. His words survive in this book but they do not resolve matters. They are alive with the fiery power that literature can give them. They work in ways that cannot be reduced to simple facts, historical reportage, or political analysis. They have power to keep the people of Judah from disappearing from history, a history long ago "transferred into the plane of poetics and transfigured into complex literary symbols."[10] These words in all their complexity enable the process of rebuilding the nation to begin.

The three endings of the book of Jeremiah honor the long process of recovery by refusing to bring closure to pain or the figure of the weeping prophet or to the God wrenched apart by the cataclysm. By ending without ending, the book refuses to smooth over or wash away the ambiguity and uncertainty of recovery. When it abstains from resolving matters and from settling the conflict and ambiguity across the book, the endings, too, create a form of literary justice. They require, like most of the book, that readers probe, question, and actively create meaning from what is before them. Jeremiah's endings make a fitting continuation of a book that exposes the wounds of the disaster to light, sets boundaries around the terrors, and invites readers to rise from the debris and live again.

12

Confusion as Meaning-Making

The Composition of the Book

Readers who have soldiered on this far may agree that, despite its terrifying and potent beauty, the book of Jeremiah presents major challenges to contemporary readers. The problems are not simply those created by the book's violence, its brutal suffering, or its fire-and-brimstone theology. Equally difficult is the book's literary shapelessness, its lack of a narrative thread or "logical" arrangement across the book, or even of a clear chronological setting out of events.[1] It is hard to think of Jeremiah as a work of transcendent art. Besides being a grab-bag of literary forms, it switches from poetry to prose, speaker to speaker, metaphor to metaphor. It jumps from themes of suffering to hope and back again to foil readers in search of a coherent structure. Even stories of Jeremiah's life and references to historical events follow little apparent organization, chronological or otherwise.

Theories about Composition

There are theories about why this is so. Biblical scholars have long laid Jeremiah's literary confusions at the feet of the writers and editors who composed it over a long period of time. According to a group of interpreters known as "source critics," the book came to be when editors combined preexisting written sources or documents. They began with Jeremiah's "authentic" poetry, that is, his own words remembered and recorded that formed the heart of the book. Next they added Baruch's biography of Jeremiah, and then, influenced by the theology of the book of Deuteronomy, composers added the sermons, and they or others put the books together in its present condition.[2]

Old Testament scholar William McKane pushes this thinking further. He believes that the process of composition was even less orderly than the source critics proposed. McKane speculates that the book came together through a more or less random collection of literary pieces by various authors. Jeremiah's original words gathered other words over decades the ways a snowball rolling down a hill gathers more snow to get larger and larger.[3]

Today these approaches to Jeremiah dissatisfy some interpreters because we have little solid evidence about who added what when. Still, these theories have contributed much to our understanding of Jeremiah because, rather than over-looking the book's confusions, they point them out and try to make sense of them. They recognize that a long process of writing and editing by many hands created the present Hebrew text. That is what endures about their work. But in my opinion, Jeremiah's literary disorder is central to its purposes.

Confusion among Survivors

Trauma and disaster studies suggest that Jeremiah's bewildering shape reflects the massive disorder that produced the book in the first place. Rather than simply arising from a random process of composition, the book's turbulence depicts the interpretive disarray in Jeremiah's audience in the aftermath of Babylonian control. Disasters create turmoil in nearly every realm of life, and that turmoil finds expression in Jeremiah's ragged contours and blue-printless architecture. The book's very conflicts and confusion require that readers become meaning-makers themselves as they try to make sense of the literature.

An Analogous Situation

A contemporary society, the Central American nation of El Salvador, provides an illuminating parallel to the social upheaval that produced the book of Jeremiah. Following its brutal civil war, El Salvador faces an interpretive dilemma that echoes the struggle in Judah after Babylonian disaster and so sheds light on the literary maze that is Jeremiah.

I glimpsed these connections when my life-long friend, missionary priest John Spain, M.M., visited my husband and me on a trip home from El Salvador in 2007. John described the continuing struggles among the Salvadoran population many years after the terrible war came to an end. John's insights come from his mission, living and working among the Salvadoran people in the decades before the war and now in its aftermath. He experienced many traumatic events first-hand, in particular the murders of friends and pastoral agents, including four church women from the United States, fellow priests, and Archbishop Oscar Romero.

Although El Salvador is now trying to emerge from that war, John reports that no single interpretation of those traumatic years has come to light, nor do people even agree about what happened. They argue, instead, about why the war happened and how they can go forward to rebuild the society. John thinks the post-war conflicts arise from the reality that "each person and group experienced the war and its aftermath differently." Many were forced to leave the country, to give up homes, animals, and land. Confined as they were in camps in the mountains across the border, this group suffered isolation and poverty. For them, interpretations of the war came from the liberation front that opposed the government. Now at the war's end, these formerly displaced people continue to keep alive their own deeply-felt "whys" of the war and of events that forced them to flee.

Other groups who remained in the war zone see things differently. Many became internal refugees and received their interpretations of events from government and media. Afterward, people in this group have not been able to express their experiences freely for fear of exposure as witnesses to atrocities or as sympathizers with the opposition. By contrast to both these groups, young people who grew up after the Peace Accords (1992) have no memories of the war and possess a fairly positive view of the future.

In the present situation, people from all these groups have come back to repopulate devastated areas. In John Spain's view, "El Salvador is still being bombarded, no longer with exploding devices falling from planes, but with interpretations and allegations that clash with the violence the people remember."[4] Common ground remains elusive in such an atmosphere. And today there are new questions of interpretation, "most cruelly, the question of whether reported events occurred at all." In the midst of this turbulence, the people must not only deal with the war's original chaos but also with warring interpretations that remain alive and cannot be subsumed into one another. The result is a bitterly divided society lacking a common language to speak about their shared calamity and lacking a forum in which to express their interpretations.

Chaotic Structure as Witness

The book of Jeremiah inscribes such confusion and offers such a forum. Its bewildering array of voices, themes, metaphors, genres, and its lack of narrative order suggest to me that similar interpretive dilemmas plagued the lives of its audience.[5] It is a public discussion that lays out the conflicting perceptions of the Babylonian disaster and their consequences for Judah. The book's cobbled-together structure itself bears witness to the Babylonian onslaught against the nation. As Pete Diamond puts it, the book is "a textuality that tears itself apart with deep contradiction."[6] Or borrowing Lawrence Langer's words relating to

Holocaust survivors, the book's confused shape conveys the "damaged mosaics of the mind, memories in pieces, memory creating a shadow over the normal."[7]

Besides replicating the interpretive turmoil of Jeremiah's first audience, the book's literary overload has another important effect. It confronts readers with the task of making sense of the confusion. The very lack of order demands that they face and answer a vast array of questions. What happened? Why did it happen? What did God have to do with it? Who was responsible for it? Is there any way forward? How shall we live now? Jeremiah's replies to these questions are multiple, and those replies vie with each another, contradict each other, and try to override each other without providing a map across the territory.[8]

Making Meaning to Survive

The book's excesses and serpentine shape contribute to its overarching intention—to generate meaning so that life may return to the people of Judah. In all its profusion, Jeremiah is a quest for meaning, a continuous search for expressions and points of view to name, understand, and live through the catastrophe. Its untidy mixture of perspectives creates conversations and arguments that force readers themselves to become analysts of a world ground to bits by the disaster. The book's fragmentation mimics the fragmented memories of the traumatized. It reproduces Judah's predicament and shows the wide range of wounds that afflict the nation. This work of literature is a moral act, for it turns readers from passive victims into agents.

Here is one example, among many, to illustrate interpretive arguments within the book that leave the task of meaning-making to the readers.

Who Deserves Power?

When the Babylonian Empire finally falls, the conquering Persian Emperor Cyrus permits exiled Jews to return home (538 B.C.E.). Their return after fifty years away creates many challenges for the rebuilding of the society. Who should have power in the aftermath of Babylonian control? Should it be exiles returning from Babylon or those who stayed in the land during the war and afterward? Who are the more authentic survivors? One text argues on behalf of the returning exiles, but the second suggests that power and authority belong to those who remained in the land under Babylonian control. The book places Jeremiah firmly in the center of both communities.

Exiles Rule (Jer 24:1-10)

In one vision, Jeremiah sees two baskets of figs, one filled with good fruit, the other with rotten fruit. The vision clearly promotes exiles alone as God's chosen one. Since these families had been among Judah's ruling elites before the invasions, they and their offspring want to regain power, status, and probably family property upon their return. Several passages authorize them as God's agent. In starkly autocratic terms, Jeremiah's vision of the figs stakes out the exiles' superiority over the ones who remained in the land, the ones who may now be occupying exiles' property (24:1-10).

> One [basket] had very good figs, like first ripe figs, but the other basket had very bad figs, so bad they could not be eaten. (24:2)

God then interprets the vision:

> The exiles from Judah whom I have sent away from this place to the land of the Chaldeans [another name for Babylonians] are like the good figs . . . I will build them, plant them, and not pluck them up. (24:5-6)

God not only stands with the exiles but also shows them exclusive preference with traditional covenant language: "I will give them a heart to know that I am the Lord; and they shall be my people and I will be their God, for they shall return to me with their whole heart" (24:7).

How can readers dispute God's choice of the exiles? In an elegant power play, Jeremiah's vision lays out a political claim in which the book's most authoritative figure declares the moral superiority of exiles over everyone else. Members of the former ruling class alone are the true Israel, the newly covenanted ones, the real chosen people whom God will build and plant. Some interpreters believe this pro-returnee propaganda trumps other perspectives found in the book.[9] The returning exiles win the power struggle and control the future.

Yet strangely, the vision of the figs blurs group identity. Among the bad figs are other elite rulers. King Zedekiah and his officials, who were also deported to Babylon, should have been counted among the "good figs" (52:8-11; 39:7). But God names them rotten figs along with the remnant in the land and those who live in the land of Egypt. They are "a disgrace, a byword, a taunt and a curse in all the places I send them" (24:8-9). If the book attempts to hand power to the Babylonian exiles, its composers obfuscate their own purposes. They neither eliminate nor diminish contrary suggestions from the book.

The Remnant Rules (40:1-6)

Other Jeremiah passages throw support behind the survivors in the land, the ones classified as rotten figs in the vision of the baskets. Jeremiah himself never goes to Babylon and publically chooses not to do so (40:1-6); God's own prophet turns out to be a "bad fig."

Jeremiah's choice to remain in the land takes place during the capture of Jerusalem. A Babylonian military captain offers Jeremiah a simple decision (40:1-6): "If you wish to come with me to Babylon, come . . . but if you do not wish to come . . . you need not come." Then, the captain repeats the terms of the choice: "See the whole land is before you; go wherever you think it is good and right to go" (40:4-5).

With explicit deliberation, Jeremiah chooses not to go to Babylon. He decides to join Gedeliah, the Babylonian appointed governor of the occupied land. The text emphasizes Jeremiah's choice by using a Hebrew verb that conveys continuity, staying, dwelling, and enduring: Jeremiah "remained" (*yšb*) with the people "left"[10] in the land (40:6). Jeremiah stays with, belongs to, and dwells among the people remaining behind. He publically rejects an opportunity to be numbered among the "good figs" that he himself identified in his vision. The book's most authoritative human dwells with the survivors in the land.

Jeremiah's dramatic decision to stay in the land follows the equally dramatic stories of his captivities where the same verb appears four times like a refrain across the chapters (chaps. 37–38):

> He remained in the cistern house (37:16)
> Remained in the court of the guard (37:21)
> Remained in the court of the guard (38:13)
> Remained in the court of the guard (38:28)

Verbal repetition hammers home Jeremiah's identification with and allegiance to the people of the land (40:6). He stuck with them and is one of them. Later he is numbered among Judean folk who flee to Egypt, the "baddest of bad figs" who forcefully carry him off with them (chaps. 42–43). To find the prophet, we have to look among the rotten figs.

Interpretive Choices

These two stories show that different groups within the book claim Jeremiah's authority for their side of the conflict, and the book refuses to resolve the dispute. It keeps both opinions. Readers must decide if the prophet's godly vision of the figs is more decisive than the story of his personal choice to remain in the land? One story challenges the other something like the interpretive confusion in post war El Salvador. This clash of perspectives may simply be the result of the desire of the book's composers to honor tradition, to tell stories of what "really happened," so they use everything they inherit no matter what. But their intentions are hidden. The results of the composers' work eclipse, mute, and dispute claims to power by any single group.

Honoring Experience

The struggle in these stories is palpable, yet both groups find themselves included in the account. The book honors their experiences. Babylonian returnees do not silence the people of the land, nor vice-versa, at least in the book. By leaving interpretations in conflict, the book represents factions and then argues with them. Refusing to settle the fracas, it does not let one point of view dominate or one answer triumph. To do so may be premature in the nation's recovery.

Rather than simplifying meaning, viewpoints multiply and create uncertainty.[11] This uncertainty, deeply embedded in the book, aids survivors of violence and disaster. It invite readers to become interpreters, potentially transforming them from passive victims into actors who make sense of their own lives. It makes them into moral agents who judge their world, actors who speak, think, imagine, and decide. Jeremiah demands that they struggle with the significance of all that has happened to their nation.

The Time Is Now!

Another way the book's confusion encourages readers to make meaning is through its muddled chronology.[12] Jeremiah confuses the times. Many passages in Jeremiah, especially in the first twenty chapters, present the disaster as a future event, as a warning that the people must change their ways or the nation will fall. But the disaster has already happened. Readers live in its aftermath, and probably even two or more generations later. Their "now" is a time trembling "on the edge of dissolution."[13] *Now* is the time to cope and begin to recover.[14]

The book generally divides time into before the disaster (chaps 1–25) and after the disaster (chaps 26–52), but beyond those loose divisions, time is askew.

The Times Are "Out of Whack"

The ancient world dated events according to the reigns of kings, as does Jeremiah. "The word of the Lord came to Jeremiah in the days of King Josiah, in the thirteenth year of his reign" (1:1-2). But when the book locates stories within the reign of kings, it ignores chronological order, making us wonder why it uses time notations at all. A brief chart illustrates the problem:

Dates in Jeremiah	
The book's opening verses (1:1-3) date the whole book after the captivity of Jerusalem in 587/6, placing readers in its aftermath. Chapters 2–20 lack clear time citations and present the disaster as a future event, though for the book's readers it has already occurred. From chapter 25 forward, date markers occur in prose narratives about Jeremiah's life.	

Chapter	Date
25	600 B.C.E.
26	605
27–28	597 under Zedekiah but events in it probably occur in 593
29	597
32	588
34	any one of three invasions, 597, 587, 582
35	609–598
36	605
37–38	588/7
39	588/7

The book shows no interest in giving readers a linear account of Jeremiah's life, nor is it trying to tell history in a step-by-step unfolding. Pete Diamond invents a word to describe Jeremiah's warped sense of time, calling it "dis-chronologization,"[15] a kind of anti-chronology.

Trauma and disaster studies suggest that Jeremiah's whacked-out dates convey their own sense of meaning. The book's dis-chronology does tell a story, but not the linear one for which modern western readers search. Rather, the messy date-line conveys the interruption of time that accompanies trauma and disaster.

Time Interrupted

"Traumatic memory is wordless and static," writes trauma expert Judith Hermann, and so initial accounts of violent events may be "pre-narrative" and "do not progress in time."[16] Time is "out of whack," stuck in fragmented, violent moments that keep repeating themselves. Recurring memories of violence replace the rhythms of the world for victims of traumatic violence. Jeremiah's lack of chronological order is mimetic, that is, it mimics the vastness of Judah's destruction and its effects upon the people. Its skewed chronology calls forth the confusion of skewed memories and signifies repeatedly that what has happened is a severing of linear order in the world.

Lawrence Langer helps here by reporting the testimony of a Holocaust survivor who managed to keep her memories of Auschwitz sealed off from the rest of her life. Langer calls this survival strategy a "doubling of memory."[17] This doubling—keeping horrible memories in a separate place in the mind—is a mode of coping that "invalidates the idea of continuity and even of chronology."[18] In the aftermath of overwhelming violence, times tumble together in a different logic. Unspeakable past events are still present, still alive, still happening at the same time as the events in the present. All realms of time converge at once. Langer calls this the "cotemporality of the past invading the present; events to be relived appear in mental space without order."[19]

Jeremiah's chronological notations depict such erosion of time and continuity with great fidelity. Past, present, and future coexist in the imaginative worlds of this book because they coexist simultaneously among disaster victims, poised as they are on the knife-edge between extermination and survival as God's people. The underlying logic of the book's anti-chronology for Jeremiah is that all times fall together within the governance of God.

Time Predictable

At the same time, Jeremiah's dates actually create other forms of "order amid chaos," to use Stulman's terms. Dates in Jeremiah's life have the additional effect of showing that the disaster was predictable and predicted. The dates establish that God informed the prophet of the disaster before it happened. There is a hidden order in a world in which all order has vanished. God knew of it and revealed it to the prophet who announced it, and so the world is not hurtling into the abyss. The disaster was predictable.

Predictability helps survival, according to Erickson, because victims of disaster "often come to feel that they have lost an important measure of control over the circumstances of their lives and are thus very vulnerable."[20] Standing on the brink of death as they do, they have a sense that the "universe is not regulated by order and continuity."[21] Or in Jeremiah's terms, they exist with "terror all around" (20:4, 10). In such a chaotic atmosphere, testimony to a divinely established order, to a predictable quality of events, can bring a sense of safety, contain the terrors, and provide a sense of solid ground underneath appearances. Jeremiah's dates reveal hidden stability in the world. They proclaim that God—not Babylonian deities nor impersonal forces—controls time.

By showing events to have been foreseeable, Jeremiah's dates contribute to what Daniel Schwarz calls "the intelligibility of history, even the place of evil in history."[22] They make the world "intelligible," readable, understandable and, in that way, create a "framework of normalcy."[23] If disastrous events were predictable, known in advance, then they might have been avoided and, so, similar catastrophes might also be avoided in the future. Whatever else the dates within Jeremiah signify, they shore up the possibility of shelter and security in disaster's aftermath because they erect boundaries around complete chaos.

Although for modern linear thinkers, Jeremiah's times add one more layer of difficulty to the book, they function as a survival strategy for an audience attempting to recover from disaster. Along with many other of its features, Jeremiah's confused structure and erratic dates honor the collapse of meaning, the dearth of hope, and the conflicts that follow in societies undone by catastrophe.

Epilogue

A Work of Hope
and Resilience

We humans cannot absorb the bitter truths of our own history, the revelation of our destructive potential, except through the mediation of art (the manifestation of our other, our constructive potential). Presented raw, the facts are rejected: perhaps not by the intellect, which accommodates them as statistics, but by the emotions—which hold the key to conscience and resolve. We numb ourselves, evading the vile taste, the stench. But whether neutralized into statistics or encountered head-on without an artist-guide (as if Dante wandered through Hell without a Virgil), the facts poison us unless we can find a way both to acknowledge their reality with our whole selves and, accepting it, muster the will to transcend it.[1]

The book of Jeremiah is a work of resilience, a survival manual, a literary anthology, and a work of theological art. It is not a factual history of events, as if that could be told. It is an emotion-soaked set of testimonies that plunge into overwhelming catastrophe and transform it, that the nation might not perish but be reborn as God's people. The whole book is a work of resilience, acknowledging reality and mustering the will to live through it and live beyond it. Every poem, story, and sermon in it addresses the disaster in some way, either to predict it, offer ways to cope with it, or to instill hope for living through it. Even as it is literature dense with uncertainty and conflict, it leads the people of Judah, as if with a scarlet thread, through the tangled mire of their suffering toward the horizon of new life.

Jeremiah's polymorphous, shape-shifting arrangement turns readers into survivors trying to make sense of the wreckage of their world. It guides them through shards of memories of violence and devastation, evokes their experiences delicately, indirectly, then more frontally with glimpses of war's multiple destructions. When it does these things, it validates the people's reality, reflects, as if in a broken mirror, their traumatized condition, reimagined in worlds of symbol and poetry. By its very representation of the nation's predicament, it forms survivors into a community able to see their lives before them and to have language to tell of them.[2] Through this book, Judah is reborn.

When I think about the descendants of the fictional families with whom I began this study, I consider that the book of Jeremiah honors the dead. But even more it serves as a survival manual for the children of those imagined victims. It is survival literature.[3] In the face of cascading needs of the destroyed nation, Jeremiah is a moral act, a healing therapy, a redeeming lifeline to survival. It places suffering within a larger context, within a world that encompasses, comforts, and gives meaning. It helps survivors to reach out beyond "embeddedness" in their overwhelmed state and to create meaning from the ashes.[4]

From the historical cauldron of dislocation and loss, the book creates literary art through "*inventive*, imaginative efforts to convey the truth of what happened."[5] It selects aspects of the disaster, tells it from different angles, tells it in symbolic terms that both illuminate and limit the expression of what has happened. Such is the creative effort of writers who scan the world looking for ways to express what cannot be expressed. Such is Jeremiah. To survive the disaster and its lingering consequences requires the remaking of language, a turning of suffering into words[6] that, in the terms of Michel Foucault, creates speech "removed from the shores of facticity."[7] It is the speech itself for which survivors struggle; new speech "is the power one is trying to seize."[8] To find language that begins to embrace historical reality is to find a kind of "redemption."

Jeremiah shows that Judah's catastrophe can be told in different ways, as mythic poetry, as prose narrative, as the life of the one prophet through prayers of lament, sermons, and letters among survivors. And yet the catastrophe is never told, cannot be told, because traumatic violence is beyond telling.[9] It can only be approached, glimpsed, struggled toward, and reframed. Perhaps Jeremiah's magnificent, unsettled literary array is the only way victims can approach disaster,[10] can read the unreadable "abyss."[11] The book takes the people of Judah into the heart of the cataclysm, and then guides them toward life, rebirth, and renewed hope in the God who has loved them "with an everlasting love" and who will again build them, and they "shall be built" (31:3-4).

The composers of Jeremiah do not know psychiatry, anthropology, or counseling techniques; they do not have the vantage points of trauma and disaster studies; and they do not have a simple design for new life. What they do have is an instinctive wisdom, a cultural knowledge of the needs of their community, and an abiding hope in the God of Judah despite all evidence to the contrary.

Their gift to victims and their offspring is to create art that takes the collapse of the known world and sets it firmly within the life of their God. These theological artists re-present and re-conceive God's relationship to them, building new worlds from the old, breaking forth into new language, and birthing toward a future that the nation is too stunned to imagine. In that distant but certain future, "their life shall be like a watered garden and they shall never languish again" (Jer 31:12).

But Jeremiah's journey toward the lush garden must first traverse disaster's wasteland and its many manifestations in this prophetic book. And when it arrives at the imagined garden it does not linger there long, because it has to revisit yet again the barren geography of catastrophe, to dwell for a time in the places of terror, grief, and shattered trust. This dwelling in the midst of devastation is the way forward and maybe the only way life can again be found, then or now.

The book of Jeremiah attempts an impossible task. There are no words able to express fully what has been lost, to describe the violent extermination of human life, of the physical world, of culture and faith. Without Jeremiah (and Ezekiel and Second Isaiah), the God of Judah would probably have died, for God's chosen people would have been dispersed and lost. At the heart of this book is resilient confidence in God, defense of God—blazing, angry, emotional, muted, weeping, furious, and always yearning for the beloved. Jeremiah's God desires love, gives love, brings new life, and reconceives the nation.

Trauma and disaster studies save the book of Jeremiah for me. Jeremiah's angry, raping, punishing God is healing because this violent theology keeps God alive in the midst of disaster, keeps God from disappearing through a "temporary stay against confusion." This God is a work of art, an expression of divine involvement when we are stuck in the mud, lost in intense pain, wandering with no compass. Above all, this what drives this God is relentless, passionate desire for relationship with the people. Jeremiah's portrait of God in its many dimensions stammers toward the unsayable. God receives many names, many characteristics in this book, yet none can satisfy, none can fully convey the experience of the divine. Jeremiah's God is the living God.

ABBREVIATIONS

AB	Anchor Bible
ABD	*Anchor Bible Dictionary.* Edited by D.N. Freedman. 6 vols. New York, 1992.
ABRL	Anchor Bible Reference Library
AnBib	Analecta biblica
AOTC	Abingdon Old Testament Commentaries
BETL	Bibliotheca ephemeridum theologicarum lovaniensium
BibOr	Biblica et orientalia
BJS	Brown Judaic Studies
CBQ	*Catholic Biblical Quarterly*
EBib	*Etudes bibliques*
EvT	*Evangelische Theologie*
HSM	Harvard Semitic Monographs
ICC	International Critical Commentary
IBC	Interpretation: A Bible Commentary for Teaching and Preaching
Int	*Interpretation*
JBL	Journal of Biblical Literature
JNES	*Journal of Near Eastern Studies*
JSOT	*Journal for the Study of the Old Testament*
JSOTSup	Journal for the Study of the Old Testament: Supplement Series
OBT	Overtures to Biblical Theology
OTE	*Old Testament Essays*
OTL	Old Testament Library
PRSt	*Perspectives in Religious Studies*
PSB	*Princeton Seminary Bulletin*
RevExp	*Review and Expositor*
SBLDS	Society of Biblical Literature Dissertation Series

SBLMS	Society of Biblical Literature Monograph Series
SJOT	*Scandinavian Journal of the Old Testament*
VT	*Vetus Testamentum*
WW	*Word and World*
WBC	Word Biblical Commentary

NOTES

Introduction

1. Kai Erikson, "Notes on Trauma and Community," *Trauma: Explorations in Memory*, Cathy Caruth, ed. (Baltimore: Johns Hopkins University Press, 1995), 184.

2. Cathy Caruth, *Unclaimed Experience: Trauma, Narrative, and History* (Baltimore: Johns Hopkins University Press, 1996), 5-6.

3. Judith Lewis Herman, *Trauma and Recovery* (New York: Basic, 1992), 7.

4. Ibid.

5. Ronnie Janhoff Bulman, *Shattered Assumptions: Toward a New Psychology of Trauma* (New York: Free, 1992), 95-104.

6. Alexander C. McFarlane and Bessel A. vander Kolk, "Trauma and Its Challenge to Society," in *Traumatic Stress: The Effects of Overwhelming Experience on Mind, Body, and Society*, Bessel A. vander Kolk, Alexander C. McFarlane, and Lars Weisaeth, eds. (New York: Guilford, 1996), 26.

7. Louis Stulman, *Order amid Chaos: Jeremiah as Symbolic Tapestry* (Sheffield: Sheffield Academic, 1998).

Chapter 1: Imagining Lives

1. Shoshana Felman, "Education and Crisis or the Vicissitudes of Teaching," in *Trauma: Exploration in Memory*, Cathy Carruth, ed. (Baltimore: Johns Hopkins University Press, 1995), 58.

2. See Erskine Clarke, *Dwelling Place: A Plantation Epic* (New Haven: Yale University Press, 2005) for one striking counterexample. This Bancroft prize-winning book tells a highly personal story of the day to day lives of slaves and slave owners in the antebellum South.

3. See especially Daniel L. Smith-Christopher, *A Biblical Theology of Exile* (Minneapolis: Fortress Press, 2002), 1-74, who criticizes historical views that vastly underplay the sufferings of Judah in the Babylonian Period.

4. Hans M. Barstad, "After the 'Myth of the Empty Land' ": Major Challenges in the Study of Neo-Babylonian Judah" in *Judah and the Judeans in the Neo-Babylonian Period*, ed. Oded Lipchits and Joseph Blenkinsopp (Winona Lake: Eisenbrauns, 2003), 3-30, considers the invasions to have been little more than a minor intrusion, not much of a disaster at all. But there is strong recognition among historians and archeologists that this time was disastrous for Judah. See Ranier Albertz, *Israel in Exile: The History and Literature of the Sixth Century b.c.e.* (Atlanta:

Society of Biblical Literature, 2003), 75; Iain Provan, V. Philips Long, and Tremper Longman III, *A Biblical History of Israel* (Louisville: Westminster John Knox, 2003); Oded Lipschits and Joseph Blenkinsopp, eds., *Judah and the Judean in the Neo-Babylonian Period* (Winona Lake: Eisenbrauns, 2003); David Stephen Vanderhooft, *The Neo-Babylonian Empire and Babylon in the Latter Prophets* (Atlanta: Scholars, 1999); Bill T. Arnold, *Who Were the Babylonians?* (Atlanta: Society of Biblical Literature, 2004); John Bright, *A History of Israel*, 4th ed. (Louisville: Westminster John Knox, 2000), 310-99.

5. Gary Alan Herion, "The Social Organization of Tradition in Monarchic Judah." Dissertation, University of Michigan, 1982, writes of the "great" and "little" traditions in monarchic Judaism.

6. Historians debate the year. Some set the fall of Jerusalem in 586.

7. These details come from chapter five of the book of Lamentations.

8. Bright, *A History*, 310.

9. See Provan et. al., *A Biblical History*, 276.

10. See Stulman, *Jeremiah*, AOTC (Nashville: Abingdon, 2005), 1-10.

11. For a succinct summary of this period, see Mark S. Smith, *The Memoirs of God: History, Memory, and the Experience of the Divine in Ancient Israel* (Minneapolis: Fortress Press, 2004), 60-63.

12. This date is recorded in the Babylonian Chronicles. See Arnold, *Who Were the Babylonians?*, 93.

13. Hans M. Barstad, "After the 'Myth of the Empty Land,'" 7-8, believes the town of Mishpah was the center of a province established by Babylon to rule the conquered people, but Vanderhooft doubts it, *Neo-Babyloninan Empire*, 8, 105.

14. On the complexity of memory, see Mark Smith, *The Memoirs of God*, especially 124-58, and Miroslav Volf, *The End of Memory: Remembering Rightly in a Violent World* (Grand Rapids: Eerdmans, 2006).

15. Arnold, *Who Were the Babylonians?* 87-95.

16. David Vanderhooft, "Babylonian Strategies of Imperial Control in the West," in *Judah and the Judeans*, ed. Lipschits and Blenkinsopp, 241.

17. Provan et. al., *A Biblical History*, 280-81.

18. Ibid., 87-105.

19. See Albertz, *Israel in Exile*, 83. Even the skeptical Barstad shares this opinion in "After the 'Myth of the Empty Land,'" in *Judah and the Judeans*, 3-20.

20. Ephraim Stern, *Archaeology and the Land of the Bible: The Assyrian, Babylonian, and Persian Periods (732-332)* vol. 2, ABRL (New York: Doubleday, 2001), 312-50.

21. See B. Oded, "Where Is the Myth of the Empty Land to Be Found? History versus Myth," in *Judah and the Judeans*, ed. Lipschits and Blenkinsopp, 65-68. Stern believes Jerusalem was not rebuilt until the Persian period, *Archaeology and the Land*, 324. Evidence for Babylonian destruction of cities and towns in Judah and adjacent regions is overwhelming. For a list of sites, see Vanderhooft, *Neo-Babylonian Empire*, 106. Eighty percent of the towns and villages in Judah were abandoned or destroyed in the sixth century according Smith-Christopher, *A Biblical Theology*, 47. See also Oded Lipschits, "Demographic Changes in Judah between the Seventh and Fifth Centuries B.C.E" in *Judah and the Judeans*, ed. Lipschits and Blenkinsopp, 323-74, for a detailed study of population changes in Judah during the Babylonian period.

22. Lisbeth Fried, "The Land Lay Desolate: Conquest and Restoration in the Ancient Near East" in *Judah and the Judeans*, ed. Lipschits and Blenkinsopp, 21-54; Charles E. Carter, "Ideology and Archaeology in the Neo-Babylonian Period: Excavating Text and Tell" in *Judah and the Judeans*, ed. Lipschits and Blenkinsopp, 318.

23. David Vanderhooft, "Babylonian Strategies of Imperial Control in the West: Royal Practice and Rhetoric," *Judah and the Judeans*, ed. Lipschits and Blenkinsopp, 252, 55, and *Neo-Babylonian Empire*, 104-14.

24. Vanderhooft, *Neo-Babylonian Empire*, 109.

25. On the benefits of testimony, see Anna Carter Florence, *Preaching as Testimony* (Louisville: Westminster John Knox, 2007.

26. See Shoshana Felman and Dori Laub, *Testimony: Crises of Witnessing in Literature, Psychoanalysis, and History* (New York: Routledge, 1992).

27. Smith-Christopher, *A Biblical Theology*, 47, asks the key question about the relationship of these biblical books to history. Why speak of the high quality of biblical literature associated with this period yet dismiss its contents that tell of immense suffering and despair as fictional?

28. See Gale A. Yee, *Poor Banished Children of Eve: Woman as Evil in the Hebrew Bible* (Minneapolis: Fortress, 2003), 111-34; David G. Garber, "Trauma, History and Survival in Ezekiel 1-24" Dissertation, Emory University (David Petersen) 2005; and Smith-Christopher, *A Biblical Theology*, 75-104.

29. On Lamentations, see Kathleen M. O'Connor, *Lamentations and the Tears of the World* (Maryknoll: Orbis, 2002; F. W. Dobbs-Allsopp, *Lamentations*, IBC (Louisville: Westminster John Knox, 2002); Nancy C. Lee, *Singers of Lamentations: Cities under Siege, from Ur to Sarajevo* (Leiden: Brill, 2002); Adele Berlin, *Lamentations: A Commentary* (Louisville: Westminster John Knox, 2002). Tod Linafelt, *Surviving Lamentations: Catastrophe, Lament, and Protest in the Afterlife of a Biblical Book* (Chicago: University of Chicago Press, 2000).

30. A phrase of Martin Buber, *Eclipse of God: Studies in the Relations between Religion and Philosophy* (New York: Harper and Row, 1952) 22-24. See Frederick L. Downing, *Elie Wiesel: A Religious Biography* (Macon: Mercer University Press, 2008).

31. For a view that challenges this dating, see Provan, "Past, Present, and Future in Lamentations III, 52-66: The Case for Precative Perfect Re-Examined," *VT* (1991) 164-65.

32. Stulman, *Order amid Chaos*, 57.

Chapter 2: Hearts of Stone

1. Vanderhooft, *Neo-Babylonian Empire*, 135.

2. See Cathy Caruth, ed., *Trauma: Explorations in Memory* (Baltimore: Johns Hopkins University Press, 1995) 11.

3. Smith-Christopher, *A Biblical Theology*, 1-26.

4. For studies of disasters and their social impacts see E. L. Quarantelli., ed., *What Is a Disaster? Perspectives on the Question* (London: Routledge, 1998); *Cross-Cultural Assessment of Psychological Trauma and PTSD*, John P. Wilson and Catherine So-kum Tan, eds. (New York: Springer, 2007).

5. Smith-Christopher, *A Biblical Theology*, 79.

6. Elaine Scarry, *The Body in Pain* (New York: Oxford University Press, 1985), 61.

7. Claude Gilbert, "Studying Disaster: Changes in the Main Conceptual Tools," *What Is a Disaster? Perspectives on the Question*, E. E. Quarantelli, ed. (London: Routledge, 1998), 16.

8. Robert A. Stallings, "Disaster and the Theory of Social Disorder," in *What Is a Disaster?*, 130, referring to Anthony Giddens, *The Consequences of Modernity* (Cambridge: Polity, 1990); and *Modernity and Self-Identity* (Cambridge: Polity, 1991).

9. Wolf R. Dombrowsky, "Again and Again: Is a Disaster What We Call a 'Disaster'?" Quarantelli, *What Is a Disaster?*, 19.

10. The oil spill in the Gulf is also a disaster, but its violence and their effects appear as if in slow motion, lacking initial violent blows to human bodies but undermining life in the sea and on the land.

11. McFarlane and van der Kolk, "Trauma and its Challenges to Society," 26.

12. Cathy Caruth, *Unclaimed Experience: Trauma, Narrative, and History* (Baltimore: Johns Hopkins University, Press, 1996), 9.

13. Ibid., 3.

14. Ibid.

15. Bessel A. van der Kolk and Onno van der Hart, "The Intrusive Past: The Flexibility of Memory and the Engraving of Trauma," in Carruth, *Trauma*, 158-82; Caruth, "Introduction II, Recapturing the Past," *Trauma*, 151.

16. Cathy Caruth, *Unclaimed Experience*, 9; See also Lawrence L. Langer, *Holocaust Testimonies: The Ruins of Memory* (New Haven: Yale University Press, 1991), 34.

17. Kai Erikson, "Notes on Trauma and Community," *Trauma: Explorations in Memory*, 183-99.

18. Scarry, *The Body in Pain*, 30-33.

19. Thanks to Jim Mengert, in response to an earlier version of this manuscript.

20. Scarry, *The Body*, 4-21.

21. W. G. Sebald, *On the Natural History of Disaster* (New York: Random, 2003).

22. Ibid., 4.

23. Ibid., 10.

24. Ibid., 24-25.

25. Ibid., 25.

26. Shoshana Felman, "Education and Crisis or the Vicissitudes of Teaching," Carruth, *Trauma*, 52; Hasia R. Diner, *We Remember with Reverence and Love: American Jews and the Myth of Silence after the Holocaust, 1945-1962* (New York: New York University Press, 2009), disputes the myth that Jews were silent following the Holocaust, but her book is not primarily about the victims themselves but about the response of American Jews to the Holocaust and its survivors.

27. Bessel A. van der Kolk, "Trauma and Memory," van der Kolk, *Traumatic Stress*, 293.

28. Caruth, *Unclaimed Experience*, 17.

29. Scarry, *The Body*, 35, 135. Similar claims are made about emotional pain and child abuse by Judith Herman, *Trauma and Recovery*; and Alice Miller, *Drama of the Gifted Child* (New York: Basic, 1979), and *For Your Own Good: Hidden Cruelty in Children and the Roots of Violence* (New York: Farrar, Straus and Giroux, 1982).

30. Dori Laub, "An Event without a Witness: Truth, Testimony, and Survival," *Testimony: Crises of Witnessing in Literature Psychoanalysis, and History*, Shoshanna Felman and Dori Laud, eds. (New York: Routledge, 1992), 78.

31. Dori Laub, "Bearing Witness of the Vicissitudes of Listening," *Testimony: Crises of Witnessing*, 67.

32. van der Kolk, "The Black Hole," *Traumatic Stress*, 12.

33. Teresa Rhodes McGee, *Transforming Trauma: A Path toward Wholeness* (Maryknoll: Orbis, 2005), 94.

34. See McGee, *Transforming Trauma*, 37-45.

35. Elzbieta M. Godziak, "Refugee Womens' Psychological Response to Forced Migration: Limitations of the Trauma Concept," (September 2004) at http://isim.georgetown.edu/Publications/ElzPubs/Refugee%20Women's%20Psychological%20Response.pdf; Boris Droždek and John P. Wilson, "Wrestling with the Ghosts from the Past in Exile: Assessing Trauma in Asylum Seekers, " *Cross-Cultural Assessment of Psychological Trauma and* PTSD, John P. Wilson and Catherine So-kum Tang, eds. (New York: Springer, 2007), 113-31.

36. van der Kolk, "The Black Hole," 26.

37. Italics original, Erikson, "Notes on Trauma and Community," 194.

38. Ibid., 198; Henry Krystal, "Trauma and Aging: A Thirty Year Follow Up," in Caruth, *Trauma*, 76-99.

39. Jean Améry, "Torture in the Holocaust," *Holocaust: Religious and Philosophical Implications*, John K. Roth and Michael Berenbaum, ed. (Saint Paul: Paragon, 1989), 170-89.

40. Ibid., 177.

41. Zachary Braiterman, *(GOD) After Auschwitz* (Princeton: Princeton University Press, 1998).

42. Ibid., 3.

43. Alexander C. McFarlane and Bessel van der Kolk, "Trauma and Its Challenge to Society," *Traumatic Stress*, 26.

44. Felman, "Education and Crisis," Caruth, *Trauma*, 58.

Chapter 3: A Relentless Quest for Meaning

1. Leslie C. Allen, *Jeremiah*, OTL (Louisville: Westminster John Knox, 2008) and others continue to hold this viewpoint.

2. William McKane, *A Critical and Exegetical Commentary on Jeremiah*, vol.1, ICC (Edinburgh: T and T Clark, 1986), l-lxxxiii.

3. We also know that the book moved from an original Hebrew version to a Greek version that may or may not have influenced the final Hebrew version, known as the Masoretic Text (MT).

4. James Boyd White, *When Words Lose Their Meaning: Constitutions and Reconstitutions of Language, Character, and Community* (Chicago: University of Chicago Press, 1985), 27.

5. Louis Stulman, *Order amid Chaos: Jeremiah as Symbolic Tapestry*, Biblical Seminar 57 (Sheffield: Sheffield Academic, 1998).

6. For a discussion of the language, see Jack R. Lundbom, *Jeremiah 1-20*, vol. 1, AB 21A (New York: Doubleday, 1999), 235.

7. Ibid., 25. Jeremiah's sermons reflect a consistent theology that the disaster occurred because the nation rejected the prophetic word.

8. See Susan J. Brison, *Violence and the Remaking of the Self* (Princeton: Princeton University Press, 2002).

9. David Grossman, "Writing in the Dark," *New York Times Magazine* (3 May 2007): 28-31.

Chapter 4: A Family Comes Undone

1. Interpreters usually name Jeremiah's domestic drama "the broken marriage metaphor," but that title is too limiting. Much more is at stake than the well-being of a husband and wife, as is often the case with a failed marriage. Although Jeremiah puts the main spotlight on the couple, children also suffer here, and the household itself collapses. Thanks to Dr. Ron Cram for this insight.

2. For a more detailed exegetical study of this material, see A. R. Pete Diamond and Kathleen M. O'Connor, "Unfaithful Passions: Coding Women Coding Men in Jeremiah 2-3 (4:2)" in *Troubling Jeremiah*, A. R. Pete Diamond, Kathleen M. O'Connor and Louis Stulman, eds., JSOTSup 260 (Sheffield: Sheffield Academic, 1999), 123-45.

3. See Mark Turner, *The Literary Mind* (New York: Oxford University Press, 1996) 13, 57.

4. I use male pronouns for God in this chapter to underscore the marital roles of the characters.

5. See our comparison of the plotlines of the two texts, Diamond and O'Connor, "Unfaithful Passions," 141-42.

6. Diamond and O'Connor, "Unfaithful Passions." For a very different understanding of the poetry in chapter 3, see Mary E. Shields, *Circumscribing the Prostitute: The Rhetorics of Intertextuality, Metaphor, and Gender in Jeremiah 3.1-4* (London: T and T Clark, 2004).

7. Across Jeremiah, Judah and Jerusalem are nearly interchangeable figures. The female poetic figure has many names: Jerusalem, Judah, the Daughter of Zion, daughter of my people. The titles offer geographic and mythic ways to speak of the people, city, and land. When God addresses Jerusalem as a woman, an ancient Near Eastern tradition of cities as feminine comes into play. Cities and nations are feminine in the ancient near East, and often personified, that is, turned into human figures, often evoking goddesses who protected cities among Israel's neighbors. See Elizabeth Boase, *The Fulfillment of Doom?: The Dialogic Interaction between the Book of Lamentations and the Pre-Exilic/Early Exilic Prophetic Literature*, (New York: T and T Clark, 2006), 53-54; Julie Galambush, *Jerusalem in the Book of Ezekiel: The City as Yahweh's Wife*, SBLDS 130 (Atlanta: Scholars Press, 1992); F. W. Doobs-Allsopp, *Lamentations*, IBC (Louisville: Westminster John Knox, 2002), 52; Kathleen M. O'Connor, *Lamentations and the Tears of the Word* (Maryknoll: Orbis, 2002), 14; Christl M. Maier, *Daughter Zion, Mother Zion: Gender, Space, and the Sacred in Ancient Israel* (Minneapolis: Fortress Press, 2008); and see Julia M. O'Brien, *Challenging Prophetic Metaphor: Theology and Ideology in the Prophets* (Louisville: Westminster John Knox, 2008).

8. The wilderness alludes to the nation's wanderings in the desert after the Exodus from Egypt, an earlier golden age.

9. See Else K. Holt, "The Fountain of Living Water and the Deceitful Brook: The Pool of Water Metaphors in the Book of Jeremiah," in *Metaphor in the Hebrew Bible*, P. van Hecke, ed., BETL 187 (Leuven: Leuven University Press, 2005), 99-117.

10. Feminist critique of this characterization is extensive. See Renita Weems, *Battered Love: Marriage, Sex, and Violence in the Hebrew Prophets* (Minneapolis: Fortress Press, 1995) and more recently O'Brien, *Challenging Prophetic Metaphor*, and Diamond and O'Connor, "Unfaithful Passions," 143-45.

11. This law may have arisen because of difficulty in determining paternity of any future children, or perhaps it relates to purity concerns about the mixing of male seed.

12. The NRSV translates "friend." This relational shift has led some interpreters to think that wife imagery disappears here and also later in 3:19 where father-daughter language reappears. The change from husband/wife to father/daughter is hard to explain, but it is clear that Jerusalem/Judah is the reference behind both wife and daughter. That a wife might refer to her husband as "father" and he to her as "daughter" makes sense in a cultural world where cities are often named as daughters of a nation. And in later passages in Jeremiah, God refers to his beloved as "Daughter Zion" (see chapter 5, "War Poems"), and here she calls him her "intimate." See O'Brien, *Challenging Prophetic Metaphor*,125-51; Shields, *Circumscribing the Prostitute,* 115-23 (who argues that this is not wife but daughter, and Lundbom, *Jeremiah 1-20*, 303 (who notes that "in Prov 2:17 the wayward woman's 'confidant of her youth' is her husband").

13. But if the address to God as father does not also mean husband, "the intimate of my youth," the verse suggests father-daughter incest prior to the woman's harlotry. Shields, *Circumscribing the Prostitute,* 44, thinks the language marks "deference between a younger woman and an older man."

14. To learn how divorce affects Wife Judah/Daughter Zion, see the book of Lamentations, which describes her as being "like a widow." See especially the first two chapters of Lamentations, and O'Connor, *Lamentations and the Tears of the World*, 17-43.

15. Many Jeremiah scholars believed the poetry of these chapters were among Jeremiah's original words because they include the northern kingdom and were thought to express

Jeremiah's hope to reunite the whole nation under King Josiah. William L. Holladay, *Jeremiah*, vol. 1, Hemeneia (Philadelphia: Fortress Press, 1986), 62-72. I think reference to the north is a later effort to place the disaster into a larger horizon of Judah's national identity, harkening back to the days when all twelve tribes were one people.

16. See Walter Brueggemann, *A Commentary on Jeremiah: Exile and Homecoming* (Grand Rapids: Eerdmans, 1998), 43.

17. Diamond and O'Connor, "Unfaithful Passions," 142.

18. "Sons" in Hebrew.

19. The readers of the text and the representatives of the nation were men, here shamed by comparison with an adulterous woman. See Diamond and O'Connor, "Unfaithful Passions," 143-45.

20. On the liturgical form, see Shields, *Circumscribing the Prostitute*, 125-28.

21. Marten W. de Vries, "Trauma in Cultural Perspective," in van der Kolk et al., *Traumatic Stress*, 410.

22. Jack Kugelmass, "Missions to the Past: Poland in Contemporary Jewish Thought and Deed," in *Tense Past: Cultural Essays in Trauma and Memory*, ed. Paul Antze and Michael Lambek (New York: Routledge, 1996), 211-12.

23. Kugelmass, "Missions to the Past," 210.

24. Showing again that the audience comprises men who alone were circumcised in ancient Israel and using male language to name the whole population. As a spiritual commitment, then, circumcising the heart can include women, but it does name the change of heart in male terms. This is not surprising in ancient Judah, where women are rarely viewed as full citizens.

25. See E. A. Goodfriend, "Adultery," *The Anchor Bible Dictionary on CD-ROM* (Oak Harbor: Logos Research Systems, 1997), for a brief discussion of adultery in the Old Testament.

26. Renita Weems, *Battered Love*; Shields, *Circumscribing the Prostitute.*

27. Weems, *Battered Love*; Diamond and O'Connor, "Unfaithful Passions." On Ezekiel's use of the marriage metaphor, see Gale A. Yee, *Poor Banished Children of Eve,* and for its appearance in Lamentations and Second Isaiah, see Kathleen M. O'Connor, "'Speak Tenderly to Jerusalem:' Second Isaiah's Reception and Use of Daughter Zion," The Thompson Lecture, *PSB* November, 1999: 281-94.

28. Words of Robert J. Lifton in Cathy Caruth, "An Interview with Robert J. Lifton," Caruth, *Trauma*, 138.

29. Gozdziak, "Refugee Women's Psychological Response," 16.

30. For examples of ways music, art, and imaginative literature helped Jews in America engage memories of the Holocaust, see, Hasia R. Diner, *We Remember with Reverence and Love: American Jews and the Myth of Silence after the Holocaust, 1945-1962* (New York: New York University Press, 2009), especially 18-149. Thanks to Mark S. Smith for this reference.

Chapter 5: Fragmented Memories of Trauma

1. Serene Jones, "'Soul Anatomy': Calvin's Commentary on the Psalms," in *Psalms in Community: Jewish and Christian Textual, Liturgical and Artistic Traditions*, ed. Harold W. Attridge and Margot E. Fassler (Atlanta: Society of Biblical Literature, 2004), 265-84.

2. Lawrence J. Kirmayer, "Landscapes of Memory," in *Tense Past: Cultural Essays in Trauma and Memory*, ed. Paul Antze and Michael Lambek (New York: Routledge, 1996), 176. See also Lawrence L. Langer, *Holocaust Memories: The Ruins of Memory* (New Haven: Yale University Press, 1991).

3. Paul Antze and Michael Lambek, eds., *Tense Past*, xix; Bessell A. Van der Kolk, Alexander C. McFarlane, and Onno Van der Hort, "A General Approach to Treatment of PTSD," in

Traumatic Stress, 417-40; Bessel A. van Der Kolk and Onno van der Hart, "The Intrusive Past: The Flexibility of Memory and the Engraving of Trauma," in *Trauma*, 158-82; and Caruth, "Introduction II: Recapturing the Past," in *Trauma*, 151.

4. Kalí Tal, *Worlds of Hurt: Reading Literatures of Trauma* (Cambridge: Cambridge University Press, 1996), 6.

5. Deborah von Fischer Samuelson, *Seven Steps to Healing: Experiential Reframing and Its Connections to Job and Jeremiah*, Project for the Doctor of Ministry Degree, Columbia Theological Seminary, 2008.

6. See Smith-Christopher, *A Biblical Theology*, 75-104; Yee, *Poor Banished Children*, 111-34; and Garber, "Trauma, History, and Survival in Ezekiel 1-24."

7. Until fairly recently, scholarly concern for historical origins of texts has veiled other aspects of the literature. In particular, many have viewed the chapters that contain the war poems (chapters 4-6; 8:16-17; 13:20-27, and 10:17-22) in broad sweeps, part of the collection of "oracles against Judah and Jerusalem" (chaps. 1–20).

8. The foe from the north first appears obliquely in Jeremiah' commission in Jer 1:13-16. Since Babylon is not to the north of Judah but to the east, scholars have made many proposals to name the foe as other enemies of Israel such as the Scythians. See John Hill, *Friend or Foe? The Figure of Babylon in the Book of Jeremiah MT*, Biblical Interpretation (Leiden: Brill, 1999) 50.

9. For Calvin, the psalms are "textual theater wherein traumatized persons can adopt identity scripts that strengthen their faith, even in the midst of the harm they are experiencing," Jones, "Soul Anatomy," 269.

10. Hill, *Friend or Foe?* For many ways to approach the figures see, Leo G. Perdue, *The Collapse of History: Reconstructing Old Testament Theology* OBT (Minneapolis: Fortress Press, 1994).

11. See Diamond et al., *Troubling Jeremiah*, for many efforts to read Jeremiah symbolically.

12. John Hill, "The Threat from the North—Reflections on a Theme Both Ancient and Modern," in *Wisdom for Life*, ed. Michael A. Kelly and Mark A. O'Brien (Adelaide: Australian Theological Forum, 2005), 6.

13. David Bourguet, *Les Mètaphores de Jérémie*, EBib 9 (Paris: LeCoffre, 1987), 117.

14. See F. W. Dobbs-Allsopp, *Weep O Daughter of Zion: A Study of the City-Lament Genre in the Hebrew Bible*, BibOr 44 (Rome: Editirce Pontificion Istituto Biblico, 1993), 87-88.

15.That she is female follows customary city and nation naming practices in the ancient world and grants her poetic status as city-woman/nation. See, most recently, Christl M. Maier, *Daughter Zion, Mother Zion: Gender, Space, and the Sacred in Ancient Israel* (Minneapolis: Fortress Press, 2008).

16. The NRSV translates the Hebrew less specifically as "evil," but "disaster" is a common meaning of *râ'âh*. The Hebrew places it at the beginning of the clause for emphasis.

17. Brueggemann, *Exile and Homecoming*, 55.

18. Historically, Jeremiah's accusation that God deceived the people may refer to Isaiah's prophecies a century earlier when Assyria was attacking Judah. Isaiah assured the Judean King Ahaz that God would protect the nation, if Ahaz stood firm and the underlying royal covenant theology (Isa 7). A century later that trust has become false certitude: God would shield them from harm no matter what they did. This is why Jeremiah accuses God of lying to them. The theology that God dwelled with them on Mount Zion and protected them is called royal covenant theology. See Bennie C. Ollegburger, *Zion the City of the Great King: A Theological Symbol of the Jerusalem Cult*, JSOTSup (Sheffield: Sheffield Academic, 1987). More recently, see Walter Brueggemann, *An Unsettling God: The Heart of the Hebrew Bible* (Minneapolis: Fortress Press, 2009), 99-123.

19. For theological analysis of God as warrior against Judah, see Stulman, *Jeremiah*, 81-85.

20. Cf. 2:1-3:25. Biddle, *Polyphony*, 20, identifies the female of God's address as Lady Jerusalem.

21. Cf. 6:3; 10:20; 30:18; 35:7, 10; 49:29.

22. In Hebrew, "to know" is often language of intimacy. Not knowing God is Hosea's complaint about God's family (Hos 2:8; 2:20; 4:1; 11:3).

23. Perdue, *Collapse of History*, 142.

24. Hill, *Friend or Foe?* Emending to the singular. Since Babylon is not to the north of Judah but to the east, scholars made many proposals to name the foe as other enemies of Israel such as the Scythians, but now it is clear that the foe is Babylon.

25. YHWH Sabbaoth means "Lord of armies."

26. The Hebrew reads "your heels undergo violence," heels being "private parts," Lundbom, *Jeremiah*, vol. 1, 686. It is well known that rape is a persistent weapon of warfare. Rape not only harms the women but was considered a form of shaming their men, who cannot protect them. See Pamela Gordon and Harold C. Washington, "Rape as Military Metaphor in the Hebrew Bible," in *Feminist Companion to the Latter Prophets*, ed. Athalya Brenner (Sheffield: Sheffield Academic, 1995), 308-25.

27. Lundbom, *Jeremiah*, vol. 1, 686, discusses the Hebrew of these verses and understands the assault as public shaming by exposure, though he also connects the verses to the sexual assaults against women common in war (Amos 1:13; Isa 3:17; Ezek 16:39-40).

28. On shame, see Amy Beth Kalmanofsky, *The Rhetoric of Horror in the Book of Jeremiah* (Ann Arbor; UMI Dissertation Services, 2005), 65-68.

29. See Susan J. Brison, *Aftermath: Violence and the Remaking of a Self* (Princeton: Princeton University Press, 2002).

30. Language of White, *When Words*, 87.

31. Brison, *Aftermath*, provides detailed testimony and analysis of the impact of rape and its consequences as well as an excellent account of the role of memory and storytelling in efforts to recover.

32. A term made part of the interpretive lexicon by Phyllis Trible, *Texts of Terror: Literary Feminist Readings of Biblical Narratives* (Minneapolis: Fortress, 1984).

33. Tal, *Worlds of Hurt*, 137; and Brison, *Aftermath*, 49-59.

34. Robert Frost, "The Figure a Poem Makes" (1939), quoted by Christopher Benfey, "The Storm over Robert Frost," *New York Review of Books* (December 4, 2008), 49.

35. Smith-Christopher, *Biblical Theology*, 80.

36. Bulman, *Shattered Assumptions*, 115-29.

37. But even when outsiders blame inhabitants' sins as the cause of tragedy, as when certain evangelists blamed New York and New Orleans, the speakers themselves are seeking order in the world to keep fear at bay by finding cause and effect.

38. Michael Lambek, "The Past Imperfect," 241. On the challenges and healing of memories, see Miroslav Volf, *The End of Memory: Remembering Rightly in a Violent World* (Grand Rapids: Eerdmans, 2006), and for theories about collective memory and their impact on the Bible, see Mark S. Smith, *The Memoirs of God: History, Memory, and the Experience of the Divine in Ancient Israel* (Minneapolis: Fortress Press, 2004), 126-40.

39. Lawrence J. Kirmayer, "Landscapes of Memory," 186.

40. From "A Childhood around 1950," a poem by Alan Williamson in *The Face of Poetry*, ed. Zak Rogow (Berkeley: University of California Press, 2005), 143.

41. Kirmayer, *Landscapes of Memory*, 176.

42. A formulation of Jones, "Soul Anatomy," 274.

Chapter 6: If Only Tears Were Possible

1. See Herman, *Trauma and Recovery*, 155.

2. See Robert Jay Lifton's chapter, "On Numbing and Feeling," in *Indefensible Weapons: The Political and Psychological Case against Nuclearism*, Robert Jay Lifton and Richard Falk (New York: Basic, 1982), 103.

3. Lifton, *Indefensible Weapons*, 101.

4. Bulman, *Shattered Assumptions,* 95, 104.

5. Robert Jay Lifton and Kai Erikson, "Nuclear War's Effect on the Mind," in *Indefensible Weapons*, 276-77.

6. Lifton and Erikson, "Nuclear War's Effect on the Mind," 276-77.

7. See Andrew Solomon, *The Noonday Demon: An Atlas of Depression* (New York: Scribner, 2001), 15-38.

8. Several biblical texts from the Babylonian Period suggest that the people of Judah experienced some forms of collective numbing. In the last two poems of the Book of Lamentations, for instance, the rage, grief, and loss of the first three poems (Lam 1–3) are replaced by an emotionally flat and abrupt style of poetry, progressively shorter poems, and the fading away of the alphabetic forms of the earlier poems. The tone is benumbed and passionless, tamped down in a kind of deadened state. It is as if the poets had no energy left to encounter or interpret their suffering, O'Connor, *Lamentations*, 58-79.

9. Jones, "Psalms in Community," 273.

10. Jones, "Psalms in Community," 280.

11. Henry Krystal, "Trauma and Aging: A Thirty Year Follow Up," in Caruth, *Trauma: Explorations in Memory*, 76-99; see Robert J. Lifton, *Death in Life: Survivors of Hiroshima*, 80.

12. The English translation numbers this material differently from the Hebrew.

13. Xuan Huong Thi Pham, *Mourning in the Ancient Near East and the Hebrew Bible*, JSOTSup 302 (Sheffield: Sheffield Academic, 1999); Saul Olyan, *Biblical Mourning: Ritual and Social Dimensions* (Oxford: Oxford University Press, 2004).

14. deVries, "Trauma in Cultural Perspective," in van der Volk, *Traumatic Stress*, 403.

15. Thomas Lynch, "Our Near-Death Experience," *New York Times*, OpEd (April 9, 2005).

16. Olyan, *Mourning Rites*, 32.

17. The English translation begins chapter 9 with the verse numbered 8:23 in the Hebrew.

18. Whether the principal speaker here is God or Jeremiah is debated, but if the speaker is Jeremiah, he speaks as if for God. For an argument that the speaker is not God, see Joseph M. Henderson, "Who Weeps in Jeremiah VIII 23 (IX1): Dramatic Speakers in the Poetry of Jeremiah," *VT* 52/2 (2002): 191-206. But see Ahida E. Pilarski, "A Study of the References to *bat-'ammî* in Jeremiah 8:18-23: A Gendered Lamentation," presented at the Annual Meeting of the Catholic Biblical Association of America, Creighton University, Omaha, August 5, 2008. Pilarski offers clear evidence that daughter terms are interchangeable in Jeremiah.

19. I have some quarrels with the usual English translations of this passage. Interpreters generally miss the gendered language, translating "daughter of my people" simply as "my people" (vv. 19, 21, 23). To disregard the more accurate "daughter" language is to fail to see that we are back in the world of the broken family, where God also appears as distraught and sorrowful.

20. But see Brueggemann, *Exile and Homecoming*, 94; J. J. M. Roberts, "The Motif of the Weeping God in Jeremiah and its Background in the Lament Tradition of the Ancient Near East," *OTE* 5 (1992): 361-74; and Pilarski, "A Study of the References to *bat-'ammî* in Jeremiah 8:18-23."

21. See Mark Biddle, *Polyphony and Symphony*, 5-13.

22. See Stulman, *Jeremiah*, 99, who credits Jeremiah with 8:18-21 and God with 9:1-3, while Lundbom, *Jeremiah 1-20*, 529-34, finds God's voice only in 19c and sees 8:22-9:1(2) as a separate poem. Joseph Henderson disagrees, followed by Nancy C. Lee in a response to a paper I gave at the Annual Meeting of the Society of Biblical Literature, 2006. These two scholars overlook the fact that personified Jerusalem/Judah, "Daughter of my people" is the same figure as the YHWH's wife in the broken family metaphor (2:1-4:2). The passage again casts husband and wife in a poem about her destruction. That God is not always the speaker of this phrase in other biblical books is not determinative here.

23. Fretheim, *Jeremiah*, 155, thinks Jeremiah is the speaker throughout but his grief "is an embodiment of God's grief."

24. 8:7, 11; 9:7; 15:7; 18:15; 23:22; and see Biddle, *Polyphony and Symphony*, 31. Henderson distinguishes between the appearance of "my people" and the phrase "daughter of my people" on the grounds that the latter refers to the wounded people and "my people" refers to the people when God is angry at them. I do not think the distinction is necessary, nor does Pilarski.

25. See 8:19, 21, 22; 9:1. Compare 4:11; 6:14, 30 and, less clearly, 6:26; 8:1; 14:17.

26. See Kathleen M. O'Connor, "The Tears of God and the Divine Character in Jeremiah 2-9" in *God in the Fray: A Tribute to Walter Brueggemann*, ed. Tod Linafelt and Timothy K. Beal (Minneapolis: Fortress, 1998), 172-85; Walter Brueggemann , *Exile and Homecoming*, 91-93.

27. Roberts, "The Motif of the Weeping God," 361-74. See also Biddle, *Polyphony*, 30.

28. Joseph Henderson, "Who Weeps," 195, makes a similar observation.

29. As an aside, there is very little depiction of former cheerfulness in the character of Jeremiah.

30. Interpreters typically overlook the daughter part of the "the daughter of my people," a common phrase for the city in Jeremiah. Granted that the figure is a way to speak of the people themselves, this is also the case whenever any collective term appears, even the more literal "Jerusalem." The feminine term evokes the many "daughter" references in Jeremiah and links this passage to the marriage metaphor. On daughters in Jeremiah, see Lundbom, *Jeremiah 1-20*, 344; and also the cogent article by Michael Floyd, "Welcome Back, Daughter of Zion," *CBQ* (2008): 465-83.

31. The *Jewish Publication Society* translation.

32. Fretheim, *Jeremiah*, 154.

33. NRSV.

34. Else K. Holt, "The Fountain of Living Water and the Deceitful Brook: The Pool of Water Metaphors in the Book of Jeremiah (MT)," in *Metaphor in the Hebrew Bible*, ed. P. van Hecke (Leuven: Leuven University Press, 2005), 99-117.

35. Language derived from Holt, "The Fountain of Living Water," 100, 115.

36. Caroline Moorehead, *Human Cargo: A Journey among Refugees* (New York: Henry Holt, 2005), 223.

37. Henderson, "Who Weeps," 204, finds it unlikely that God speaks both angry and sympathetic remarks, but trauma and disaster studies urge the conclusion that it is exactly such turmoil and inconsistency that follows cataclysm. The logic here is poetic not linear, and it is consistent with emotional states of victims.

38. Fretheim, *Jeremiah*, 164-66.

39. Abraham Heschel, *The Prophets*, vol. 2 (New York: Harper Colophon, 1975), 59-78.

40. Lundbom, *Jeremiah 1-2*, 549, thinks Jeremiah is the speaker in verse 10 and God in verse 11, even though he translates both verses in the first person and there are no syntactical clues to suggest a change of speaker.

41. Depending on the translation of the first verse, God either weeps following Hebrew, Greek, or Syrica, or as in the NRSV translations, God commands the people to weep and lament. I see no reason to challenge the Hebrew and other versions. God continues to speak from the previous poem (9:7-9), and surely only God can be the one who makes Jerusalem a rubble (9:11).

42. The mourning women may or may not have been professionals. Some think they occupied an official position in towns and villages; others believe their role was more informal. Women's association with mourning in the Bible and other ancient near eastern texts is well attested, according to Olyan, *Mourning Rites*, 50. Whether or not they were officially sanctioned would probably not have mattered to families of the deceased. Today it does matter to women in search of women's history. Mourning rituals may have been one of the few places women assumed leadership in public rituals. Some cultures today employ professional mourners as a way to care for the bereaved and to honor the dead.

43. Lundbom, *Jeremiah 1-20*, 559.

44. Sidra Koven Ezrahi, *By Words Alone: The Holocaust in Literature* (Chicago: Chicago University Press, 1980), 146.

45. Judith Herman, *Trauma and Recovery*, 133–213.

46. Jones, "The Psalms in Community," 280-81.

Chapter 7: Telling a Life

1. Gerhard von Rad, *Old Testament Theology*, vol. 2 (New York Harper and Row, 1965), 207.

2. For accounts of Ezekiel's supposed madness, see David J. Halperin, *Seeking Ezekiel: Text and Psychology* (University Park: Pennsylvania State University Press, 1993) for readings that view the strangeness as literary response to trauma, see Smith-Christopher, *A Biblical Theology*, 75-104; Yee, *Poor Banished Children*, 111-34; and Garber, "Trauma, History and Survival in Ezekiel."

3. Dana Greene, "Biography and the Search for Meaning," *National Catholic Reporter*, May 5, 2006.

4. Ibid.

5. Paul Antze and Michael Lambek, *Tense Past*, xxii,

6. Jack R. Lundbom, *Jeremiah 1-20: A New Translation with Introduction and Commentary*, AB 21A (New York: Doubleday, 1999), *Jeremiah 21-36: A New Translation with Introduction and Commentary*, AB 21B (New York: Doubleday, 2004), and *Jeremiah 36-52: A New Translation with Introduction and Commentary*, AB 21C (New York: Doubleday, 2004); William L. Holladay, *Jeremiah 1: A Commentary on the Book of the Prophet Jeremiah Chapters 1-25*, Hermeneia (Philadelphia: Fortress Press, 1986) and *Jeremiah 2: A Commentary on the Book of the Prophet Jeremiah Chapters 26-52*, Hermeneia (Philadelphia: Fortress Press, 1989); and J. Skinner, *Prophecy and Religion: Studies in the Life of Jeremiah* (Cambridge: Cambridge University Press, 1922).

7. Walter Brueggemann, "The Book of Jeremiah: Portrait of the Prophet," in *Interpreting the Prophets*, ed. James Luther Mays and Paul J. Achtemeier (Philadelphia: Fortress Press, 1987), 13-29, and *The Theology of the Book of Jeremiah*, Old Testament Theology (Cambridge: Cambridge University Press, 2007), 27-35; Timothy Polk, *The Prophetic Persona: Jeremiah and the Language of the Self*, JSOTSup 32 (Sheffield: Sheffield Academic, 1984); Terence Fretheim, *Jeremiah*, Smyth and Helwys Bible Commentary (Macon: Smyth and Helwys, 2002); Robert P. Carroll, *Jeremiah: A Commentary*, OTL (Philadelphia: Westminster, 1986); Corrine Carvalho, "Layers of Meaning: Priesthood in Jeremiah MT," in *The Priests in the Prophets: The Portrayal of*

Priests, Prophets, and Other Religious Specialists in the Latter Prophets, ed. Lester L. Grabbe and Alice Ogden Bellis (London: T and T Clark, 2004), 149-76.

8. See Pete Diamond, "Introduction" in *Troubling Jeremiah*, esp. 3.

9. Terence E. Fretheim, "Caught in the Middle: Jeremiah's Vocational Crisis, *WW* 4/22 (Fall 2002): 351-60.

10. I am not the first person to make this suggestion. In the middle of the last century, German scholar Heinz Kremers, "Ledensgemeinschaft mit Gott im Alten Testament," *EvT* 13 (1953): 122-40, noticed parallels between Jeremiah's suffering and the fate of the people and saw his life as an anticipation of the passion of Jesus. This article speaks about the importance of Jeremiah's suffering but with unfortunate Christological intentions. In rushing to the New Testament, he skips over Jeremiah's significance for the book's own audience and inappropriately "baptizes" the Old Testament. But I want to retrieve some of Kremer's insights to understand how these stories help victims of the Babylonian catastrophe. Gerhard von Rad called the prophet's life a *via dolorosa*, a way of sorrow, a kind of passion narrative in his *Old Testament Theology*, 2 vols. (New York: Harper and Row, 1962), 206-8. For a more appropriate study of Jeremiah's influence on Matthew's Gospel, see Mark F. Whitters, "Jesus in the Footsteps of Jeremiah," *CBQ* (2006): 229-47.

11. See Kathleen M. O'Connor, *The Confessions of Jeremiah: Their Interpretation and Role in Chapters 1-25*, SBLDS 94 (Atlanta: Scholars, 1988), 118-22.

12. Jeremiah appears here as a prophet like Moses whose career also lasts forty years, from the thirteenth year of King Josiah's rule (627 B.C.E.) to the eleventh year of Zedekiah's rule (587 B.C.E., Jer 1:1-3). Kathleen M. O'Connor, "Jeremiah," in *The Oxford Bible Commentary*, ed. John Barton and John Muddiman (Oxford: Oxford University Press, 2001), 490.

13. For example, the ruin of Jeremiah's loin cloth (13:1-11) and the smashing of the jug before the witnessing elders (19:1-15).

14. See Jon D. Levenson, *Restoration and the Resurrection of Israel: The Ultimate Victory of the God of Life* (New Haven: Yale University Press, 2006), 48-51; Lundbom, *Jeremiah 1-20*, 757-58; Fretheim, *Jeremiah*, 249.

15. Ibid.

16. Ibid., 248.

17. Erikson, "Notes on Trauma and Community," 189; Marten W. deVries, "Trauma in Cultural Perspective," in *Traumatic Stress*, 398-413.

18. Marvin Sweeney thinks Jeremiah's celibacy is a model of Judah's punishment by drought in Jer 14:1-22. See his notes to the *Jewish Study Bible Tanak Translation* (Oxford: Oxford University Press, 2004), 958. That may be so, but we do not know if the drought is a metaphoric description for the barren world left by the invasions, or whether it was an additional trauma suffered by the people.

19. Whether Jeremiah is imprisoned in the stocks, in a cell, or in some other form of imprisonment is not clear from the Hebrew. To be held in the "stocks" overnight adds physical torture and public humiliation to imprisonment.

20. Chapter 26 introduces the second half of the book and engages a different set of circumstances from the many poetic oracles of the book's first half. In fits and starts the second half (chaps. 26-52) focuses largely on matters of survival and reflects on the place of Judah's disaster in the divine plan for the nations. The prophetic message in contention is no longer whether Judah will repent in time to avert collapse. After chapter 20, the book generally assumes the disaster to be a present reality rather than a coming catastrophe. Narratives of Jeremiah's capture become less mythic, more "historic" sounding, because as the events occur, God is not the principal speaker. The poetry, by contrast, casts the catastrophe in a mythic world in which God

is one of the main speakers. At the level of the book's loose, arcing narrative, the second part assumes the disaster has occurred. By and large, it speaks less of the invasions and captivities as coming events, and concerns itself with how to survive and explain the disaster, O'Connor, *Confessions*, 145-47, and O'Connor, "Jeremiah," *Oxford*, 509.

21. Chapter 26, for example, severely shrinks the temple sermon to two verses (26:2-3) and adds a complicated story about the community's response (vv. 7-25). The chapter also ignores Jeremiah's condemnation of false worship, so central to the sermon, and instead tells of the prophet's impudence in announcing the destruction not only of the temple but here primarily of the city (26:6,11,15): "I will make this house like Shiloh, and I will make this city a curse for all the nations of the earth" (26:6). For a discussion of these changes see Kathleen M. O'Connor, " 'Do not Trim a Word': The Contributions of Chapter 26 to the Book of Jeremiah," *CBQ* (1989): 617-30.

22. Fretheim, *Jeremiah*, 368.

23. Ahikam is a member of the Shaphan family, highly placed leaders who support Jeremiah across the book. For a family tree, see Lawrence Boadt, *Jeremiah 26-52, Habbakuk, Zephaniah, Nahum*, Old Testament Message 10 (Wilmington: Michael Glazier, 1982), 15.

24. O'Connor, "Jeremiah," *Oxford*, 510-11.

25. O'Connor, "Do Not Trim," 629. See 27:7, 22; 29:4-7, 10-14, for Jeremiah's instructions to endure.

26. This story occurs in the collection of hopeful passages called the "Little Book of Consolation" (chaps. 30–33). Although the story focuses on a symbolic action, I include it because it takes place in captivity.

27. Walter Brueggemann, "Faith at the *Nullpunkt*," in *The End of the World and the Ends of God: Science and Theology on Eschatology*, ed. John Polkinghorne and Michael Welker (Harrisburg: Trinity International, 2000), 143-54.

28. Some interpreters see these stories as two versions of the same event, but the two chapters have different purposes and can be read as a continuous narrative. See Mark Roncace, *Jeremiah, Zedekiah, and the Fall of Jerusalem* (New York: T and T Clark, 2005) for a wonderful literary study of these chapters.

29. Some interpreters see them as variants on the same events, but that is not clear.

30. Some escaped during the siege and resettled in Benjamin. See Stern, *Archaeology*, 312-50. Benjamin is also the location of Jeremiah's hometown, Anathoth.

31. The cistern also connects Jeremiah's captivity with the story of Joseph in the book of Genesis. Joseph's brothers leave him to die in the cistern (*bôr*) and from there sell him into slavery in Egypt (37:24, 28). Later Potiphar imprisons Joseph in a cistern (Gen 40:15) and from there he finally escapes (41:14). The allusion to the story of Joseph cloaks Jeremiah's imprisonment in the cistern with ancient meaning. The word joins his captivity to that of an ancestor who knows similar peril and escapes imprisonment to flourish another day. Jeremiah's story thereby gains the aura of ancestral authority and promises hope of survival to the people also trapped in the pit of suffering.

32. Jeremiah's identification with the people in the land is cemented by chapter 40, another account of release. The Babylonians remove the fetters from Jeremiah's hands and tell him to choose between going to Babylon or remaining in the land: "See the whole land is before you, go wherever it is good and right to go." The text twice uses the verb *yāšab* in describing his choice. He joins Gedeliah, the Judean official appointed by Babylon to govern the occupied land "and remained with him among the people" (40:5-6).

33. See chapter 13 below.

34. On the ambiguity of Zedekiah's character in these narratives, see Roncace, *Jeremiah, Zedekiah, and the Fall.*

35. This use of "remain" (*yāšab*) seems to contradict my previous claim about this word and maybe it does. But its specific sense here is to urge the people to stop defending Jerusalem and to surrender to Babylon in order to survive.

36. Note the similar plight of the king in 38:22, and the possible connection with the speaker in Lamentations 3:55 where *bôr* appears again. See von Rad, *Old Testament Theology*, 208.

37. Ebed-Melech means "Servant of the King," but which king, earthly or heavenly?

38. On the way readers create coherence, see Turner, *The Literary Mind*, 13.

39. Clifford Geertz, "The Impact of the Concept of Culture on the Concept of Man," *The Interpretation of Cultures: Selected Essays* (New York: Basic, 1973), 45.

Chapter 8: Survive by Praying

1. 20:14-18 is a curse rather than a lament, though some interpreters include it in the final confession. See O'Connor, *The Confessions of Jeremiah: Their Interpretation and Role in Chapters 1-25*, SBLDS 94 (Atlanta: Scholars, 1988), 75-80.

2. Leslie C. Allen, *Jeremiah*, OTL (Louisville: Westminster John Knox, 2008), 145, denies biographical status to the confessions because they lack explicit settings in Jeremiah's life. But their first person speech, no matter how conventional, sets the prayers in his life, even if they are added by later editors of the book.

3. Fretheim, *Jeremiah*, 187. See also Allen, *Jeremiah*, 144.

4. See Walter *Baumgartner's* classic discussion, *Jeremiah's Poems of Lament* (Sheffield: Almond, 1988).

5. William S. Morrow, *Protest against God: The Eclipse of a Biblical Tradition*, Hebrew Bible Monographs 4 (Sheffield: Sheffield Phoenix, 2006), provides an excellent study of the lament form across the Bible.

6. See Walter Brueggemann's essay, "The Formfulness of Grief," *The Psalms and the Life of Faith* (Minneapolis: Fortress Press, 1995), 84-97.

7. For exegetical studies of the confessions, see O'Connor, *The Confessions*; A. R. Diamond, *The Confessions of Jeremiah in Context: Scenes of Prophetic Drama*, JSOTSup 45 (Sheffield: Sheffield Academic, 1987); and Mark Smith *The Laments of Jeremiah and their Contexts*, SBLMS 42 (Atlanta: Scholars, 1990).

8. On functions of the form, see O'Connor, *Lamentations and the Tears of the World*, 9-11.

9. Walter Brueggemann, "The Formfulness of Grief," and Fretheim, *Jeremiah*, 187.

10. With the possible exception of 15:19, but see below.

11. Translations are mine.

12. Josep Dubbink,"Getting Closer to Jeremiah: The Word of YHWH and the Literary-Theological Person of a Prophet," in *Reading the Book of Jeremiah: A Search for Coherence*, ed. Martin Kessler (Winona Lake: Eisenbrauns, 2004), 25-40.

13. See Walter Brueggemann, *Like Fire in the Bones: Listening for the Prophetic Word in Jeremiah* (Minneapolis: Fortress Press, 2006).

14. When Jeremiah insists on his fidelity before God, he defends prophecy. The confessions are a kind of "prophet-odicy," a kind of prophetic self-defense. Such a defense is necessary because disasters undermine the credibility of social and religious institutions, but Jeremiah has been a true and faithful speaker for God. His confessions not only defend him against false prophets who prophesy "peace, peace when there is no peace" (6:14; 8:11); they also reclaim and reconstitute prophecy itself. Jeremiah's prayers are the evidence that prophecy still burns brightly.

15. So also Allen, *Jeremiah*, 145.

16. Quoted by Christopher Benfey, "The Storm Over Robert Frost," *New York Review of Books* (December 4, 2008), 50.

17. On self-blame as a survival strategy after child abuse, see Alice Miller, *The Drama of the Gifted Child* (New York: Basic, 1979), and *For Your Own Good* (New York: Farrar, Strauss and Giroux, 1982).

18. The Hebrew root *pth* carries sexual nuances in Judg 14:15; 15:16 as does *hzq* in Deut 22:25; Prov 7:13; Isa 4:1; 2 Sam 13:1; Judg 19:25, 29. See my argument in *The Confessions*, 70-71; Allen, *Jeremiah*, 230; and Stulman, *Jeremiah*, 198-200.

19. For further discussion of these two categories, see Morrow, *Protest against God*, 42-45 and 76-81.

20. For example, Lam 3; Pss. 9-10; 44; 77; 94). Because some laments mix singular and plural voices, the singular voice seems capable of standing for everyone.

21. Carleen Mandolfo, *God in the Dock: Dialogic Tension in the Psalms of Lament*, JSOTS 357 (Sheffield: Sheffield Academic, 2002), 50, suggests that distinguishing between individual and collective speech does little to affect the impact of the passage.

22. Pete Diamond, *The Confessions*, 190, agrees that there must be that there must be "wider significance" beyond the prophet himself "to account for their [the prayers] preservation in the tradition."

23. Louis Stulman, "Jeremiah as a Messenger of Hope in Crisis," *Int* 62 (2008): 5-20; Henning Graf Reventlow, *Liturgie und prophetisches Ich bei Jeremiah* (Gütersloh: Gütersloher, 1966); Erhard Gerstenberger, "Jeremiah's Complaint: Observations on Jer 15:10-21," *JBL* (1963): 393-408.

24. The Hebrew verb, *šûb*, means to turn around, to turn back.

25. Mark S. Smith, *The Laments*, 49, notes that "the prophet's fate stands as a central example of the difficulties in the relationship between Yahweh and Israel."

26. In addition to other lament psalms, similar resistance to the rhetoric of human responsibility appears in other biblical books. Second Isaiah announces comfort and reinterprets the disaster as far more punishment than the people deserved for their sins: "You have suffered double for all your sins" (Isa 40:1). Even if they sinned, their suffering is out of proportion, overdone, and the fault of Babylon. And Job, the classic God-resister, utterly rejects the blame his friends heap upon him as he challenges God's justice at every turn.

Chapter 9: Encoding Catastrophe

1. Bulman, *Shattered Assumptions*, 4.

2. For a list of these passages, see Louis Stulman, *The Prose Sermons of the Book of Jeremiah: A Redescription of Correspondences with the Deuteronomist Literature in the Light of Recent Text-Critical Research*, SBLDS 83 (Atlanta: Scholars, 1982), vi.

3. Schwartz, *Imagining the Holocaust*, 32.

4. Stulman, *Order amid Chaos*, 52.

5. Robyn Fivush and Beth Seelig, "Interdisciplinary Responses to Trauma: Memory, Meaning, and Narrative," in *Interdisciplinary Responses to Trauma: Memory, Meaning, and Narrative*, ed. Robyn Fivush and Beth Seelig, Academic Exchange 5 (Atlanta: Emory University, 2005), 5.

6. Fivush and Seelig, "Interdisciplianry Responses," 5.

7. Ibid.

8. Tal, *Worlds of Hurt*, 6.

9. Stulman, *Jeremiah*, 86, addresses the first fifteen verses because source critics have claimed that it is the historic core of the sermon to which other verses were added. For readers of the book who have survived the invasions, however, the whole sermon works as a unified piece that addresses their historical context in several ways. Like Else Kragelund Holt, "Jeremiah's Temple Sermon and the Deuteronomists: An Investigation of the Redactional Relationship between Jeremiah 7 and 26," *JSOT* 36 (1986): 73-87, I understand the sermon in the final form of the book to be a retrospective account of the nation's fall.

10. Judah borrowed its sense of the temple's significance from its neighbors in the Ancient Near East. In stories about neighboring Canaanite gods (Ugaritic Baal Cycle), the gods lived on Mount Saphon, also known as "the Mountain of the North," and their presence protected the people. When this theology comes into Israel through Isaiah of Jerusalem and through Davidic Covenant theology, the Jerusalem temple on Mount Zion became God's abode among them.

11. And the temple's destruction also disrupts economic life, because it was an economic center, a place of commerce, exchange, and employment. See Lizabeth Fried, "The Land Lay Desolate," 22.

12. Shiloh was home to the priestly family of Eli and the place of Samuel's call (1 Sam 1-3; Josh 18:1; Judg 18:31; 21:19). Regarding archeology of the site see Lundbom, *Jeremiah* 1-20, 486.

13. The sermon may be addressed primarily to the deportees (7:15; 8:3) but its repetition of references to "place," that is the Jerusalem temple (7:5, 7, 14), its address to "all you people of Judah who enter the gates to worship," its reference to Judah and the streets of Jerusalem (7:34, 8:2), and its description of the destruction of the land and the piling up of corpses seems firmly grounded in the land. I think the sermon attends to the different experiences of the disaster among those surviving in the land and those deported to Babylon.

14. Erickson, "Notes on Trauma and Community," 194.

15. This list of curses so well describes a society destroyed by invasion and occupation. Moses' long list of curses reverses and expands Moses shorter list of blessings (Deut 28:1-4). I think Deuteronomy also needs to be studied as survival literature.

16. Erickson, "Notes on Trauma and Community," 195.

17. Not carrying a burden involves more than a prohibition of heavy lifting; it forbids business labors that violate the Sabbath command to rest and hallow the day. See also Lundbom, *Jeremiah 1-20*, 806.

18. Fretheim, *Jeremiah*, 262-65.

19. But see Brueggemann, *Exile and Homecoming*, 166-67; Fretheim, *Jeremiah*, 265.

20. Brueggemann, *Exile and Homecoming*, 165-67.

21. Stulman, *Order amid Chaos*, 177.

22. However, the practice of Sabbath "blossoms" only during the Exilic or Post Exilic period. Its observance seems to have gained central importance only after the loss of the temple.

23. Fivush and Seelig, "Interdisciplinary Responses to Trauma," 5, make their claims about narrative, but I apply their observations to prose sermons.

24. Stulman, *Order amid Chaos*, 185.

Chapter 10: Rekindling Hope

1. An earlier version of ideas in this chapter appeared in Kathleen M. O'Connor, "Jeremiah's Two Visions of the Future," *Utopia and Dystopia in Prophetic Literature*, ed. Ehud ben Zvi, Finnish Exegetical Society in Helsinki (Göttingen: Vandenhoeck and Ruprecht, 2006), 86-104.

2. The book of consolation is variously identified as chapters 30–31 or 30–33. But 32–33 continue in the prose narrative style of chapters 26–29. See Allen, *Jeremiah*, 33; Holladay, *Jeremiah*, vol. 2, 155-56; and Fretheim, *Jeremiah*, 411.

3. Martin Kessler, "Jeremiah Chapters 26–45 Reconsidered," *JNES* 27 (1968): 81-88.

4. Steve James Schweitzer, "Exploring Utopian Space of Chronicles: Some Spatial Anomalies," a paper presented at the Catholic Biblical Association Annual Meeting, San Francisco, 2003. Jeremiah is not writing a utopia as a full blown literary form as in Thomas Moore's *Utopia*, but utopian thinking exists in biblical texts and utopian theory offers help in understanding the power of the imaginary world.

5. Schweitzer, "Utopian Space."

6. Fretheim, *Jeremiah,* 416.

7. Most likely chapters 30–33 address exiles, as many interpreters recognize, for they promise a journey home. But I think the vision includes internal refugees as well.

8. John J. Collins, "Models of Utopia in the Biblical Tradition," in *"A Wise and Discerning Mind": Essays in Honor of Burke O. Long,* ed. Saul M. Olyan and Robert C. Culley, BJS (Providence: Brown University Press, 2000), 67.

9. Steven James Schweitzer, "Reading Utopia in Chronicles" (PhD Dissertation, University of Notre Dame, 2005), 29-64.

10. Ibid., 150; Louis Marin, *Utopics: Spatial Play,* Contemporary Studies in Philosophy and the Human Sciences, (Atlantic Heights: Humanities, 1984), 84; Schweitzer, "Reading Utopia," 4.

11. See Saul M. Olyan, *Disability in the Hebrew Bible: Interpreting Mental and Physical Differences* (Cambridge: Cambridge University Press, 2008).

12. See Barbara Bozak, *"Life Anew": A Literary Theological Study of Jer 30-31,* AnBib 122 (Rome: Pontifical Biblical Institute, 1991). Bozak also attends to *variations* in addresses between masculine and feminine in chapters 30–31.

13. Because they are names also associated with fallen the northern kingdom of Israel, some interpreters explain their presence here as an expression of Jeremiah's pre-exilic hope for a reunited nation under King Josiah. See Holladay, *Jeremiah* 2, 160-71.

14. David Dobbs, "The Post-Traumatic Stress Trap," *Scientific American* (April 2009): 68.

15. Israel/Jacob is father of the twelve tribes and the patronymic ancestor of "all the families of Israel" (31:1), Rachel (31:15)—Jacob's most beloved wife—is quintessential mother of all Israel, and Ephraim is her (grand)son.

16. Roland Boer, *Novel Histories: The Fiction of Biblical Criticism,* Playing the Text 2 (Sheffield: Sheffield Academic, 1997), 113.

17. See Brueggemann, *A Commentary on Jeremiah* , 286-88.

18. See Phyllis Trible, *God and the Rhetoric of Sexuality,* OBT (Philadelphia: Fortress Press, 1968), 40-50, for a brilliant and now classic study of this poem.

19. See the many possibilities of translation in Gerald L. Keown, Pamela J. Scalise, and Thomas G. Smothers, *Jeremiah 26-52,* WBC (Dallas: Word, 1995), 122-23.

20. O'Connor, "Jeremiah," 514.

21. But see Rodney R. Hutton, "Are the Parents Still Eating Sour Grapes? Jeremiah's Use of the *Māšāl* in Contrast to Ezekiel," *CBQ* (2009): 275-85.

22. Or "their master," Holladay, *Jeremiah,* vol 2., 198.

23. For different interpretations of this passage, see Walter Brueggemann, *A Commentary on Jeremiah,* 293-95.

24. Roland Boer, *Novel Histories,* 120.

25. Ibid., 113.

26. Louis Marin, *Utopics,* 81-82.

Chapter 11: Running Out of Strength

1. Walter Brueggemann, *Like Fire in the Bones*, 86.
2. Shoshana Felman, *The Juridical Unconscious: Trials and Traumas in the Twentieth Century* (Cambridge: Harvard University Press, 2002), 8. See also Shoshana Felman and Dori Laub, *Testimony*, and Elissa Marder, "Trauma and Literary Studies: Some Enabling Questions in Fivush and Seeling, in *Interdisciplinary Responses*, Across Academe 5 (Atlanta: Emory University Academic Exchange, 2005), 9-17.
3. Felman, *Juridical Unconscious*, cited by Elissa Marder, "Trauma and Literary Studies," 16.
4. Ibid.
5. On these, see Louis Stulman, *Jeremiah*, 349-87; Lundbom, *Jeremiah 37-52*, 181-510; Alice Ogden Bellis, *The Structure and Composition of Jeremiah 50:2-51:38* (Lewiston: Mellon, 1995).
6. Diamond, "Jeremiah," 612.
7. Stulman, *Jeremiah*, 384-87.
8. Jack Kugelmass, "Missions to the Past: Poland in Contemporary Jewish Thought and Deed," in *Tense Past: Cultural Essays in Trauma and Memory*, ed. P. Antze and M. Lambek (New York: Routledge, 1996), 210, writes about "secular" rituals of remembrance," "performances of the past" in which American Jews visit Holocaust locations in Poland. These visits are rituals that "piece together the icons of the past," "reclaim . . . and reassemble them" to inscribe meaning in the present.
9. Ibid, 211.
10. Diamond, "Interlocutions," 49.

Chapter 12: Confusion as Meaning-Making

1. See discussions in Martin Kessler, ed., *Reading the Book of Jeremiah: A Search for Coherence* (Winona Lake: Eisenbrauns, 2004).
2. The process is even more drawn out than this. Current thinking is that first there was a Hebrew version of the book, then a Greek version with many additions and variations, and then another Hebrew version.
3. William McKane, *A Critical and Exegetical Commentary on Jeremiah*, ICC (Edinburgh: T and T Clark, 1986).
4. "The political parties and the National Assembly have made the most progress in trying to get opposing politicians to work together since the Peace Accords (1992). However, on the economic, social, and ideological level there are still great divisions in the El Salvadoran society." Words of John Spain, M.M. in a private email (July 20, 2007).
5. See Louis Stulman, *Jeremiah*, 32.
6. A. R. Pete Diamond, "Deceiving Hope: The Ironies of Metaphorical Beauty and Ideological Terror in Jeremiah," *Scandinavian Journal of the Old Testament* (2003).
7. Lawrence L. Langer, *Holocaust Testimonies: the Ruins of Memory* (New Haven: Yale University Press, 1991) 34.
8. See. Diamond, "Interlocutions."
9. Fretheim, *Jeremiah*, 19; Robert P. Carroll, *Jeremiah*, OTL (Philadelphia: Westminster, 1986), 69-82; Carolyn J. Sharp, *Prophecy and Ideology in Jeremiah: Struggles for Authority in Deutero-Jeremianic Prose* (London: T and T Clark, 2003).
10. The second Hebrew verb ('š'r), translated "left" relates to the theologically loaded term, "remnant."

11. White, *When Words*, 34.

12. For a thorough chart of the chronological chaos of Jeremiah texts and the dates to which they are assigned, see Lundbom, *Jeremiah 37-52*, 582-85, and especially see the discussion of A. R. Pete Diamond, "Jeremiah," in *Eerdman's Commentary on the Bible*, ed. J. D. G. Dunn and J. W. Rogerson (Grand Rapids: Eerdmans, 2003), 545-46.

13. White, *When Words*, 31, writing about Homer's *Iliad*.

14. Allen, *Jeremiah*, 14-18.

15. Diamond, "Jeremiah," 546, also notes that the dates "represent a significant tactic of time management from chaps. 21–52," but he does not elaborate on what that might mean.

16. Judith Herman, *Trauma and Disaster*, 175.

17. Langer, *Holocaust Testimonies*, 5; Diamond, "Jeremiah," 545-46.

18. Ibid., 3.

19. Ibid.

20. Kai Erickson, "Notes on Trauma and Community," 194.

21. Ibid., 195-96.

22. Schwartz, *Imagining the Holocaust*, 7.

23. Langer, *Holocaust*, 9.

Epilogue

1. Denise Levertov, "Paradox and Equilibrium," *New and Selected Essays*, New York: New Directions, 1992), 141-42. My thanks to Dana Greene for this reference.

2. Ibid., 54.

3. See Tod Linafelt's discussion of Lamentations as survival literature, *Surviving Lamentations: Catastrophe, Lament, and Protest in the Afterlife of a Biblical Book* (Chicago: University of Chicago Press, 2000).

4. McFarlane and van der Kolk, "Trauma and Its Challenge," 29.

5. Schwarz, *Imagining the Holocaust*, 36.

6. Laub, "An Event without a Witness," 78.

7. Quoted by Donna J. Young, "Remembering Trouble: Three Lives, Three Stories," in *Tense Past*, 41.

8. Ibid.

9. Caruth, *Trauma: Explorations in Memory*, 1-12, and especially *Unclaimed Experience*. On the Holocaust testimonies, see Giorgio Agamben, *Remnants of Auschwitz: The Witness and the Archive* (New York: Zone, 1999), 11-14. Thanks to Davis Hankins for this reference.

10. See James E. Young, *Writing and Rewriting the Holocaust: Narrative and the Consequences of Interpretation* (Bloomington: Indiana University Press, 1988), 89.

11. Walter Brueggemann, *Like Fire in the Bones: Listening for the Prophetic Word in Jeremiah* (Minneapolis: Fortress Press, 2006), 1-26.

SELECTED BIBLIOGRAPHY

Jeremiah/Bible

Albertz, R. *Israel in Exile: The History and Literature of the Sixth Century b.c.e.* Studies in Biblical Literature 3. Atlanta: Society of Biblical Literature, 2003.

Allen, L. C. *Jeremiah: A Commentary.* OTL. Louisville: Westminster John Knox, 2008.

Attridge, H. W. and Fassler, M. eds. *Psalms in Community: Jewish and Christian Textual, Liturgical, and Artistic Traditions.* Atlanta: Society of Biblical Literature, 2004.

Arnold, B. T. *Who Were the Babylonians?* Archaeology and Biblical Studies 10. Atlanta: Society of Biblical Literature, 2004.

Barstad, H. M. "After the 'Myth of the Empty Land': Major Challenges in the Study of Neo-Babylonian Judah." In *Judah and the Judeans in the Neo-Babylonian Period,* edited by O. Lipschitz and J. Blenkinsopp, 3-20. Winona Lake: Eisenbrauns, 2003.

Baumgartner, W. *Jeremiah's Poems of Lament.* Sheffield: Almond, 1988.

Bellis, A. O. *The Structure and Composition of Jeremiah 50:2-51:38.* Lewiston: Mellon, 1995.

Berlin, A. *Lamentations: A Commentary.* OTL. Louisville: Westminster John Knox, 2002.

Biddle, M. E. *Polyphony and Symphony in Prophetic Literature: Rereading Jeremiah 7-20.* Studies in Old Testament Interpretation 2. Macon: Mercer University Press, 1996.

Boadt, L. *Jeremiah 26-52, Habakkuk, Zephaniah, Nahum.* Old Testament Message 10. Wilmington: Michael Glazier, 1982.

Boase, E. *The Fulfillment of Doom? The Dialogic Interaction between the Book of Lamentations and the Pre-Exilic/Early Exilic Prophetic Literature.* Library of Hebrew Bible/Old Testament Studies 437. New York: T and T Clark, 2006.

Bourguet, D. *Les Mètaphores de Jérémie.* EBib 9. Paris: Le Coffre, 1987.

Barbara, B. *"Life Anew": A Literary Theological Study of Jer 30-31.* AnBib 122. Rome: Pontifical Biblical Institute, 1991.

Bright, J. *A History of Israel.* 4th ed. Louisville: Westminster John Knox, 2000.

Brueggemann, W. "The Book of Jeremiah: Portrait of the Prophet." In *Interpreting the Prophets,* edited by J. L. Mays and P. J. Achtemeier, 113-39. Philadelphia: Fortress Press, 1987.

———. *A Commentary on Jeremiah: Exile and Homecoming.* Grand Rapids: Eerdmans, 1998.

————. "Faith at the *Nullpunkt.*" In *The End of the World and the Ends of God: Science and Theology on Eschatology*, edited by J. Polkinghorne and M. Welker, 143-54. Harrisburg: Trinity International, 2000.

————. "The Formfulness of Grief." In *The Psalms and the Life of Faith*, edited by Patrick Miller, 84-97. Minneapolis: Fortress Press, 1995.

————. *Like Fire in the Bones: Listening for the Prophetic Word in Jeremiah.* Minneapolis: Fortress Press, 2006.

————. *The Theology of the Book of Jeremiah.* Old Testament Theology. New York: Cambridge University Press, 2007.

Carroll, R. P. *Jeremiah: A Commentary.* OTL. Philadelphia: Westminster, 1986.

Carter, C. E. "Ideology and Archaeology in the Neo-Babylonian Period: Excavating Text and Tell." In *Judah and the Judean in the Neo-Babylonian Period*, edited by O. Lipschitz and J. Blenkinsopp, 301-22. Winona Lake: Eisenbrauns, 2003.

Carvalho, C. "Layers of Meaning: Priesthood in Jeremiah MT." In *The Priests in the Prophets: The Portrayal of Priests, Prophets and Other Religious Specialists in the Latter Prophets*, edited by L. L. Grabbe and A. Ogden Bellis, 149-76. London: T and T Clark, 2004.

Clarke, E. *Dwelling Place: A Plantation Epic.* New Haven: Yale University Press, 2005.

Clements, R. E. *Jeremiah.* IBC. Atlanta: John Knox, 1988.

Collins, J. J. "Models of Utopia in the Biblical Tradition." In *"A Wise and Discerning Mind": Essays in Honor of Burke O. Long*, edited by Saul M. Olyan and Robert C. Culley, 67. BJS. Providence: Brown University Press, 2000.

Diamond, A. R. P. "Deceiving Hope: The Ironies of Metaphorical Beauty and Ideological Terror in Jeremiah." *SJOT* 17/1 (2003): 34-48.

————. "Interlocutions: The Poetics of Voice in the Figurations of YHWH and His Oracular Agent, Jeremiah." *Int* 62/1 (January 2008): 48-63.

————. "Introduction." In *Troubling Jeremiah*, edited by A. R. P. Diamond, K. M. O'Connor, L. Stulman, 15-31. JSOTSup 260. Sheffield: Sheffield Academic, 1999.

————. "Jeremiah." In *Eerdman's Commentary on the Bible*, ed. J. G. D. Dunn and J. W. Rogerson, 545-46. Grand Rapids: Eerdmans, 2003.

Diamond, A. R. P., and K. M. O'Connor. "Unfaithful Passions: Coding Women Coding Men in Jeremiah 2-3 (4:2)." In *Troubling Jeremiah*, edited by A. R. P. Diamond, K. M. O'Connor, L. Stulman, 123-45. JSOTSup 260. Sheffield: Sheffield Academic, 1999.

Diamond, A. R. P., and Louis Stulman. eds. *Jeremiah (Dis)Placed: New Directions in Writing/Reading Jeremiah.* Library of Hebrew Bible/Old Testament Studies 529. New York: T and T Clark, 2011.

Dobbs-Allsopp, F. W. *Lamentations.* IBC. Louisville: John Knox, 2002.

Dubbink, J. "Getting Closer to Jeremiah: The Word of YHWH and the Literary-theological Person of a Prophet." In *Reading the Book of Jeremiah: A Search for Coherence*, edited by Martin Kessler, 25-40. Winona Lake: Eisenbrauns, 2004.

Floyd, M. H. "Welcome Back, Daughter of Zion." *CBQ* (July 2008): 484-504.

Franke, C. and O'Brien, J. M., eds. *The Aesthetics of Violence in the Prophets.* New York: T and T Clark, 2010.

Fretheim, T. E. *Jeremiah.* Smyth and Helwys Bible Commentary. Macon: Smyth and Helwys, 2002.

————. "Caught in the Middle: Jeremiah's Vocational Crisis." *WW* (Fall 2002): 351-60.

Fried, L. S. "The Land Lay Desolate: Conquest and Restoration in the Ancient Near East." In *Judah and the Judean in the Neo-Babylonian Period*, edited by O. Lipschitz and J. Blenkinsopp, 21-54. Winona Lake: Eisenbrauns, 2003.

Furst, R. C. "Prophecy as a Narrative World: A Study of the World Constructing Conventions and Narrative Techniques in Hosea 1-3." PhD Diss., Montréal: Université de Montreal, 2004.

Galambush, J. *Jerusalem in the Book of Ezekiel: The City as Yahweh's Wife*. SBLDS 130. Atlanta: Scholars, 1992.

Garber, D. "Trauma, History, and Survival in Ezekiel 1-24" PhD Diss (David Petersen). Atlanta: Emory University, 2005.

Gerstenberger, E. "Jeremiah's Complaint. Observations on Jer 15:10-21." *JBL* (1963): 393-408.

Goodfriend, E. A. "Adultery." *The Anchor Bible Dictionary on CD-ROM*. Oak Harbor: Logos Research Systems, 1997.

Gordon, P., and H. C. Washington. "Rape as Military Metaphor in the Hebrew Bible." In *A Feminist Companion to the Latter Prophets*, edited by A. Brenner, 308-25. Sheffield: Sheffield Academic, 1995.

Green, B. *How Are the Mighty Fallen? A Dialogical Study of King Saul in 1 Samuel*. JSOTSup 365. Sheffield: Sheffield Academic, 2003.

Halperin, D. J. *Seeking Ezekiel: Text and Psychology*. University Park: Pennsylvania State University Press, 1993.

Henderson, J. M. "Who Weeps in Jeremiah VIII 23 (IX 1): Identifying Dramatic Speakers in the Poetry of Jeremiah." *VT* 52 (2002): 191-206.

Herion, G. A. "The Social Organization of Tradition in Monarchic Judah." PhD Diss., Ann Arbor: University of Michigan, 1982.

Heschel, A. J. *The Prophets*. 2 vols. New York: Harper and Row, 1969.

Hill, J. "The Threat from the North—Reflections on a Theme Both Ancient and Modern." In *Wisdom for Life*, edited by M. A. Kelly and M. A. O'Brien, 35-44. ATF 14. Adelaide: Australian Theological Forum, 2005.

———. *Friend or Foe? The Figure of Babylon in the Book of Jeremiah MT*. Biblical Interpretation Series 40. Leiden: Brill, 1999.

Holt, E. K. "The Fountain of Living Water and the Deceitful Brook: The Pool of Water Metaphors in the Book of Jeremiah." In *Metaphor in the Hebrew Bible*, edited by P. Van Hecke, 99-117. BETL 187. Leuven: Leuven University Press, 2005.

———. "Jeremiah's Temple Sermon and the Deuteronomists: An Investigation of the Redactional Relationship between Jeremiah 7 and 26." *JSOT* 36 (1986): 73-87.

Holladay, W. L. *Jeremiah 1: A Commentary on the Book of the Prophet Jeremiah Chapters 1-25*. Hermeneia. Philadelphia: Fortress Press, 1986.

———. *Jeremiah 2: A Commentary on the Book of the Prophet Jeremiah Chapters 26-52*. Hermeneia. Philadelphia: Fortress Press, 1989.

Hutton, R. R. "Are the Parents Still Eating Sour Grapes? Jeremiah's Use of the *Māšāl* in Contrast to Ezekiel." *CBQ* (2009): 275-85.

Jones, S. " 'Soul anatomy': Calvin's commentary on the Psalms." In *The Psalms in Community: Jewish and Christian Textual, Liturgical, and Artistic Traditions*, edited by H. W. Attridge and M. E. Fassler, 265-83. Leiden: Brill, 2004.

Kalmanofsky, A. B. "The Rhetoric of Horror in the Book of Jeremiah." Ph.D. Diss. Ann Arbor: UMI Dissertation Services, 2005.

Keown, G. L., Scalise, P. J., and Smothers, T. G. *Jeremiah 26-52*.WBC. Dallas: Word, 1995.

Kessler, M. "Jeremiah Chapters 26-45 Reconsidered." *JNES* 27 (1968): 81-88.

Kremers, H. "Ledensgemeinschaft mit Gott im Alten Testament." *EvT* 13 (1953): 122-40.

Lapsley, J. E. "A Feeling for God: Emotions and Moral Formation in Ezekiel 24:15-27." In *Character Ethics and the Old Testament: Moral Dimensions of Scripture*, edited by M. D. Carroll R. and J. E. Lapsley, 93-102. Louisville: Westminster John Knox, 2007.

Lee, N. C. *Singers of Lamentations: Cities under Siege, from Ur to Sarajevo.* Leiden: Brill, 2002.

Leuchter, M. *Josiah's Reform and Jeremiah's Scroll: Historical Calamity and Prophetic Response.* Hebrew Bible Monographs 6. Sheffield: Phoenix, 2006.

Levenson, J. D. *Restoration and the Resurrection of Israel: The Ultimate Victory of the God of Life.* New Haven: Yale University Press, 2006.

Linafelt, T. *Surviving Lamentations: Catastrophe, Lament, and Protest in the Afterlife of a Biblical Book.* Chicago: University of Chicago Press, 2000.

Lipschits, O., and J. Blenkinsopp, eds., *Judah and the Judeans in the Neo-Babylonian Period.* Winona Lake: Eisenbrauns, 2003.

Lundbom, J. R. *Jeremiah 1-20: A New Translation with Introduction and Commentary.* AB 21A. New York: Doubleday, 1999.

———. *Jeremiah 21-36: A New Translation with Introduction and Commentary.* AB 21B. New York: Doubleday, 2004.

———. *Jeremiah 37-52: A New Translation with Introduction and Commentary.* AB 21C. New York: Doubleday, 2004.

McKane, W. *A Critical and Exegetical Commentary on Jeremiah* vol 1. ICC. Edinburgh: T and T Clark, 1986.

Maier, C. M. *Daughter Zion, Mother Zion: Gender, Space, and the Sacred in Ancient Israel.* Minneapolis: Fortress Press, 2008.

Mandolfo, Carleen. *God in the Dock: Dialogic Tension in the Psalms of Lament.* JSOTSup 357. Sheffield: Sheffield Academic, 2002.

Marin, Louis. *Utopics: Spatial Play.* Contemporary Studies in Philosophy and the Human Sciences. Atlantic Heights: Humanities, 1984.

Morrow, W. *Protest against God: The Eclipse of Biblical Tradition.* Hebrew Bible Monographs 4. Sheffield: Sheffield Phoenix, 2006.

O'Brien, J. M. *Challenging Prophetic Metaphor: Theology and Ideology in the Prophets.* Louisville: Westminster John Knox, 2008.

O'Connor, K. M. "A Family Comes Undone (Jer 2:1-4:2)." *RevExp* (Spring 2008): 201-8.

———. "Building Hope upon the Ruins in Jeremiah." In *The Bible in the American Future,* edited by Robert Jewett with Wayne L. Alloway Jr. and John G. Lacey, 146-61. Eugene: Cascade, 2009.

———. "The Book of Jeremiah: Reconstructing Community after Disaster." In *Character Ethics and the Old Testament,* edited by M. Daniel Carroll R. and Jacqueline E. Laspley, 81-92. Louisville: Wesminster John Knox, 2008.

———. "'Do Not Trim a Word': The Contributions of Chapter 26 to the book of Jeremiah." *CBQ* (October 1989): 617-30.

———. "Jeremiah." In *The Oxford Bible Commentary,* edited by John Barton and John Muddiman, 487-528. Oxford: Oxford University Press.

———. "Jeremiah's 'Prophetic Imagination': Pastoral Intervention for a Shattered World. " In *Shaking Heaven and Earth: Essays in Honor of Walter Brueggemann and Charles B. Cousar,* edited by K. M. O'Connor, Christine Yoder, Elizabeth Johnson, and Stanley P. Saunders, 59-72. Louisville: Westminster John Knox, 2005.

———. "Jeremiah's Two Visions of the Future." In *Utopia and Dystopia in Prophetic Literature,* edited by Ehud ben Zvi, 86-104. Finnish Exegetical Society in Helsinki. Göttingen: Vandenhoeck and Ruprecht, 2006.

———. *Lamentations and the Tears of the World.* Maryknoll: Orbis, 2002.

———. "Lamenting Back to Life." *Int* (January 2008): 34-47.

———. "Reclaiming Jeremiah's Violence." In *The Aesthetics of Violence in the Prophets*, ed. C. Franke and J. M. O'Brien, 37-49. New York: T and T Clark, 2010.

———. "'Speak Tenderly to Jerusalem': Second Isaiah's Reception and Use of Daughter Zion." *PSB* (November 1999): 281-94.

———. "Teaching Jeremiah." *PRSt* (Fall 2009): 273-88.

———. "The Tears of God and the Divine Character in Jeremiah 2-9." In *God in the Fray: A Tribute to Walter Brueggemann*, edited by T. Linafelt and T. K. Beal, 172-85. Minneapolis: Fortress Press, 1998.

———. *Lamentations and the Tears of the World*. Maryknoll: Orbis, 2002.

Ollenburger, B. C. *Zion the City of the Great King: A Theological Symbol of the Jerusalem Cult.* JSOTSup. Sheffield: Sheffield Academic, 1987.

Olyan, S. M. *Biblical Mourning: Ritual and Social Dimensions.* Oxford: Oxford University Press, 2004.

———. *Disability in the Hebrew Bible: Interpreting Mental and Physical Differences.* Cambridge: Cambridge University Press, 2008.

Pham, X. H. T. *Mourning in the Ancient Near East and the Hebrew Bible.* JSOTSup 302. Sheffield: Sheffield Academic, 1999.

Polk, T. *The Prophetic Persona: Jeremiah and the Language of the Self.* JSOTSup 32. Sheffield: Sheffield Academic, 1984.

Provan, I .W. "Past, Present and Future in Lamentations III, 52-66: The Case for Precative Perfect Re-Examined." *VT* (1991): 164-65.

Provan, I. W., V. P. Long, and T. Longman III. *A Biblical History of Israel.* Louisville: Westminster John Knox, 2003.

von Rad, G. *Old Testament Theology.* 2 vols. New York: Harper and Row, 1965.

Reventlow, H. G. *Liturgie und prophetisches Ich bei Jeremiah.* Gütersloh: Güttersloher, 1966.

Roberts, J. J. M. *The Bible and the Ancient Near East: Collected Essays.* Winona Lake: Eisenbrauns, 1992.

Roncace, M. *Jeremiah, Zedekiah, and the Fall of Jerusalem.* Library of Hebrew Bible/Old Testament Studies 423. New York: T and T Clark, 2005.

Schweitzer, S. J. "Exploring Utopian Space of Chronicles: Some Spatial Anomalies." Paper presented at the Catholic Biblical Association Annual Meeting, San Francisco, 2003.

Sharp, C. J. *Prophecy and Ideology in Jeremiah: Struggles for Authority in Deutero-Jeremianic Prose.* London: T and T Clark, 2003.

Shields, M. E. *Circumscribing the Prostitute: The Rhetorics of Intertexuality, Metaphor, and Gender in Jeremiah 3.1-4.4.* JSOTSup 387. New York: T and T Clark International, 2004.

Skinner, J. *Prophecy and Religion: Studies in the Life of Jeremiah.* Cambridge: Cambridge University Press, 1922.

Smith, M. S. *The Laments of Jeremiah and Their Contexts.* SBLMS 42. Atlanta: Scholars, 1990.

———. *The Memoirs of God: History, Memory, and the Experience of the Divine in Ancient Israel.* Minneapolis: Fortress Press, 2004.

Smith-Christopher, D. *A Biblical Theology of Exile.* OBT. Minneapolis: Fortress Press, 2002.

Stern, E., and A. Mazar. *Archaeology of the Land of the Bible: The Assyrian, Babylonian, and Persian Periods, 732-332 BCE, vol II.* ABRL. New York: Doubleday, 2001.

Stulman, L. *Jeremiah.* AOTC. Nashville: Abingdon, 2005.

———. "Jeremiah as a Messenger of Hope in Crisis." *Int* (January 2008): 15-20.

———. *Order amid Chaos: Jeremiah as Symbolic Tapestry.* Biblical Seminar 57. Sheffield: Sheffield Academic, 1998.

————. *The Prose Sermons of the Book of Jeremiah: A Redescription of Correspondences with the Deuteronomist Literature in the Light of Recent Text-Critical Research*. SBLDS 83. Atlanta: Scholars, 1982.

Sweeney, M. "Jeremiah, notes." In *The Jewish Study Bible: Tanak Translation*, edited by Adele Berlin and Marc Zvi Brettler, 917-1041. Oxford: Oxford University Press, 2004.

Trible, P. *Texts of Terror: A Literary-Feminist Readings of Biblical Narratives*. OBT. Philadelphia: Fortress Press, 1984.

Weems, R. J. *Battered Love: Marriage, Sex, and Violence in the Hebrew Prophets*. OBT. Minneapolis: Fortress Press, 1995.

Whitters, M. F. "Jesus in the Footsteps of Jeremiah." *CBQ* (October 2006): 229-47.

Van Hecke, P. ed. *Metaphor in the Hebrew Bible: Theology and Ideology in the Prophets*. BETL. Leuven: Leuven University Press, 2005.

————. *The Neo-Babylonian Empire and Babylon in the Latter Prophets*. HSM 59. Atlanta: Scholars, 1999.

Whitters, M. "Jesus in the Footsteps of Jeremiah." *CBQ* (2006): 229-47.

Yee, G. A. *Poor Banished Children of Eve: Women as Evil in the Hebrew Bible*. Minneapolis: Fortress Press, 2003.

Trauma, Disaster, and Related Studies

Agamben, G. *Remnants of Auschwitz: The Witness and the Archive*. New York: Zone, 2000.

Améry, J. "Torture in the Holocaust." In *Holocaust: Religious and Philosophical Implications*, edited by J. K. Roth and M. Berenbaum, 170-89. Saint Paul: Paragon, 1989.

Antze, P., and M. Lambek. *Tense Past: Cultural Essays in Trauma and Memory*. New York: Routledge, 1996.

Antze, P., M. Lambek, and O. Van der Hort. "A General Approach to Treatment of PTSD." In *Traumatic Stress: The Effects of Overwhelming Experience on Mind, Body, and Society*, edited by B. A. van der Kolk, A. C. Mc Farlane, and L. Weisaeth, 417-40. New York: Guilford, 1996.

Braiterman, Z. *(GOD) After Auschwitz: Tradition and Change in Post-Holocaust Jewish Thought*. Princeton: Princeton University Press, 1998.

Brison, S. J. *Aftermath: Violence and the Remaking of the Self*. Princeton: Princeton University Press, 2002.

Bulman, R. J. *Shattered Assumptions: Toward a New Psychology of Trauma*. New York: Free, 1992.

Caruth, C. "Introduction II, Recapturing the Past." In *Trauma: Explorations in Memory*, edited by C. Caruth, 151-57. Baltimore: John Hopkins University Press, 1995.

————. *Unclaimed Experience: Trauma, Narrative, and History*. Baltimore: Johns Hopkins University Press, 1996.

Danieli, Y. "Assessing Trauma across Cultures from a Multigenerational Perspective." In *Cross-Cultural Assessment of Psychological Trauma and PTSD*, edited by J. P. Wilson and C. S. Tang, 65-89. New York: Springer, 2007.

De Vries, M. W. "Trauma in Cultural Perspective." In *Traumatic Stress: The Effects of Overwhelming Experience on Mind, Body, and Society*, edited by B. A. van der Kolk, A. C. Mc Farlane, and L. Weisaeth, 398-413. New York: Guilford, 1996.

Diner, H. R. *We Remember with Reverence and Love: American Jews and the Myth of Silence after the Holocaust, 1945-1962*. New York: New York University Press, 2009.

Dobbs, D. "The Post-Traumatic Stress Trap." *Scientific American* (April 2009): 64-69.

Dombrowsky, W. R. "Again and Again: Is a Disaster What We Call a 'Disaster'?" In *What Is a Disaster? Perspectives on the Question*, edited by E. L. Quarantelli, 19-31. London: Routledge, 1998.

Downing, F. L. *Elie Wiesel: A Religious Biography*. Macon: Mercer University Press, 2008.

Droždek, B., and J. P. Wilson. "Wrestling with the Ghosts from the Past in Exile: Assessing Trauma in Asylum Seekers." In *Cross-Cultural Assessment of Psychological Trauma and PTSD*, edited by J. P. Wilson and C. S. Tang, 113-31. New York: Springer, 2007.

Erikson, K. "Notes on Trauma and Community." In *Trauma: Explorations in Memory*, edited by C. Caruth, 183-99. Baltimore: Johns Hopkins University Press, 1995.

Ezrahi, S. D. *By Words Alone: The Holocaust in Literature*. Chicago: University of Chicago Press, 1980.

Felman, S. "Education and Crisis or the Vicissitudes of Teaching." In *Trauma: Explorations in Memory*, edited by C. Caruth, 13-60. Baltimore: Johns Hopkins University Press, 1995.

———. *The Juridical Unconscious: Trials and Traumas in the Twentieth Century*. Cambridge: Harvard University Press, 2002.

Felman, S., and D. Laub. *Testimony: Crises of Witnessing in Literature, Psychoanalysis, and History*. New York: Routledge, 1992.

Fivush, R., and B. Seelig. *Interdisciplinary Responses to Trauma: Memory, Meaning, and Narrative*. Atlanta: Academic Exchange, 2005.

Geertz, C. *The Interpretation of Cultures: Selected Essays*. New York: Basic, 1973.

Gilbert, C. "Studying Disaster: Changes in the Main Conceptual Tools." In *What Is a Disaster? Perspectives on the Question*, edited by E. L. Quarantelli, 11-18. London: Routledge, 1998.

Anthony Giddens. *The Consequences of Modernity*. Cambridge: Polity, 1990.

———. *Modernity and Self-Identity*. Cambridge: Polity, 1991.

Gozdziak, E. M. "Refugee Women's Psychological Response to Forced Migration: Limitations of the Trauma Concept." Online: http://isim.georgetown.edu/Publications/ElzPubs/Refugee%20Women's%20Psychological%20Response.pdf.

Herman, J. L. *Trauma and Recovery*. New York: Basic, 1992.

Kirmayer, L. J. "Landscapes of Memory: Trauma, Narrative, and Dissociation." In *Tense Past: Cultural Essays in Trauma and Memory*, edited by P. Antze and M. Lambek, 173-98. New York: Routledge, 1996.

Krystal, H. "Trauma and Aging: A Thirty Year Follow Up." In *Trauma: Explorations in Memory*, edited by C. Caruth, 76-99. Baltimore: Johns Hopkins University Press, 1995.

Kugelmass, J. "Missions to the Past: Poland in Contemporary Jewish Thought and Deed." In *Tense Past: Cultural Essays in Trauma and Memory*, edited by P. Antze and M. Lambek, 199-214. New York: Routledge, 1996.

Langer, L. L. *Holocaust Testimonies: The Ruins of Memory*. New Haven: Yale University Press, 1991.

Laub, D. "An Event without a Witness: Truth, Testimony, and Survival." In *Testimony: Crises of Witnessing in Literature Psychoanalysis, and History*, edited by S. Felman and D. Laud, 75-92. New York: Routledge, 1992.

———. "Bearing Witness of the Vicissitudes of Listening." In *Testimony: Crises of Witnessing in Literature Psychoanalysis, and History*, edited by S. Felman and D. Laub, 57-74. New York: Routledge, 1992.

Lifton, R. J. *Death in Life: Survivors of Hiroshima*. New York: Random House, 1968.

———. "On Numbing and Feeling." In *Indefensible Weapons: The Political and Psychological Case against Nuclearism*, edited by R. J. Lifton and R. Falk, 100-110. New York: Basic, 1982.

Lifton, R. J., and K. Erikson. "Nuclear War's Effect on the Mind." In *Indefensible Weapons: The Political and Psychological Case against Nuclearism*, edited by R. J. Lifton and R. Falk, 274-78. New York: Basic, 1982.

Lynch, T. "Our Near-Death Experience," *New York Times*, OpEd (April 9, 2005).

McFarlane, A. C. and B. A. Van der Kolk, B. A. "Trauma and Its Challenge to Society." In *Traumatic Stress: The Effects of Overwhelming Experience on Mind, Body, and Society*, edited by B. A. van der Kolk, A. G. McFarlane, and L. Weisaeth, 24-46. New York: Guilford, 1996.

McGee, T. R. *Transforming Trauma: A Path toward Wholeness*. Maryknoll: Orbis, 2005.

Miller, A. *Drama of the Gifted Child: The Search of the True Self*. New York: Basic, 1979.

———. *For Your Own Good: Hidden Cruelty in Child-Rearing and the Roots of Violence*. New York: Farrar, Straus and Giroux, 1983.

Moorehead, C. *Human Cargo: A Journey among Refugees*. New York: Henry Holt, 2005.

Nelson, H. L. *Damaged Identities, Narrative Repair*. Ithaca: Cornell University Press, 2001.

Quarantelli, E. L., ed. *What Is a Disaster?: Perspectives on the Question*. London: Routledge, 1998.

Samuelson, D. "Seven Steps to Healing: Experiential Reframing and Its Connections to Job and Jeremiah." Doctor of Ministry Project, Columbia Theological Seminary, 2008.

Schwartz, D. R. *Imagining the Holocaust*. New York: St. Martin's, 1999.

Sebald, W. G. *On the Natural History of Destruction*. New York: Random House, 2003.

Scarry, E. *The Body in Pain: The Making and Unmaking of the World*. New York: Oxford University Press, 1985.

Solomon, A. *The Noonday Demon: An Atlas of Depression*. New York: Scribner, 2001.

Stallings, R. A. "Disaster and Theory of Social Order." In *What Is a Disaster?: Perspectives on the Question*, edited by E. K. Quarantelli, 127-45. London: Routledge, 1998.

Tal, K. *Worlds of Hurt: Reading Literatures of Trauma*. Cambridge: Cambridge University Press, 1996.

Trible, P. *God and the Rhetoric of Sexuality*. OBT. Philadelphia: Fortress Press, 1968.

van der Kolk, B. A. "Trauma and Memory." In *Traumatic Stress: The Effects of Overwhelming Experience on Mind, Body, and Society*, edited by B. A. van der Kolk, A. G. McFarlane, and L. Weisaeth, 293-301. New York: Guilford, 1996.

van der Kolk, B. A., and A. C. McFarlane. "The Black Hole of Trauma." In *Traumatic Stress: The Effects of Overwhelming Experience on Mind, Body, and Society*, edited by B. A. van der Kolk, A. G. McFarlane, and L. Weisaeth, 3-23. New York: Guilford, 1996.

van der Kolk, B. A., and O. Van der Hart. "The Intrusive Past: The Flexibility of Memory and the Engraving of Trauma." In *Trauma: Explorations in Memory*, edited by C. Caruth, 158-82. Baltimore: John Hopkins University Press, 1995.

van der Kolk, B. A., and A. C. McFarlane, eds. *Traumatic Stress: The Effects of Overwhelming Experience on Mind, Body, and Society*. New York: Guilford, 1996.

Volf, M. *The End of Memory: Remembering Rightly in a Violent World*. Grand Rapids: Eerdmans, 2006.

White, J. B. *When Words Lose Their Meaning: Constitutions and Reconstitutions of Language, Character, and Community*. Chicago: University of Chicago Press, 1985.

Wilson, J. P. "Preface." In *Cross-Cultural Assessment of Psychological Trauma and PTSD*, edited by J. P. Wilson and C. S. Tang, vii-xvii. New York: Springer, 2007.

Wilson, J. P., and C. S. Tang, eds. *Cross-Cultural Assessment of Psychological Trauma and PTSD*. New York: Springer, 2007.

Young, J. E. *Writing and Rewriting the Holocaust: Narrative and the Consequences of Interpretation*. Bloomington: Indiana University Press, 1988.

Miscellaneous

Benfey, C. "The Storm over Robert Frost." *New York Review of Books* (December 4, 2008): 49.

Boer, R. *Novel Histories: The Fiction of Biblical Criticism*. Sheffield: Sheffield Academic, 1997.

Buber, M. *Eclipse of God: Studies in the Relations between Religion and Philosophy*. New York: Harper and Row, 1952.

Downing, F. L. *Elie Wiesel: A Religious Biography*. Macon: Mercer University Press, 2008.

Geertz, C. *The Interpretation of Cultures: Selected Essays*. New York: Basic, 1973.

Grossman, D. "Writing in the Dark." *New York Times Magazine* (May 13, 2007): 28-31.

Greene, D. "Biography and the Search for Meaning." *National Catholic Reporter* (5 May 2006). *http://natcath.org/NCR_Online/archives2/2006b/050506/050506t.php*

Levertov, D. "Paradox and Equilibrium." In *New and Selected Essays*. New York: New Directions, 1992.

Marin, L. *Utopics: Spatial Play*. Contemporary Studies in Philosophy and the Human Sciences. Atlantic Heights: Humanities, 1984.

Turner, M. *The Literary Mind*. New York: Oxford University Press, 1996.

Williamson, A. "A Childhood Around 1950." In *The Face of Poetry*, edited by Zak Rogow, 143. Berkeley: University of California Press, 2005.

INDEX OF SCRIPTURAL PASSAGES

INDEX OF NAMES AND SUBJECTS

Halperin, David J., 152n2
Henderson, Joseph M., 150n18, 151n22, 151n24, 151n28, 151n37
Herion, Gary Alan, 8, 142n5
Herman, Judith Lewis, 68, 132, 141n3, 144n29, 150n1, 152n45, 160n16
Heschel, Abraham, 65
Hill, John, 148n8, 148n10, 148n12, 149n24
history
    great story, 7; history, little stories, 7–12; history, problems, 14–16
Holladay, William L., 147n15, 152n6, 157n2, 158n13, 158n22
Holocaust, 2, 24, 25, 26, 64, 65, 67, 128, 133, 159n8
Holt, Else K., 64, 146n9, 150n34–36, 157n9
hope, 103–13, 125, 136
Hutton, Rodney R., 158n21

interpreting to survive. *See* reframing violence

Jehoiachin, 13, 100, 121
Jehoiakim, 13, 75
Jeremiah, life of, 69–91, 125, 135
Jeremiah, as iconic figure, 70, 73–74, 87–91
Jeremiah, as rejected prophet, 70–72, 78, 82, 90, 96
Job, 83, 84, 156n26
Jones, Serene, 47, 147n1, 148n9, 149n42, 150n9–10, 152n6
Josiah, 12, 131, 146n15, 153n12, 158n13

Kalmanofsky, Amy Beth, 149n28
Keown, Gerald L., 159n19
Kessler, Martin, 155n12, 158n3, 159n1
Kirmayer, Lawrence J., 147n2, 149n39, 149n41
Kremers, Heinz, 153n10
Krystal, Henry, 145n38, 150n11
Kuglemass, Jack, 147n22–23, 159n8

Lambek, Michael, 47, 147n22, 147n2–3, 149n38, 152n4, 159n8
laments, 29, 60, 65, 81–89, 116
Langer, Lawrence, 127, 133, 142n16, 147n2, 159n7, 160n17, 160n23
language
    breakdown of, 2–24, 33, 57; quest for, x, 33, 38–39, 44, 72, 88, 93, 115–16, 135; metaphoric, 7, 9, 10, 33, 35–36, 45–49, 52, 54, 60–61, 65, 67, 69, 73, 81, 82, 84, 88, 90–91, 102, 105, 111, 114, 115, 120, 127–129, 125, 136–37; misogynist, 43–44; symbolic. *See* language, metaphoric
Laub, Dori, 143n26, 144n30–31, 159n2, 160n6
Lee, Nancy C., 143n29, 150n22
Levenson, Jon D., 153n14
Lifton, Robert J., 59, 147n28, 150n2–3, 150n5–6, 150n11
Linafelt, Tod, 143n29, 151n26, 160n3
Lipschits, Oded, 141n4, 142n21
literary justice, 116–19, 123
literary structure, 29–32, 125–34, 135
liturgy, 40–42, 88, 94, 96–98, 120
"Little Book of Consolation," 32, 103–13
Longman, Tremper, III, 142
Lundbom, Jack R., 67, 145n6, 146n12, 149n26–27, 151n22, 151n30, 151n40, 152n43, 152n6, 153n14, 157n12, 157n17, 159n5, 160n12
Lynch, Thomas, 61, 150n15

McFarlane, Alexander C., 26, 141n6, 144n11, 145n43, 147n3, 160n4
McGee, Teresa Rhodes, 144n33–34
McKane, William, 30, 126, 145n2, 159n3
Maier, Christl M., 146n7, 148n14
Mandolfo, Carleen, 156n21
Marder, Elissa, 159n2
Marin, Louis, 158n10, 158n26

meaning
  making, 31, 41, 44, 70, 120, 123,
    125–34; quest for, 29–34, 44, 71,
    91, 100, 102, 103, 116
memory
  of violence, 2, 22–23, 47–49, 53,
    56–57, 96, 104, 134, 135; nature
    of, 57
Miller, Alice, 144n29, 156n17
Moses, 71, 93, 99, 100, 111, 112
Moorehead, Caroline, 64, 151n36
moral act, the book as, 29, 43, 57, 69, 80,
  148–49
Morrow, William S., 155n5, 156n19
mourning
  customs, 60–61, 98; women, 60, 66–68

numb, becoming, 22–23, 25, 26
numbing, psychic, 59–60, 66, 68

O'Brien, Julia M., 146n7, 146n10, 146n12
O'Connor, Kathleen M., 143n29,
  145n2n5, 146n6–7, 146n10, 146n14,
  147n17, 147n19, 147n27, 150n8,
  151n26, 153n11–12, 154n20–21,
  154n24–25, 155n1, 155n7–8, 157n1,
  158n20
Olyan, Saul, 61, 150n13, 150n16, 152n42,
  158n8, 158n11
oracles against the nations, 44, 115–21

parataxis, 52
Perdue, Leo G., 148n10
Pham, Xuan Huong Thi, 150n13
Pilarski, Ahida E., 150n18, 150n20,
  151n24
Polk, Timothy, 152n7
Prediction, 58, 94, 100, 133–34
Provan, Ian, 142n4, 142n9, 142n17,
  143n31
prophetic
  oracles, 70; sign acts, 70–73, 117–18

Quarantelli, E. L., 143n4, 143n7, 143n9

Rachel, 107–10
rape, 2, 49, 54–57, 87, 107, 149n26
readers. *See* audience
rebuilding, 17, 27, 31, 35, 68, 71, 102,
  104–6, 122, 128
reframing violence, x, 47–48, 94, 99–100,
  102, 110–12, 120–21, 130–31
repentance, 39, 41, 61, 88–89, 96, 98, 100,
  102, 108–10, 153n20
resilience, 17, 25, 44, 93, 102, 135–38
resisting God, 85–87, 90–91
retraumatize, 23, 35, 96, 115
rhetoric of responsibility, 40, 43–45, 50,
  52, 55 56, 62, 68, 71, 72, 83, 84, 93,
  100–101, 119–20
ritual, 37, 41, 53, 61, 73
Reventlow, Henning Graf, 156n23
Roberts, J. J. M., 63, 150n20, 151n27
Rogerson, J. W., 160n12
Roncace, Mark, 154n28, 155n34
Roth, John K., 145n39

Sabbath, 94, 98, 100–102, 157n17, 157n22
Samuelson, Deborah von Fischer, 48, 121
Scalise, Pamela J., 158n19
Scarry, Elaine, 23, 143n6, 144n18,
  144n20, 144n29
Schwarz, Daniel, 134
Schweitzer, Steven James, 158n4–5,
  158n9–10
Sebald, W. G., 23–24, 144n21
Seelig, Beth, 94, 156n5–6, 157n23, 159n2
sermons, 34, 70, 74, 93–102, 125
Sharp, Carolyn J., 159n9
Shields, Mary E., 146n6, 146n12–13,
  147n20, 147n26
Shiloh, 95–96, 154n21, 157n12
simplifying. *See* reframing
Skinner, J., 152n6
Smith, Mark S., 142n11, 142n14, 147n30,
  149n38, 155n7, 156n25
Smith-Christopher, Daniel, 20, 141n3,
  142n21, 143n27–28, 143n3, 143n5,
  148n6, 149n35, 152n2

CPSIA information can be obtained
at www.ICGtesting.com
Printed in the USA
LVHW020430150819
627675LV00014B/270